Rhetoric, Uncertainty, and the University as Text: How Students Construct the Academic Experience

Rhetoric, Uncertainty, and the University as Text: How Students Construct the Academic Experience

Edited by

Andrew Stubbs

2007

UNIVERSITY OF
REGINA

CANADIAN PLAINS
RESEARCH CENTER

Canadian Plains Research Center
University of Regina
Regina, Saskatchewan S4S 0A2
Canada
Tel: (306) 585-4758
Fax: (306) 585-4699
E-mail: canadian.plains@uregina.ca
http://www.cprc.uregina.ca

Library and Archives Canada Cataloguing in Publication

Rhetoric, uncertainty, and the university as text : how students construct the academic experience / edited by Andrew Stubbs.

Includes bibliographical references.
ISBN 978 0 88977 203 8

1. English language Rhetoric Study and teaching. 2. Academic writing. 3. Teacher student relationships. 4. Classroom environment. I. Stubbs, Andrew James II. University of Regina. Canadian Plains Research Center

LB2325.R44 2007   808'.0420711   C2007 906329 2

Cover design: Donna Grant, Canadian Plains Research Center

We acknowledge the financial support of the Government of Canada through the Book Publishing Industry Development Program (BPDIP) for our publishing activities. We acknowledge the support of the Canada Council for the Arts for our publishing program.

Printed in Canada

This book is dedicated to the memory of Randall Popken

TABLE OF CONTENTS

ACKNOWLEDGEMENTS

I'd like to thank Nancy Welta, Coordinator of the Student Development Centre, University of Regina, who made the resources of SDC available during the preparation of this volume. In particular, the attention given to the ever-burgeoning task of bringing the manuscript to final form by Richelle Leonard and Laura Herperger made this project a pleasure and, indeed, possible. To my students over the years, who took the risk of opening their writing to me, my indebtedness is beyond words: I continue to learn from you.

Introduction

> And so I proceed: what does university responsibility represent? This
> question presumes that one understands the meaning of "responsibility," "uni-
> versity" — at least if these two concepts are still separable.
>
> The university, what an idea!
>
> It is a relatively recent idea. We have yet to put it aside, and it is already
> being reduced to its own archive, to the archive of archives, without our having
> quite understood what had happened with it.
>
> Jacques Derrida, Eyes of the University, p. 83

> You cannot get to new horizons without grasping the essence of complex-
> ity theory. The trick is to learn to become a tad more comfortable with the awful
> mystery of complex systems, to do fewer things to aggravate what is already
> a centrifugal problem, resist controlling the uncontrollable, and to learn to use
> key complexity concepts to design and guide more powerful learning systems.
> You need to tweak and trust the process of change while knowing it is unpre-
> dictable.
>
> Michael Fullan, Change Forces with a Vengeance, p. 21

RHETORIC, UNCERTAINTY, AND THE UNIVERSITY AS TEXT...

Scene 1: "I was meeting my first-year writing class — about fifteen students — for the first time. For a first 'activity' (not for grading), I asked them to
think about themselves as writers, jot down impressions. Then I went around
the room asking them to read what they'd written. A lot was predictable: 'I
want to improve my writing'; 'I need to learn more grammar'; etc. But one student, mischievously, went to the board and wrote: 'I am a pour righter'.

"What this student did, I realized later, wasn't admit failure but act *out*
— i.e., rhetorically — his perception of the university's perception of him. He
had internalized the message the culture had been sending him for years. He

'got' it, which means his confession was a kind of triumph. It takes some savvy to see self-deprecation as a means to power. In this case, appropriately enough, over language."

Scene II: "I was carving a pumpkin with my daughter — her first Halloween, her first trick-or-treat. As the face became more detailed, it began to assume personality. It was supposed to go outside on the veranda, part of our usual display. But my daughter was nervous about marauding 'boy gangs' who struck in the night, smashing and wrecking. She argued for keeping it inside, safe.

"For whatever reason, it was decided the pumpkin had to take its chances. I remember working on a funeral speech, to be delivered next morning, after the carnage was discovered. Miraculously, ours was the lone pumpkin to make it through. I remember sidewalks and lawns strewn with debris, pumpkin corpses everywhere, but ours hadn't been touched. Why? To this day I have no idea."

These "scenes" offer a way to see teaching and learning as both place and process. "Place," here, means game space: competing sides cooperate — antagonistically — to effect a result. "Process" then implies strategy, a linked series of moves, drawn from a larger menu of options, leading to an outcome. The outcome, of course, is fitted to a binary, "win/lose." Or as we say in the teaching game, "succeed/fail."

In the first scene, the "pour righter" uses his zero status to turn the rules back on the (institutional) setting. A martyr figure, or Socratic eiron who refuses to oppose his enemy's sentence of death, he writes his failure to write. In the second scene, the pumpkin, despite — or because of — its frailty, prevails over huge odds. It doesn't have to do much, really, just be there. In both situations, what enables victory, or survival, is the capacity for self-effacement, or passivity. (One thinks of the Bruce Willis character in the M. Night Shyamalan film *Unbreakable*. David Dunne, a lifetime under-achiever, gains power after being, inexplicably, the sole survivor of a train wreck.)

How do the "pour righter" and "pumpkin" scenarios, one a classroom experience, the other a kind of urban legend, converge? In each case we have a setting, within which is inscribed a player. Think of setting as "outer field," here represented as restrictive or threatening. The "inner field" is the player, or player's performance, which contests the setting. Observe, however: 1) this performance doesn't seem to change anything (it supports the status quo); but 2) it turns on an ironic reversal.

Rhetoric, Uncertainty, and the University as Text... approaches the classroom along these lines, i.e., in terms of the geometry of placement. The outside/inside trope is adopted from Kenneth Burke (1945, 1962), who in *A Grammar of Motives* reflects on the "container and the thing contained": "Using 'scene' in the sense of setting, or background, and 'act' in the sense of action, one could say that 'the scene contains the act.' And using 'agents' in the sense of actors, or acters, one could say that 'the scene contains the agents'" (p. 3):

> It is a principle of drama that the nature of acts and agents should be consistent with the nature of the scene. And whereas comic and grotesque works may deliberately set these elements at odds with one another, audiences make allowance for such liberty, which reaffirms the same principle of consistency in its very violation. (p. 3)

Burke assumes "consistency" between these two zones, but this includes "violation," so symmetry is replicated in non-symmetry. Presumably, the "acter" (like the student) stands against a "background" discourse that has originated elsewhere and prior to his/her arrival on the scene. The acter resists the domination of the scene via what Michel Serres (1982), in his analysis of post-Baconian physics, calls the "command obedience couplet": "One commands nature by obeying it.... Since nature is stronger than we are, we must bend to its law, and it is through its orders it turns its forces against order" (p. 21).

Teaching and learning are placements, in Burke's sense, since they are tied to ideas of location and action, what he calls scene and act. Institutions "contain" classrooms; classrooms contain — engender — social (inter)actions. Some aspects of this process are obedient to rule, some are not. And the unexpected can lead to knowledge — if, as bell hooks (1994) claims, teaching is excess (i.e., "transgression"). Plainly, too, classrooms, as spaces, are fluid. In effect, classrooms behave like texts and, like any text, can be read and misread. Here is another analogy to the classroom as a tightly figured spatial graphic, Wallace Stevens's "Anecdote of the Jar."

> I placed a jar in Tennessee,
> And round it was, upon a hill.
> It made the slovenly wilderness
> Surround that hill.

The wilderness rose up to it,
And sprawled around, no longer wild.
The jar was round upon the ground
And tall and of a port in air.

It took dominion everywhere.
The jar was gray and bare.
It did not give of bird or bush,
Like nothing else in Tennessee.

The jar is an anomaly ("like nothing else in Tennessee"), but the "slovenly" wilderness surrounding it is pacified, civilized by it. Still, the roundness of nature is an attribute of the roundness of the jar. The first line seems to tell us Tennessee has been there all along, the jar comes later. But, of course, all we have in front of us is text, i.e., the words on the page. And text is, like the jar, the opposite of nature; it is made by human hands and, in turn, makes everything inside it virtual. In the end, can we really tell what is out and what is in? Or what is solid ("The jar was round upon the ground") and what is intangible, transparent: a sign, a lens ("a port in air")?

Using Burke, we might formulate a kinship between rhetoric and uncertainty, a kinship that emerges when we treat experience, in particular classroom experience, as a socio-linguistic "appearance." If the classroom, with its multiple and dynamic layers of information, misinformation, and disinformation, is a text to be read as well as lived, then, allegorically speaking, everyone involved is a jar in Tennessee. To gain power in any scene, including learning communities, one needs to see from far away and close up (overview and particulars). Fullan (2003): "People in learning communities learn to 'talk back', and to be skeptical about imposed ideas. They are in a better position to question external solutions. But we don't want people to turn inward, which is groupthink" (p. 30).

> Going back to our metaphor, you have to move back and forth from the balcony to the dance floor, over and over again throughout the day, week, month, and year. You take action, step back and assess the results of action, reassess the plan, then go to the dance floor and make the next move. (Heifetz & Linsky, qtd. in Fullan, 2002, p. 100)

Once "complexity" or doubleness of vision is factored in, we put a premium on re-vision as the crucial element in classroom exchange, not only in teaching and learning but as a component of text. This is embodied in the rhetorical idea of ratios: Burke's "scene-act ratio" (etc.); Harold Bloom's (1973) "revisionary ratios"; Deanne Bogdan's (1992) feminist re-reading (*Re-educating the Imagination*) of Northrop Frye. To claim that scene impacts how we think of writing, and in particular how we tell "good" from "bad" writing, is to follow a postmodern, post-process, social constructionist trail. The university as "idea" in Derrida's sense, and the classroom as rhetorically constructed, leads to Weisser and Dobrin's (2001) conception of writing as environment.

In *Ecocomposition*, Weisser and Dobrin treat environment as natural as well as social space, ecosystem and institution (the places we inherit, i.e., remember, versus the places we compose). It is also linked to pluralism, diversity, and the ways textual spaces enable us to be conscious of these, conscious of being scripted by places even as we more-or-less successfully inhabit them. And this awareness becomes not only an attitude, or ethical stance, but the main content of the lesson. "We teach our students about context and convention" (Weisser & Dobrin, 2001, p.19):

> Context is the situated place where writing happens. Not just the physi-
> cal environment where a writer writes, but the environment of writing, the
> ideological environment, the cultural environment, the social environment,
> the economic environment, the historical environment. If writing takes place, it
> takes place in context. (p. 19)

Given the reversible, mirroring relation of outer to inner, we should anticipate a similar exchange between context and writing, so "place" enters text as a mark of meaning, as a sign of how to read "into," as well as write new texts. Sure enough, Edward M. White (1995): "The very word topic comes from the Greek word for 'Place,' suggesting that the thinking process is a kind of geographic quest..." (qtd. in Weisser and Dobrin, p. 19). In short, place is commentary as well as "invention" in the classical sense, and it offers a method ("arrangement," in the classic canon) of joining knowledge and act.

This brings us back to the classroom, where questions of what to know and what to do are routinely faced. How, then, does the student, especially the student as writer, address the pressures of the classroom, both dodge the bullet and hopefully, in due course, survive, even succeed? The answer is, through a trick — or call it a rhetorical device: don't resist, bow to circumstance, accept the finality of defeat.

At least, this defines the student as rhetor, as one in place. The tactic has a kinship, as noted earlier, with Socratic irony: one fetishizes ignorance. Such a game move enables the lesser force to gain the upper hand, and not just in a hostile environment, such as students often imagine universities to be. It also gives power over the instrument of language itself. Marguerite Duras (1993) in *Writing*:

> To write.
> I can't.
> No one can.
> We have to admit: we cannot.
> And yet we write. (p. 32)

Duras uses the impossibility of writing to instigate new writing. Writing's failure is replicated through a series of writing "non-actions." This we see in the almost incantatory repetitions of "no" ("No one," "can't," "cannot"). But the string of negations culminates in the detour "And yet...." The site of writing is marked by conflict: termination and profusion. Writing begins where it ends.

Writing's primary lesson may well be that since it cannot exist in the first place, it is inexhaustible. While this may seem unduly abstract, it is not far off what students intuitively feel once they are exposed to university writing tasks. This insecurity can be attributed not to any lack of grammar training or knowledge of the rules of form. It is, rather, the nature of writing itself. Such knowledge — if it is knowledge — is available to students and "accomplished" writers alike, which levels the playing field. In fact, this is where the whole focus on writing as ecology has its impact. Anis Bawarshi (2001): "Writing is not only about learning to adapt, socially and rhetorically, to various contexts via genres; it is also about reproducing these contexts at the same time as we are enacting ourselves, our social practices, and our relations to others within them" (p. 78). Right from the get-go, *everyone* is affected by the same *generic* anxieties of writing. It is one of the ironies of writing, and the writing life, that writing's origin is botched. It is afflicted by contrariness. Now, this is not normally how we address issues of "basic" literacy and how to develop it. Yet seeing the classroom as a rhetorically configured "inventory" of communication strategies seems to support this conclusion. On the plus side, the shared experience of stress and rupture can, possibly, bring learners and teachers together.

It becomes possible, then, to approach the classroom in terms of its patterns or, more specifically, commonplaces (which are always local). Or, as Thomas B. Farrell (1993) identifies these, "norms" ("of rhetorical culture"):

> Appearances come to us as configurations, as ensembles of objects, habitats, paths, tools, tasks, icons, and more or less recognizable characters that engage and reassure us with their own emergent familiarity. For the most part, most of the time, most of us are at home in the world of appearances. The stability of the familiar and the persistence of the recognizable lend a solidity to one another. Yet it is in their very particularity that appearances can begin to seem ambiguous or even equivocal and incomplete. When we have some stake, or interest, in the array of things around us, for instance, we are not likely to be concerned with an underlying cause or a larger, more inclusive general opinion. For the particularity of things has become a provocation. We cannot leave well enough alone. We also disagree about things. We may try to ignore them. We may take issue as regards what they mean. Eventually — perhaps sooner than we wish — we may have to own up to them, make judgments about them, and act on them. This is the tension that Aristotle captures with his rhetorical mood of *contingency*. Here we suddenly have the unsettledness of appearances, wherein differences are crystallized in opposed directions which may be resolved one way or the other. (p. 27)

Notice how quotidian, domestic, Farrell's visualization of rhetoric is, yet the "routines" of rhetorical culture are breached by "contingency." The point is that the classroom opens to uncertainty, to "opposed directions," in a similar way.

But doubleness and duplicity have been endemic to rhetoric since Aristotle named it, in the first sentence of his *Rhetoric*, the "counterpart" of dialectic (1354a). He also posited the enthymeme as rhetoric's version of the syllogism (1355a), which limits rhetorical pronouncements to probability rather than, as in dialectic, necessity. Students who take to heart such orientation-day directives as "Work hard and you'll succeed," who then work hard but do poorly, are witnesses to the craftiness of the enthymeme. The advice is, of course, true *and* false, since generally hard work pays off, but in particular cases the claim may not apply. We come to the moral ambivalence that has attached to rhetoric since Plato's *Gorgias*: the skilled speaker can inspire right or wrong action.

Another way of seeing the writing class is as the place — maybe one of the few places — where objective ("scientific") and ironic (literary/poetic) ways of knowing intersect. Writing courses are expected not only to impart knowledge but also refine skills, since it seems to be agreed that writing is not just something to know but something to do. Knowledge, in its "pure" or academic state, thus relies on, or gets entailed in, less explicitly academic considerations such as "experience" (as in "the student experience" or "the quality experience").

All of this has to do with the various ways writing prompts a split vision, making this split a requirement of learning. Into this dire yet potentially rewarding feedback loop, where institutional text and student text interrupt and modify each other, is where the essays in this volume take us. Call this a move to the interior, which may feel uncomfortable at first (though, again, we learn from situations as situations surround, consume us: we study history from inside history). The good news is that while viewpoints collide, and blur, the demand for rigor intensifies, and this can be taken as an opportunity. So we focus on the breaks and new combinations: acknowledging the double bind gives it epistemic value, and makes it, hopefully, productive for the learning writer.

Naturally, the doublet with which one is most familiar is "teaching-learning" itself. Twinning these operations leads, again, to the idea that knowledge and experience are rhetorical formulae, not something anyone can own, or contain. Richard McKeon (1997): "Rhetoric is an instrument of continuity and of change, of tradition and revolution. The history of rhetoric is the history of a continuing art undergoing revolutionary changes" (p. 2). On the same wavelength, Thomas O. Sloan (1997) associates rhetoric with the discovery of opposition, discord:

> The first principles of whatever might be considered rhetoric's intellectual habit stem from openness to contrariness, even to perversity, and from the ancient dialogic practice of generating arguments on both sides of the question. This is the position that — though I've put it in the technical terms of rhetoric — I find central to the great documents of humanism. (p. 11)

Viewing the classroom as a "rhetorical culture," in Farrell's terms, is like looking in a mirror. In a mirror, items duplicate each other (in strength) and reverse each other, which is to say continuity is always inhabited by difference. The mirror is also a metaphor for the incongruent counterparts of "objective" nature and culture. (The border between those two circles is the indefinable space where Freud's Sphinx lurks). Alternatively, it could be said knowledge building involves two tropes, not always reconcilable. These are, as we say, truth (to nature) and community (a construction of art).

On second thought, they may be reconcilable, but only at certain times, and only for the moment. Our point is that teaching-learning, as a double inscription, is a gateway to other problematic doublings. Some have been hinted at: public versus private discourse, literal versus figural ways of seeing, open versus closed organizations. Overall, we think in binaries because a textually situated universe compels us to. And what we think of as the normal gets affixed to what we might rather suppress: chaos. But rhetoric is provocative. The essays presented here attempt to uncover creative moments of reversal in the classroom. This is where what we may have overlooked, at second glance, comes back to haunt and inspire us.

HOW STUDENTS CONSTRUCT THE ACADEMIC EXPERIENCE

Rhetoric, Uncertainty, and the University as Text... is a gathering of first-person commentaries (observations, reflections, polemics) on the classroom experience by writing teachers from Canadian and American universities. The focus is the classroom as a socio-rhetorical construct, which means taking into account the unique, locally resonant features of various classroom sites. Such features emerge from institutional, disciplinary, and year-level differences and involve socio-cultural, political, as well as interpersonal factors. What is intriguing is the *movement* of knowledge in the classroom, but it is also important to examine the experience of transformation (continuity and difference, direction and misdirection) in classroom situations. The overall aim is to extend our sense of the malleability, indeed volatility, of the classroom as an event in the lives of those invested in its evolution and sustainability. We want to examine in a hands-on way the structures of change, and the critical moments of disruption, collision — in effect uncertainty — in classroom processes.

Change may seem a loose term, since it touches everything from the day-to-day routines of classroom management, to the inner and outer power relations of classroom, institution, surrounding community, not to mention course content and its delivery. But notice the extremes, the overt and covert/off-stage and on-stage movement of classroom discourse, allowing for an unstable vision of the classroom at work. Any mobility threatens the teaching-learning site, bringing the trickster, the Derridean pharmakon (Neel, 1988, pp. 79-99), to the fore. Instruction intrigues with trickery in that it is kill or cure, as we have known all along: knowledge is born of suffering; it can be constructive (cure cancer) or threatening (destroy cities). In any case, (r)evolution, with all its various postmodern slippages and breakages, can be taken as constitutive of the classroom event.

The essays are arranged in strategic combinations, such as student versus teacher viewpoints, real versus virtual classroom communities: the aim is to convey a sense of educational environments as bifurcated. Change, from one angle, is "natural," if unpredictable, a pattern one grows into, or an abyss one stumbles on, in the course of giving or taking a class. But it is also invented, a social fiction, and therefore something we would desire and, by extension, something that ideally we should take responsibility for. The next questions are 1) who affirms, resists, benefits, or suffers from change (or, conceivably, the absence of change) and 2) how does awareness of change frustrate or facilitate dialogue? Note, too, that change is linked with notions of progress: there is always pressure to go forward, to improve or increase knowledge, to refine our talents for expression. But there is also retreat, nostalgia for old positions maybe (as in "back to basics"), which on the positive side can lead to re-examination of what we do and re-formulation of how to do it.

Transformation involves risk and gain, but it is something we as teachers ordinarily attribute value to, not just an objective condition worth observing (though it is that) but an experience we feel instructors and students *ought* to undergo. This of course identifies transition — i.e., its recognition and engagement — with successful classroom goals: call these empowerment, liberation. Accordingly, the collection can be taken as a dialogue on a set of recurring themes that shift as we talk; but if the subject keeps changing, then the subject of "change" is subject to change, i.e., subject to itself. That is to say, it is "metacognitive"; in "Metacognition in Writing: Facilitating Writer Awareness," Neal J. Anderson stresses its critical role in the development of literacy:

> Metacognition can be defined simply as thinking about thinking. Understanding and controlling cognitive processes may be one of the most essential skills that classroom teachers can develop in writers. Rather than focusing writer attention solely on paragraph development or producing an essay, educators can structure a learning atmosphere where thinking about what happens in the writing process will lead to stronger writing skills. (p. 19)

The theme is taken up in several ways in the three ensuing essays, Julie Jung taking as her point of departure the student writer's preliminary feelings of impairment or disempowerment in "Vulnerable Writers at Work." Jung's classroom evokes instability as a teaching instrument, enabling students to deal with "competing realities" (p. 45) and escape the traps of a too ready and easy "coherence" or "inevitability" (p. 45). This subversive way of relating to text drives Andrew Stubbs and Michael Whitehead in " 'Since the Dawn of Time...': Thinking/Writing in the Gaps." Here, the instants of disruption become not threats entirely but opportunities for revelation and revaluation — the moments when, metacognitively, text is revealed to itself.

Jung notes how such a practice enables students to overcome "silence" (p. 45); for Stubbs and Whitehead, it helps students repel dangerously hyperbolic, monolithic claims in favour of allowing for "friction between ideas" (p. 77). One question that keeps coming up is, can students learn from the equivocal aspects of classroom experience and academic discourse, which the classroom in theory models. It is tempting to think of first-year students primarily (who are under the most acute circumstances of transition). But any student may be said to be in the perilous space between there and here, to be *living* transition from course to course and year-level to year-level.

When we talk of space, of place, of competing discipline codes, we are raising the issue of genre, Randall Popken's subject in "Uncertainty and the Acquisition of Academic Writing: A Pedagogy of Genre Destabilization." Students, for instance, do not simply inherit the unknown, as if it is — as in *X-Files* — "out there," waiting to expose or devour them. They also, presumably, need to *invent* the unknown, discover gaps, *internal* separations between factions, viewpoints, in a subject area in order to launch inquiry. As Popken points out, there is what students bring to the classroom *already*, what generic knowledge they pre-possess, not necessarily expressed in "a purely theoretical language, inspired solely by an interest in truth" (Derrida, 2004, p. 99). For Popken, this creates an opportunity for education to *undo* ways of knowing, so learning, for him, aims to "destabilize":

> In contrast to Prince's proposal for a stable, scaffolded syllabus for students entering the genres of academic life, I prefer the exact opposite: to destabilize students' discursive experience. That is, whereas Prince's model is based on assumptions of discursive certainty, I argue for the necessity of discursive uncertainty. (p. 101)

Classroom interactions, which initially strike us as part of the background, as merely particular and occasional, become, once uncertainty is factored in, the main lesson to be acquired. Treating the classroom as scene and text, again, is what opens the student to the metacognitive domain, which in turn becomes the hallmark of the best educational practice. We are learning how a classroom "thinks," which segues naturally to Robert Luke's analysis of the classroom as virtual space in "Process Report://computing.interactive.classrooms." Luke's description of a personal experience of virtual — i.e., "self-reflective educational space" (p. 112) — emphasizes ways that the scene as text is both medium and message. This is an interactive process whereby students are empowered "to critically examine and more directly inform the educational process by interacting with the course material as it is" (p. 112).

That technology re-inscribes, and gives force to, ideas of community, interaction, even intimacy accentuates the way environment performs a constitutive role in the process of learning. The levelling associated with "computing.interactive.environments" is one where teachers and students can change places, trade roles. It is worth noting how these essays are inflected by first-person narration, which enables the authors to act out the kinds of reflexivity they want students to perform. They present, publicly, moments of rupture, even error in their own practices, which lead to revaluations of these practices; instructor turns into learner, learner into teacher, as we spot the Other/double of their text, the one yet to be written.

The moment of doubt may be shattering yet groundbreaking, and it has something to do with the creative re-routing of the teaching process. Bill Heath, Kim Fedderson, Frederick Holmes, and Jeanette Lynes look back on their work with "'alternative' forms" (p. 152) of writing in a literature-based course in "Learning Journals at Lakehead: Four Pedagogical Perspectives." Emphasis is on "increasing students' sense of accountability and responsibility for their own writing," which run parallel to instructors' ongoing "re-negotiating of our own positions" (p. 152). Heath, Fedderson, Holmes, and Lynes are interested in correspondences between their varied, multi-textual, interactive approach to writing tasks, which emerged from the collaborative nature of the project. The "outlaw" aspect of journal writing contributed to students' growing discovery of personal agency.

Similarly, William Thelin and Wendy Carse, in "Disruption Fairy Tales and Unsettling Students," talk about writing in a literary context. Again we see a collaborative lesson plan evolving, subject to internal critique and re-direction. Results are not always predictable, and part of the issue is prior knowledge and prior expectations, both students' and instructors'. Looking back, Thelin and Carse report "…we had not counted on something important: the relatively comfortable relationships students had with fairy tales" (p. 155). Like Heath et al., they find that an interesting problem arises in the connection, or lack of connection, between popular and academic. They find that resistance to crossing the gap inhibits writing and teaching. This happens in spite of the counter-emphasis on negotiating difference implied by the collaborative nature of their project.

We begin to see the classroom as a continuing narrative of teacher-student contacts, in effect a metatext: polysemous, open-ended, a text that belongs to no one and everyone. Popken says, "destabilization is necessary for students acquiring academic genres because it reproduces the natural 'interlanguage' situation of written language acquisition" (p. 101). Imagine a student text that is deliberately, relentlessly uncertain about its status as text — that is "gapped," muddled but irrepressible — yet tied to place(s) and time(s). It would look partial, tentative, asymptotic — always verging on but never quite arriving at a final (published) state. But publication makes its own *non-sequitur*, real-world demands on authors, since it is a pressure from outside that marks a piece of writing as a rhetorically constructed and situated.

Keep in mind that student writing, ordinarily, is writing written not to be published; in fact, it is shrouded by the same deficit term, "mere," that usually prefaces rhetoric itself. This is a condition that, ironically, is brought about with the compliance of students. It denies the gaps that disfigure and configure "mainstream," professional — including professorial — utterance. Apparently one needs to get not just at text but at its unconscious; i.e., one needs, again, to read double, to read not just for declared meanings but for symptoms, points of cover-up, subterfuge. These factors show through a text when we see the prefatory negation: "*un*certainty," "*de*stabilization." One needs to see the institution, the community, inside the utterance.

Given that student writing, once it is re-imagined as written to be read, i.e., published, are we not obligated to identify it in generic terms? The trouble with the "exercise" approach to writing instruction, with its focus on sentence structure or paragraph form, is that it removes the reader from the contract. What happens when students are challenged with real-world writing scenarios? Seeing student writing as a genre would turn uncertainty from an obstacle to a mark of a specific textuality, but to accomplish this, we need to make a place for personal-style narratives. This is Judy Hunter's purpose in "The Personal and the Academic: Construction of School and Self in First-Year University Writing." Hunter makes a case for taking seriously personally-focussed writing in her discussion of a refugee student's predicament in her English as a Second Language class. Hunter describes students with "extensive previous English language education..." (p. 173). Upping the ante, she claims these students "needed not another grammar course, but refinement — instruction, guidance, and practice in the use of English in the university" (p. 173). Start with the social engagement, the communal discourse.

The cracks and confusions, the slips in private discourse, now become a way of mediating publics. Jaqueline McLeod Rogers invokes Sherrie Gradin's notion of "social expressivist" (p. 187). In "Provisional Knowing and Exploratory Narrative: Positioning Uncertainty in Academic Inquiry," Rogers claims: "A stance of self-consciousness rather than confidence is often intellectually appropriate to the process of sorting out old assumptions from fresh understandings" (p. 185). Key to this growth is narrative, with its power to connect observer and site. Rogers: "Narrative is a form of thinking and writing that enables the making of personal and provisional observations about human situations" (p. 186).

From the role of narrative in the construction of the classroom as social space, we move back to drama's role in this process with Robert S. Vuckovich's "The Arts of Rhetorical Deception and Modification" and Carrie E. Nartker's "'All the World's a Stage': Performance, Audience, and A Room of One's Own." Both explore the classroom as a rhetorical/dramatic space, which turns the classroom back to what it already is (i.e., it regresses to what it has been all along), namely a three-dimensional entity. It is an architecture, which is to say a scene of performance, which does not make knowledge vanish, but puts knowledge where Burke would place it: in the dramatic action. The deformity we associate with student writing is, again, not just the writer's fault but the writer's responsibility: it is a quality of the mechanism, of writing itself. The way to get at this attribute of writing is to experience it through the teacher, who conscientiously uses the classroom as a site of ethical trickery; for Vuckovich, the teacher as trickster is the teacher as rhetor:

> ...I, as instructor, presented myself duplicitously as one who knows and does not know. To define myself in terms of opposing predicates is, to say the least, a rhetorical ploy. Burke...affirms the practicality of enlisting opposites, because toying with opposites is an invitation to the students to participate. Non-participation was not an option. My show of ignorance acted as an opportunity for the students to participate. (p. 196)

Alternatively, the classroom generates a dramatic pre-script that students must learn to avoid writing in order to discover a personal stage, and multiple roles. This translates into problems of power relations between the (student) writer and reader, in effect a real-life/real-writer problem of "publication." For Nartker, the problem emerges from a faulty conception of audience, the fault lying not in confusion *per se* but in a failure to take complexity into account, the latent double message in the instructor's performance:

> Students in composition classes are really writing for an audience of one, the instructor. However, the instructor "constructs" herself as a multiple audience — as a critic who has multiple views. When an instructor reads a paper, she is looking at it from perspectives of all the people she creates in her head to make sure the paper is written clearly enough for many different people to understand. Perhaps, then, the student's anxieties are not unfounded. (p. 212)

We arrive back at a sense of the cooperation between the site of knowing and knowing itself, a relationship that is no doubt ideal, but that allows, in Martin Buber's terms, the "I" (first person/writer) and "Thou" (second person/reader) through cooperation to generate objective meaning, a third person. We come to the classroom as a local site of radical encounter, which is nothing other than a meeting between I and Other leading to a "phenomenology of sociality" (Levinas, 1999, p. 103). We keep, in other words, finding ways of giving the phenomenon of uncertainty agency, making it productive as opposed to silencing, or, better, incorporating silence into the texts we both live inside and create as outcomes. The dynamic, and economic, factor within writing — and learning — surfaces, generically, in acts of re-vision, a re-seeing that comes to the fore most readily in self-writing. This theme of the exemplary, and functional, role of the personal is announced a number of times here, and its broader applications include the affirmation of the imaginary in the construction of knowledge — again, the epistemic function of literary form.

The critical difference is therefore not between incapable and capable writers, or the illiterate and literate, or whatever other binary we might want to invoke. It is between writers who do not acknowledge the frontiers that press against writing and those who do, and so accept the "unpredictable" nature of writing as change. For teachers, as we have seen, this acknowledgement might be in the form of an acceptance of the text students bring to class, i.e., the pre-text. To do this they need to see beyond the class, to see the borderlines of the class, the points of interface with outer environments, in short, to let the outside in. This would be a step to recognizing the estrangement students feel in various ways regarding normal classroom operations.

At first glance, this ulterior or pre-text seems inordinately fragile and, of course, it is inflected by a range of social, cultural, economic, etc., factors. Robert Runte, Barry Jonas, and Tom Dunne identify the intimidation factor precisely in "Falling Through the Hoops: Student Construction of the Demands of Academic Writing":

> Intimidated by the diction and convoluted style of the academic reading that confronts [the student], she has become convinced that academic writing is something distinct from normal communication and completely beyond her own writing abilities. And yet this student is perfectly capable of holding her own in classroom discussion or of writing in other contexts. It is her perception of the academic writing task as alien, arbitrary, and daunting that undermines her achievement. (p. 221)

For Runté et al., such *pre*scriptions oversimplify — they are simultaneously reductive and overreaching. Paradoxically, they are the work of students capable of high achievement, who nonetheless romance academic writing by placing it in some esoteric void, a space beyond the pale.

Underachievement, the expectation of failure, is a text, consciously contrived, and a strong text at that, that mediates the student's relationship to the university. It is, in Robert C. Twigg's terms, a "coping" strategy. In Twigg's "Second Chances: A Study of the Coping Strategies of Undergraduate University Students" we see that, paradoxically the "weakness" of student writing is revealed not by error but hyperbole. The grand scheme, the once-and-for-all truth, is marked by technical jargon. It is undistinguished by nuance, concreteness, or audience sensitivity.

To read, we discover, is to read the seams in the quilt, which involves re-reading not just reading, which in turn privileges the second glance over the first. Twigg's study is about "second chances." A group of students, who "should have been required to withdraw from university for two semesters," were allowed to register. The official reason for this extension of grace was a 'computer programming error'" (p. 239). The opportunity for students to succeed was provided by trying again. Note that it is based on a glitch — an institutional anomaly.

The second glance may strike students as an intrusion, an interruption in the kind of "natural" consensus they most desire. What the second time round can expose is the lurking situational forces that encourage their overdetermined idea of the university as an "experience" in the first place. In reality, as we become aware later, "operating on the edge of chaos means also resisting the temptation to impose too much order" (Fullan, 2003, p. 26). Interruption, as practiced by Coleridge's visitor from Porlock, may be the fundamental work of writing and its teaching.

We arrive at a notion of instructor intervention in student processes not simply as beneficial, or necessary, but as constituting a kind of third dimension, an instrument that reshapes the parties — writer and reader — to the conversation. This sense of a third "person" is partly supplied by the classroom, real or virtual. After all, the classroom as scene shifts to the classroom as instrument (Burke's "agency"): place supplies the tissue of connection, and the motive to engage, a role performed by rhetoric. Rhetoric, then, is fear and desire — both at once. Possibly the classroom is a shifting set of lenses through which to look at the real, but eventually these lenses turn inward (like, in the end, Burke's pentad), so we just see other windows, and, through these, ourselves peering in.

— Andrew Stubbs

References

Aristotle. (1954). The rhetoric and poetics of Aristotle. Trans. W. Rhys Roberts and Ingram Bywater. New York: Random House, The Modern Library.

Bawarshi, A. (2001). The ecology of genre (pp. 69-80). Christian Weisser and Sidney I. Dobrin (Eds). Ecocomposition: Theoretical; and pedagogical perspectives. Albany: State University of New York Press.

Bloom, H. (1973). The anxiety of influence: A theory of poetry. Oxford: Oxford University Press.

Bogdan, D. (1992). Re-educating the imagination: Toward a poetics, politics, and pedagogy of literary engagement. Toronto: Irwin.

Buber, M. (1970). I and thou. New York: Scribner.

Burke, K. (1945, 1962). A grammar of motives. Berkeley: University of California Press.

Derrida, J. (2004). Eyes of the university. Trans. Jan Plug and others. Stanford: Stanford University Press.

Duras, M. (1993). Writing. Trans. Mark Polizzotti. Bridge: Lumen Editions.

Farrell, T. (1993). Norms of rhetorical culture. New Haven: Yale University Press.

Fullan, M. (2003). Change forces with a vengeance. London: Routledge Falmer.

hooks, b. (1994). Teaching to transgress: Education as the practice of freedom. New York: Routledge.

Levinas, E. (1999). The proximity of the other. Alterity and transcendence (pp. 97-109). M. B. Smith (Trans.). New York: Columbia University Press.

McKeon, R. (1987). The uses of rhetoric in a technological age: Architectonic productive acts. Rhetoric: Essays in invention and discovery (pp. 1-24). M. Backman (Ed.). Connecticut: Ox Bow Press.

Neel, J. (1988). Plato, Derrida, and writing. Carbondale and Edwardsville: Southern Illinois University Press.

Sloan, T.O. (1997). On the contrary: The protocol of traditional rhetoric. Washington: The Catholic University of America Press.

Serres, M. (1982). Hermes: Literature, science, philosophy. Josue V. Harari and David F. Bell (Eds.) Baltimore and London: The Johns Hopkins University Press.

Stevens, W. (1981). The Collected Poems of Wallace Stevens. New York: Alfred K. Knopf.

Weisser, C. and Dobrin, S. (2001). Ecomposition: Theoretical and pedagogical perspectives. Albany: State University of New York Press.

Metacognition in Writing: Facilitating Writer Awareness

Neil J. Anderson
Brigham Young University

What do writers do to facilitate mastery of writing? What can teachers of writing courses do to facilitate the development of writing skills among the learners in their classes? The focus of this chapter is to examine the role of metacognition in writing as a tool for facilitating writer awareness. The following five issues are dealt with in the chapter: (1) Definitions of metacognition, (2) A model of metacognition, (3) Relationships between metacognition and cognition, (4) The role of metacognition in learning how to learn, and (5) The teacher's role in developing metacognition in writers.

DEFINITIONS OF METACOGNITION

On a National Public Radio broadcast from Washington, D.C., on Friday, March 19, 1999, Snigdha Prakasha reported on the Stock Market Game, an activity to help children become familiar with how the stock market functions. A sixth grader explained what she was learning from playing the game. She said, "this game makes me think how to think" (Prakasha, 1999).

Metacognition can be defined simply as thinking about thinking. Understanding and controlling cognitive processes may be one of the most essential skills that classroom teachers can develop in writers. Rather than focusing writer attention solely on paragraph development or producing an essay, educators can structure a learning atmosphere where thinking about what happens in the writing process will lead to stronger writing skills. Developing metacognitive awareness may also lead to the development of stronger cognitive skills in writing.

The development of metacognition centers around attended processing versus unattended processing during learning. As writers attend to what they are trying to accomplish and focus on the strategies that can help them write better, they are able to make improvements in their work as writers. The improvements in writing lead to better learning as well as an increased confidence in writing. The active role that the writer has in the learning process is a focus of attended processing. Metacognition is central to coordinating learning processes. Attended processing is a key to learning how to learn.

Caine and Caine (1991) define metacognition as "thinking about the way that we think, feel, and act" (p. 160). They emphasize that metacognition

> helps us to learn in much more depth because we begin to recognize and capitalize on personal strengths while improving or allowing for weaknesses. We are also better able to appreciate what is really important to us, and so access our own intrinsic motivation. (p. 160)

Goodrich Andrade and Perkins (1998) define metacognition as "being aware of and controlling one's own thinking in order to think and learn better" (p. 68). This definition emphasizes the truly active nature of learning. Control over one's thinking can lead to better thinking and learning. Goodrich Andrade and Perkins state that "research shows repeatedly that students who monitor and regulate their own thinking tend to be better at solving problems, writing, [and] reading" (p. 69).

Sternberg (1998) provides three important distinctions highlighting the role of metacognition. First, metacognition is diverse. He emphasizes that metacognition "includes both understanding and *control* [italics added] of cognitive processes" (p. 128). This is an important distinction for writing teachers to keep in mind because writers may demonstrate their understanding in what looks like similar ways but in reality it could be in different ways. Not all writers approach a writing task in exactly the same way. If we only look at the products that writers produce, it may appear that everyone approaches writing in the same way. Not everyone solves the same problem in exactly the same way. If we only look at the solutions that learners give to a problem, it may appear that those who reach the same solution have solved the problem in the same way. There are multiple ways to think through the solutions to a learning task or to approach a writing assignment. Much of the literature has examined metacognition as if it were a unitary skill or ability.

Second, Sternberg urges educators to keep two issues distinct when examining the role of metacognition: understanding of learners' metacognition and knowing how to act on the understanding. This is important because we cannot assume that because we understand metacognition we know what to do. And, the reverse is true: we may have some very good suggestions of what writers can do and not understand the metacognitive processes that they have used. This information is particularly important for teachers in the classroom. We cannot rely on our cognitive understanding of the processes of which we are trying to make our learners aware. Teachers and researchers must also use metacognitive skills to reflect on what they are learning about the processes utilized by their learners.

Third, the interaction of metacognition with other characteristics of a learner is of vital importance. We must be aware of the varied abilities of the writers we work with. We must be aware of factors such as learning style and preferred learning strategies. The writers' personalities will also interact with their metacognitive abilities.

Sitko (1998) provides an excellent review of the research in metacognitive processes and writing. Expert and novice writers approach writing differently. Expert writers are much more aware of highly interactive processes of goal setting, generating ideas, and organizing material involved in writing. Revising and editing processes of expert writers also differ from those of novice writers. The conscious control of writing processes is a central aspect of metacognitive instruction in writing.

Activities in the classroom that allow writers to reflect on what they are doing and how they approach learning will lead to improved learning. Understanding what constitutes metacognition will allow teachers to incorporate more metacognitive activities in the learning process.

A MODEL OF METACOGNITION

Metacognition combines various attended thinking and reflective processes. Figure 1 (on the following page) illustrates the interaction of these processes.

Metacognition can be divided into five primary components: (1) preparing and planning for effective learning, (2) deciding when to use particular strategies, (3) knowing how to monitor strategy use, (4) learning how to orchestrate various strategies, and (5) evaluating strategy use and learning.

Preparing and *Planning* for Effective Learning
As writers take time to focus their attention on learning, they can make improvements in their writing. Taking time to prepare the learning

Figure 1. A Model of Metacognition

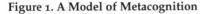
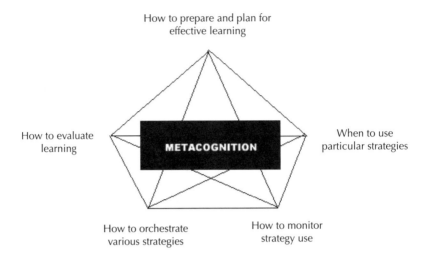

How to prepare and plan for
effective learning

How to evaluate
learning

METACOGNITION

When to use
particular strategies

How to orchestrate
various strategies

How to monitor
strategy use

environment and plan what needs to be accomplished makes a significant difference in learning. Preparing and planning also includes setting learning goals. The setting of goals should include having some indication of how the writers will know when they have accomplished the goal. The more clearly articulated the goal, the easier it will be for the writers to judge whether progress is being made.

Writers who are aware of what the writing task entails and what information must be used to accomplish the task are more successful in completing the task. Poor writers often state that they do not know how to begin the writing process. Writing teachers can teach students how to prepare and plan, how to set appropriate writing goals, and how to begin a writing task.

Sitko (1998) suggests that there may be a pedagogical implication for the preparing and planning strategies of metacognitive development. She points out that "it may be instructive to pause a moment to consider what beliefs and practices students may need to 'unlearn'" (p. 100). Teachers need to examine the types of writing assignments in which they engaged their writers. A clear focus on an audience other than the teacher often requires that writers "unlearn" their tendency to write for a specific audience. The teacher may evaluate the work, but who would best benefit from the writing of a student? Some writers need to "unlearn" that one-shot-writing is often not effective. Revision is an important part of writing. While teaching the metacognitive strategies of preparing and planning, teachers have an ideal context to address these issues.

Deciding When to Use Particular Strategies

Knowing when to use particular writing strategies is an important aspect of metacognition. Many poor writers don't recognize when to incorporate the use of learning strategies. The metacognitive ability of deciding when to use particular strategies indicates that the writer is thinking and making conscious decisions about the learning process. "Effective learning therefore seems to involve a critical attitude regarding our current level of knowing, which prompts us to ask questions, test ourselves, seek alternate opinions, and so forth" (Bransford, 1979, p. 201). Zimmerman and Bandura (1994) emphasize that "[g]ood self-regulators do better academically than poor self-regulators even after controlling for other potentially influential factors" (p. 846).

Knowing How to Monitor Strategy Use

One metacognitive skill is the ability to monitor current levels of under-standing. Good writers are able to recognize when they do not understand and stop in order to do something about it. Poor writers typically do not stop to monitor. Whimbey (1976) points out that for the poor learner "the pattern of gradual, sequential construction of exact meaning is totally foreign. One-shot thinking is the basis on which the poor [learner] makes interpretations and draws conclusions" (p. 86).

Learning How to Orchestrate Various Strategies

During the learning process, good writers do not use one strategy at a time but will use multiple strategies simultaneously. Knowing how to orchestrate the use of more than one strategy is an important metacognitive skill. Coordinating, organizing, and making associations among the various strategies available to a writer are major distinguishing features between strong and weak learners.

Strategy use does not occur in isolation. Often we discuss the use of a strategy as if it happens all by itself. An analogy of an orchestra may be helpful in viewing the use of strategies and especially how metacognition is used in order to improve learning. I play the string bass. The string bass really is not a very beautiful instrument when played alone. There is real value in having a variety of instruments playing together to make beautiful music. When I practice by myself, I can imagine in my mind the sound of the other instruments in the orchestra. I am aware of how the sound of my instrument fits into the overall beauty of the music. There is an interdependency of instruments in an orchestra. Understanding the interdependency of the string bass with the violins, violas, cellos, and other instruments in the orchestra is a very important learning experience. Likewise, understanding the interdependency of learning strategies while engaged in a writing task is an important learning experience.

Chamot, Barnhardt, El-Dinary, and Robbins (1999) suggest that certain strategy combinations are typical. For example, they state that goal setting and goal checking should always be used together. They emphasize the importance of metacognitive awareness in the use of these two evaluation strategies in particular.

> If learners set goals, they need to check whether they met their goals; otherwise, there is no point in setting goals. Evaluating progress towards their goals can give learners confidence if progress is being made. When students are not meeting their goals, then they may need to reflect on their plans and their actions for reaching their goals. (Chamot et al., 1999, pp. 32-33)

Englert, Raphael, Anderson, Anthony, and Stevens (1991) focus on combinations of strategies in their Cognitive Strategy Instruction in Writing model. They state:

> Writing is a complex process that must be regulated by writers themselves. The process of planning a paper, for example, involves several thinking and self-questioning strategies, such as identifying one's audience, ...determining one's purpose, ...activating background knowledge, ... and organizing brainstormed ideas.... During drafting, writers take the ideas gathered in planning and translate those ideas to conform to their audience and purpose; relevant ideas are included and expanded in the written draft, while irrelevant ideas are discarded. During editing, writers edit their draft to ensure that writing objectives are met, giving attention to their intended audience... and to their purpose.... Finally, in revising, students implement their editing plans to add, delete, substitute, and modify their textual ideas. This literature suggests that writing instruction must further students' metacognitive knowledge of the strategies and self-talk for planning, organizing, drafting, editing, and revising their ideas. Accordingly, writing curricula must be designed to cue appropriate strategy use related to planning, drafting, editing, and revising expository texts. (p. 341)

This highlights the essential nature of teaching students the metacognitive skills of orchestrating various writing strategies. Being metacognitively aware of strategy use allows a writer to use strategies in an integrated way as opposed to thinking that they occur in isolation.

Evaluating Strategy Use and Learning

Learners must be able to evaluate whether what they are doing is effective. Poor writers often do not evaluate the success or failure of strategy use. Bransford's (1979) work supports the importance of evaluating. He points out that

> poor [writers] may not only lack the skills to apply their existing knowledge to comprehension of new information; they may also be lacking in sensitive criteria for assessing their comprehension. Helping them learn to learn therefore involves changing their approach to comprehension tasks. (p. 199)

Part of the metacognitive skill of evaluating is tied to the writer's ability to recognize weaknesses in their work. "Too often, it seems, we place the greatest emphasis on what people know at the moment, rather than on their ability to realize gaps in their current knowledge and hence learn effectively" (Bransford, 1979, p. 202).

Knowing how and when to revise and edit one's writing is not an easy task but clearly demonstrates the metacognitive activity of evaluation. Schriver (1993) identifies five issues that can guide thinking about revising. First, "seeing, characterizing, and solving text problems are distinct revising activities" (p. 150). Schriver points out that writers may be able to see a problem in a text they have written but that does not mean that they know how to fix it. Second, "writers often have more difficulty seeing problems in their own text than seeing them in text created by someone else" (p. 151). Revising one's own work is much more challenging than revising the work of someone else. Perhaps the closer that writers are to the text the more challenging it is to identify the problems that may exist. Next, "writers' definitions for revision influence what they attend to and ignore" (p. 152). The writer's goals will effect what is revised and how it is revised. Fourth, "a writer's task definition for revision is self created and socially constructed" (p. 153). The relationship between the author and the audience influences how the revisions are addressed. The author uses the social setting of the writing process as a basis for determining what and how to revise the written word. Finally, "writers can benefit from instruction that helps them to revise by design rather than by default" (p. 154). Schriver points out that students tend to revise sentence by sentence by default rather than by choice. Instead of revising on a global basis, the sentence level and surface level changes are typically what occupy the writer's attention during the revising stage of producing a text.

The Interaction of Metacognitive Skills

Each of these five metacognitive skills interacts with the other. Metacognition is not a linear process moving from preparing and planning to evaluating. More than one metacognitive process may be happening at a time during a writing task. This highlights once again how the orchestration of various strategies is a vital component to writing. Allowing writers opportunities to think about how they combine various strategies facilitates the improvement of strategy use.

RELATIONSHIPS BETWEEN METACOGNITION AND COGNITION

An example from the writing classroom will illustrate the difference between cognition and metacognition. Writing a summary of material read is a cognitive skill. Understanding what goes into the summary and how long the summary should be are direct cognitive skills. Knowing how to write the summary and when a summary is needed and why are metacognitive skills.

Schraw (1998) points out the distinctions between cognition and meta-cognition. He indicates that cognition is needed in order to perform a task. Individuals use cognitive skills each time they undertake to accomplish a task. Metacognition is needed in order to understand how a task is performed. Individuals use metacognitive skills each time they think through the process of a task. Schraw indicates that there are two components of metacognition: knowledge of cognition and regulation of cognition. Knowledge of cognition "refers to what individuals know about their own cognition or about cognition in general" (p. 114). Regulation of cognition "refers to a set of activities that help students control their learning" (p. 114). Some researchers do not make distinctions between cognition and metacognition (Schraw, 1998).

You cannot have metacognition of something for which you don't have cognition. In order for metacognitive skills to be developed, writers must have the cognitive skills to reflect on. Teachers often push higher order thinking skills when there is no thinking in the first place. Sternberg and Spear-Swerling (1996) outline seven cognitive skills that should be developed prior to or along with metacognitive skills so that the writer has something to reflect on. The seven cognitive skills are listed in Table 1.

Table 1. Seven Cognitive Processes

1. Recognizing and defining the existence of a problem
2. Process selection
3. Representation of information
4. Strategy formulation
5. Allocation of resources
6. Solution monitoring
7. Evaluating solutions

Source: Sternberg and Spear-Swerling, 1996, pp. 24-30.

Notice the similarities here between these cognitive processes and the model of metacognition provided in Figure 1. Preparing and planning are metacognitive skills that relate to the cognitive skill of recognizing and defining. Knowing when to use a particular strategy involves reflection on the cognitive skill of process selection. Representation of information and strategy formulation are cognitive skills that are tied to the metacognitive process of monitoring strategy use. The cognitive skills of allocation of resources and solution monitoring relate to the metacognitive skill of orchestrating strategy use. Evaluating solutions is a cognitive process as well as a metacognitive process. The evaluation itself utilizes cognitive abilities, but knowing when and how to evaluate are metacognitive abilities.

Schraw (1998) reports three divisions of knowledge of cognition: declarative, procedural, and conditional knowledge. It is important for teachers in a writing context to understand this distinction because depending on what we want writers to focus on will determine the type of metacognitive focus in the classroom. Declarative knowledge refers to "knowing 'about' things" (Schraw, 1998, p. 114). Writers who demonstrate a high degree of declarative knowledge are aware of themselves as writers and what influences their performance. This type of metacognitive awareness would be demonstrated in a writer consciously preparing the writing environment prior to sitting down to write — for example, knowing that you prefer to write using a word processor or a pen/pencil and paper, what time during the day you work best as a writer, where you like to sit, and whether you like to have music playing as you work. Each of these activities demonstrates declarative knowledge.

Procedural knowledge is defined as "knowing 'how' to do things"

(Schraw, 1998, p. 114). Writers who demonstrate procedural knowledge know how to begin writing. They are aware of what strategies work best for them to begin generating ideas, they know how to edit their work, they know how to solicit input and feedback from their peers.

Conditional knowledge refers to "knowing the 'why' and 'when' aspects of cognition" (Schraw, 1998, p. 114). This is important because the writer knows when to change strategies and adjust to the different learning environments or stimuli.

Cognitive skills often operate at an unconscious level. We are unaware of what is happening as we perform a task. Automaticity is key to many cognitive tasks. Metacognition, on the other hand, requires a consciousness of what is happening as we perform a task. This difference between unconsciousness and consciousness relates to the unattended versus attended processing referred to earlier.

Sternberg points out the delicate balance between automaticity in strategy use and being metacognitively aware of strategy use. I have pointed out elsewhere (Anderson, 1994) that when an ability is highly automated, awareness of what one is doing is extremely difficult. A professional sports player may not be the best teacher of that sport. The tennis professional may not be aware at all of how far apart her feet are when she serves the ball. She may not be aware of the angle of her arm or how she grips the racket. These skills have all become highly automated in the development of her ability to play tennis. Good writers are often unaware of what they do as they work their way through a writing task.

Sternberg states that "although metacognitive activities may be quite useful in many aspects of... learning, they are not necessarily always called for. Students need to learn to automatize, which means, in practice, learning to bypass certain conscious metacognitive activity" (p. 129). Before automaticity is developed, metacognitive awareness of what one is doing can facilitate the use of the cognitive ability. Metacognitive awareness can accelerate the learning of a skill and move the writer closer to automaticity in accomplishing the skill.

Let me share how I "discovered" the principle of automaticity. As a graduate student at the University of Texas at Austin, I often drove my car to school. One beautiful fall afternoon I left campus to drive home. It was late in the afternoon, about 6:00 p.m. The sky was a crystal clear blue. I listened to the radio and enjoyed the drive home. My mind wandered as I thought about the beauties of the day and about the tasks I was working on.

As I drove into the driveway of my home and shut off the car, I sat in amazement. I was almost overcome with a sense of fear. I didn't remember crossing the bridge. I didn't remember stopping at any red lights. I didn't remember taking the exit from the freeway. I didn't remember turning on my blinkers, although I am confident that I did because it was my habit to do so. What if every other driver on the road that afternoon had had the same experience I had? Isn't this a bit dangerous?

I didn't give the matter additional thought as I entered my home and put the day of university studies behind me.

The next morning I left early to teach my 8:00 a.m. writing course. As I left the house it was raining. I jumped into the car and got it started. I turned on the windshield wipers and nothing happened! What? No wipers? How am I going to drive to campus without wipers? I realized that I would be late for class if I didn't just get started.

I backed out of the driveway. Before I had even made it to the first corner, I had to shut off the radio. (It was still on from the pleasant drive home the previous afternoon.) As I turned each corner, I was very much aware of turning on my blinkers. My speed was very slow as other cars whizzed by me in the rain. I realized that if I sat very low in the seat I had a bit of visibility directly under the edge of the windshield wiper. I also rolled down the window in order to see the white lines of my lane on the highway pavement.

There I sat, driving very slowly on the interstate, getting drenched from the rain, sitting low in my seat trying to navigate my way to campus. I remember passing several dead armadillos. I remember being very much aware of the weight of my foot on the accelerator. When I arrived at the campus parking lot, I was exhausted!

After I taught my class, I began to reflect on these two driving experiences and the connection of automaticity became very clear to me.

When conditions are proper, with no interference, we sail along with perfect comfort, not thinking about what we are doing. Automaticity takes control of the "regular" events we complete. When conditions become less than favorable, we suddenly become very conscious of what we are doing. I wouldn't have been able to tell you what I did the afternoon I drove home under perfect conditions. But if you were to ask me what I did the morning of the rainstorm, driving with no windshield wipers, I would have been able to tell you everything I did and give great detail about every inch of highway between my home and the university.

Cognitive skills are the automatic processes that we use when we are learning. This level of thinking is unconscious. When we incorporate a metacognitive component to learning we force our learners to be aware of what they are doing. We make their learning visible. Writers should be encouraged to monitor their automatic processes so they can reflect on what they are thinking and doing.

Smith (1990) highlights the importance of thinking by pulling together a list of 77 verbs that are related to thinking. Table 2 lists these 77.

Table 2. Seventy-seven Verbs Related to Thinking

analyze	deduce	intend	reason
anticipate	deem	introspect	recall
apprehend	deliberate	invent	reflect
argue	determine	judge	remember
assert	devise	know	review
assume	discover	meditate	revise
attend	divine	muse	ruminate
believe	emphasize	opine	schematize
calculate	estimate	organize	scheme
categorize	examine	plan	speculate
classify	expect	plot	suggest
cogitate	explain	ponder	suppose
comprehend	fabricate	postulate	suspect
conceive	fantasize	predict	systematize
concentrate	foresee	premeditate	theorize
conceptualize	guess	presume	understand
conjecture	hypothesize	presuppose	wonder
consider	imagine	project	
contemplate	induce	propose	
create	infer	rationalize	

Source: Smith, 1990, pp. 1-2.

This list highlights the variety of verbs we use in English to refer to cognitive processes. Each of these terms refers to an aspect of cognition. Smith (1990) indicates that these words describe the "activities of people, not of their brains…. The language of thinking is not about brains, but about people" (p. 2, 4). Smith continues to emphasize the importance of thinking as it relates to writers being engaged in activities. He states that "thinking is a presupposition of reading [and] writing" (p. 4).

Smith (1990) does not share the belief that metacognition can facilitate learning. He states:

> Monitoring, reviewing, reflecting, and revising are regarded as "meta-cognitive" skills, involving thinking about thinking, which is regarded as a higher kind of thinking than thinking about anything else. "Observing" and "controlling" one's own thought processes are supposed to be different and

superior modes of thinking, not practiced by many people because they have not learned how. But once again these are all fictitious and prejudicial concepts, favored by people with vested interests in finding ways of categorizing individuals — usually school-children — in discriminatory ways. No one needs to learn how to think about the consequences of their own thought, although we all have differing propensities to become analytical (and self-critical) in particular circumstances.

Besides, we cannot observe our own thought processes. We are not aware of them, and they cannot be inspected in oneself or in anyone else. They are obscured in a world of neurological and chemical flux which no one can read or translate. What we are aware of when we listen to the inner voice of introspection is a product of our own thought — and no one is deaf to that voice.

How could "thinking about thinking" be different from thinking about anything else? We usually know when we do not understand something, or when we have solved a problem, at least to our own satisfaction. If we do not know these things on a particular occasion, it is not because we lack certain skills; we just do not understand sufficiently what we are trying to do (or we are not paying enough attention, which is a matter of our disposition in particular circumstance, rather than lack of a special skill). (p. 26)

I see two interesting arguments that Smith presents against the concept of metacognition: (1) that because we cannot observe our cognitive processes metacognition is not possible, and (2) that we know when we don't understand and we do something about it. My role as a classroom teacher and as a teacher educator has provided experiences that cause me to disagree with Smith. First, as I get learners to become more metacognitively aware of what they are doing and why, they begin to "observe" what before was unobservable to them. Getting the learners to focus on what is happening behind and underneath their thinking allows them to observe what they do. Also, some poor learners do not stop and repair their learning when they do not understand. They do not monitor their learning and stop to fix it when they are faced with challenges. Smith's work highlights the wide variety of words and terms that we use to describe the cognitive processes that are used on a daily basis. My belief is that thinking about our thinking is a different kind of thinking. It takes writers into a different realm of thinking. Writers become conscious of what are often unconscious processes. They recognize that they need to utilize a particular set of strategies in order to satisfactorily complete a writing task. Thinking about thinking moves writers to a new level of thinking. They are now moving to a level of learning how to learn.

THE ROLE OF METACOGNITION IN LEARNING HOW TO LEARN

Caine and Caine (1991) point out that reflection on learning is not a simple process. They divide reflection into three main types: reflection on feedback from others, reflection without assistance, and personal awareness of deep meanings. Reflection on feedback from others allows a learner to compare what she is doing against what others do. Caine and Caine suggest that guided modeling and approximation play an essential role in this area of reflective learning. This is particularly important for novice writers who need to learn how to write or improve their writing. A model provided by the teacher and/or other student writers plays an important role in reflective learning. Reflection without assistance requires a greater self-awareness and the ability to self-correct. Caine and Caine indicate that this reflective ability is "an invaluable tool for teachers or teacher trainees to use in their interactions with students" (p. 160). This type of reflection requires an ability to step back and view your own actions and then make appropriate changes. Think-aloud protocols can be used as a pedagogical tool to teach writers this type of reflective learning. Think-aloud protocols will be discussed in detail in the next section of this chapter. Personal awareness of deep meanings is the third type of reflection identified by Caine and Caine. Reflection in this category suggests that we can identify the deep meanings that influence the ways we respond and change as people. Being aware of how we are utilizing our strengths and weaknesses as writers can help us to improve our writing.

Chamot, Barnhardt, El-Dinary, and Robbins (1999) emphasize the central role that metacognition plays in learning. They state that

> the goal of learning strategies instruction is to assist students in developing awareness of their own metacognition and thus control of their own learning. Learners who are aware of their own learning processes, strategies, and performances are able to regulate their learning endeavors to meet their own goals. In other words, they become increasingly independent and self-regulated learners. (pp. 2-3)

Helping writers become independent learners who can monitor and regulate their writing is a role that teachers can play in the classroom. Through the development of metacognitive practices in the writing classroom, teachers can move writers to be more independent.

The development of metacognitive skills appears to transfer from one area of learning to others. This is a key aspect of learning how to learn.

Schraw (1998) points out that "cognitive skills tend to be encapsulated within domains or subject areas, whereas metacognitive skills span multiple domains, even when those domains have little in common" (p. 116). However, it is important to point out that explicit instruction of metacognitive skills is essential for transfer to occur. Goodrich Andrade and Perkins (1998) point out that "knowledge and skills are inert, meaning that students possess them but do not think to use them unless they are explicitly instructed to do so" (p. 86). The transfer of metacognitive skills is an important point for teachers to be aware of because these skills that can be taught in the classroom go far beyond the subject-specific cognitive skills that are taught. The classroom teacher who focuses on integrating metacognitive and cognitive skills will teach learners far more than content-specific knowledge. Schraw encourages teachers to focus on the development of general cognitive skills through increased metacognitive awareness. He argues that with the development of metacognitive awareness, rather than subject-specific knowledge, teachers can help learners improve their own learning.

What is important for writing teachers to keep in mind is that assisting writers to control their learning is a valuable pedagogical activity. This control is developed through "regulation of cognition" (Schraw, 1998, p. 114). The regulation of cognition is learned through development of one's metacognitive skills. Refer back to Figure 1. Preparing and planning, teaching when to use strategies, monitoring strategy use, teaching how to orchestrate strategy use, and evaluating strategy use are all regulatory skills which writing teachers can teach students and thus assist them in the development of their metacognitive skills.

THE TEACHER'S ROLE IN DEVELOPING METACOGNITION IN WRITERS

For some writers, writing is intimidating. Metacognitive skills can be taught to writers that can result in increased performance and result in the writer's being less intimidated. In the context of writing, students may have excellent knowledge of the mechanics of writing (i.e., spelling, punctuation, formatting of a paper) and yet lack the ability to write a message which accomplishes its purpose. The teacher's role can consist of creating a classroom culture of thinking and using metacognitive skills to improve learning. Sitko (1998) states that "metacognitive instruction is a natural environment for active learning in writing" (p. 113).

Teachers, both at the preservice and inservice levels, need to be shown how to integrate the teaching of metacognitive awareness into the writing curriculum. Sternberg and Spear-Swerling (1996) provide ten principles and seven pitfalls in the teaching of thinking. Table 3 lists the ten principles. Table 4 lists the seven pitfalls.

Table 3. Ten Principles in the Teaching of Thinking

1.	In the everyday world, the first and sometimes most difficult step in problem solving is the recognition that a problem exists.
2.	In everyday problem solving, it is often harder to figure out just what the problem is than to figure out how to solve it.
3.	Everyday problems tend to be ill structured.
4.	In everyday problem solving, it is not usually clear just what information will be needed to solve a given problem, nor is it always clear where the requisite information can be found.
5.	The solutions to everyday problems depend on and interact with the contexts in which the problems are presented.
6.	Everyday problems generally have no one right solution, and even the criteria for what constitutes a best solution are often not clear.
7.	The solutions of everyday problems depend at least as much on informal as on formal knowledge.
8.	Solutions to important everyday problems have consequences that matter.
9.	Everyday problem solving often occurs in groups.
10.	Everyday problems can be complicated, messy, and stubbornly persistent.

Source: Sternberg and Spear-Swerling, 1996, pp. 103-112.

Table 4. Seven Pitfalls in the Teaching of Thinking

1.	The teacher is the teacher and the student is the learner.
2.	Thinking is the students' job and only the students' job.
3.	The most important thing is to decide on the correct program.
4.	What really counts is the right answer.
5.	The solutions to everyday problems depend on and interact with the contexts in which the problems are presented.
6.	Mastery-learning principles can be applied to learning to think, just as they can be applied to anything else.
7.	The job of a course in thinking is to teach thinking.

Source: Sternberg and Spear-Swerling, 1996, pp. 113-121.

These principles and pitfalls can be points of focus for classroom teachers. Using these ideas during the development of writing course goals and instructional objectives will make learners more metacognitively aware of how to implement the principles and overcome the pitfalls. Notice the first principle Sternberg and Spear-Swerling (1996) list: In the everyday world, the first and sometimes most difficult step in problem solving is the recognition that a problem exists. Think back to Smith's (1990) argument that learners know when they don't understand. Sternberg and Spear-Swerling suggest here that the recognition may not be as obvious as Smith leads us to believe. Notice pitfall 4: What really counts is the right answer. Teachers can facilitate learning by helping learners move beyond looking for right answers to examining appropriate strategies for arriving at answers.

Schraw (1998) suggests four ways to increase metacognition in the classroom: promoting general awareness of metacognition, improving knowledge of cognition, improving regulation of cognition, and fostering environments that promote metacognitive awareness. Related to the area of promoting general awareness of metacognition, he suggests that teachers model the processes they use as they accomplish certain tasks. The more that we as teachers move beyond teaching the cognitive skills of writing and instead highlight the processes of writing, the more aware our students will be of how to use metacognitive strategies in their own writing. Also, he emphasizes that teachers should allocate class time to discuss metacognitive strategies in spite of the demands of an exacting curricula. The time spent in the development of metacognitive skills will help to develop stronger learners who are better prepared to monitor their own learning.

Improving knowledge of cognition is a second way that Schraw suggests that teachers can increase metacognition in the classroom. He provides a strategy evaluation matrix (SEM) that teachers can use to improve student knowledge of cognition. Table 5 (on the following page) contains a strategy evaluation matrix from Schraw, which I have adapted for the context of integrated reading/writing. The matrix includes information on five metacognitive strategies. We are provided with the strategy, information on how to use it, when to use it, and what to use it for. Teachers can improve knowledge of cognition by developing student metacognitive awareness with instruments like the SEM. Planned, regular instruction on different cognitive strategies is an important feature of this model.

A third suggestion by Schraw (1998) for increasing metacognition in the classroom is to improve the regulation of cognition. He suggests the use of what he calls a regulatory checklist (RC). Table 6 (on the following page)

Table 5. A Strategy Evaluation Matrix

Strategy	How to Use	When to Use	Why to Use
Skim	Search for headings, highlighted words, summaries.	Prior to reading an extended text.	Provides conceptual overview, helps to focus one's attention.
Slow down	Stop, read, and think about information.	When information seems especially important.	Enhances focus of one's attention.
Activate prior knowledge	Pause and think about what you already know. Ask what you don't know.	Prior to reading or an unfamiliar task.	Makes new information easier to learn and remember.
Mental integration	Relate main ideas. Use these to construct a theme or conclusion.	When learning complex information or a deeper understanding is needed.	Reduces memory load. Promotes deeper level of understanding.
Diagrams	Identify main ideas, connect them, list supporting details under main ideas, connect supporting details.	When there is a lot of interrelated factual information.	Helps identify main ideas, organize them into categories. Reduces memory load.

Source: Schraw, 1998, p. 120.

Table 6. A Regulatory Checklist

Planning

1.   What is the nature of the task?

2.   What is my goal?

3.   What kind of information and strategies do I need?

4.   How much time and resources will I need?

Monitoring

1.   Do I have a clear understanding of what I am doing?

2.   Does the task make sense?

3.   Am I reaching my goals?

4.   Do I need to make changes?

Evaluating

1.   Have I reached my goal?

2.   What worked?

3.   What didn't work?

4.   Would I do things differently next time?

Source: Schraw, 1998, p. 121.

gives an example of a regulatory checklist. Three main categories comprise the checklist: planning, monitoring, and evaluating. Schraw reports research by King that concludes that "explicit prompts in the form of checklists help students to be more strategic and systematic when solving problems" (p. 121).

A final suggestion from Schraw (1998) for how to increase metacognition in the classroom is to foster conducive environments. Teachers should establish an environment where learners are focusing not only on mastery of the material but on performance and how student performance can lead to increased competence. This type of learning environment provides an atmosphere for development of a wider range of strategies, encouragement to use the strategies, and acquisition of greater metacognitive knowledge.

THINK-ALOUD PROTOCOLS

Think-aloud protocols are frequently used to assist in the development of metacogntive awareness in learners. A think-aloud protocol is produced when one verbalizes his or her thought processes while completing a task or immediately after having completed a task (Ericsson & Simon, 1984; Olson et al., 1984). Think-aloud protocols have been used primarily as a research tool. Very few classroom teachers use them as a pedagogical tool, yet they work extremely well in explicitly addressing the role of metacognitive strategy awareness in the classroom.

Think-aloud protocols can be divided into three sub-categories: self-report, self-observation, and self-revelation. Self-report is a generalized statement about one's own typical behavior. Self-observation requires that the specific processes used to accomplish a particular task be reported simultaneously or within a very short period of time (introspection) or through probing for information soon after completing the task (retrospection). Self-revelation is a disclosure of thought processes in a stream of consciousness while the information is in the focus of the learner's attention. Self-revelation data are basically unedited and unanalyzed; by contrast, this suggests that self-observation might be at least partially analyzed or subject to a bit of reflection.

The use of think-aloud protocols is not without criticism. Tomlinson (1984) advises researchers to be aware when retrospective protocols are gathered, because subjects may rely on their background knowledge and opinions of a topic to fill in void areas where they cannot remember what they were actually thinking. Tomlinson also points out that sometimes subjects forget that their task is to report on the mental process they have used to complete a task and not interpret or explain what they have done.

Dobrin (1986) poses four objections to think-aloud protocols. First, he is concerned with possible methodological flaws, such as those mentioned above. Second, inferences are made from protocol analyses about whole processes. These inferences are made from traces of mental processes. Dobrin contends that reports do not show that the traces are large enough to make inferences about the mental processes that occur. Third, there is no mechanism to determine whether a trace is relevant to the actual process being described. Finally, Dobrin concludes that the studies that have used protocols have not provided enough information that common sense does not already offer.

Afflerbach (1986) advises that think-aloud protocols may not give helpful information if the process under investigation is automatic. "Automatic processes bypass working memory, and hence are not available for verbal reports" (p. 1). When the strategies or steps followed in a process have become automatic, we no longer think about what we are doing; we simply do the task.

Evans (2000) states that he is "sceptical of the value of introspective reporting, but sympathetic to use of verbal protocol analysis" (p. 4). He cautions against asking people to rely on their memories or to interpret the processes they have used while engaged in a task. He encourages the use of think-aloud protocols. "Here, the participant is not asked to remember, report, describe, or interpret anything but merely to externalize explicit thought by verbalizing it. Protocol analysis is particularly useful for discovering the locus of attention, the goals that people are following, and the order in which subprocesses are applied" (Evans, 2000, p. 5). He states that it is the responsibility of the researcher, not the participant, to make sense of the protocols and identify the strategies that have been used.

In spite of any weaknesses, the use of think-aloud protocols provides valuable insight into a rich source of data that is inaccessible to observation and would otherwise be lost. Ericsson and Simon (1980) emphasize that

> for more than half a century ... the verbal reports of human subjects have been thought suspect as a source of evidence about cognitive process.... . [Yet] verbal reports elicited with care and interpreted with full understanding of the circumstances under which they are obtained, are a valuable and thoroughly reliable source of information about cognitive process.... . They describe human behavior that is as readily interpreted as any other human behavior. (p. 247)

USING THINK-ALOUD PROTOCOLS IN THE WRITING CLASSROOM

Goodrich Andrade and Perkins (1998) encourage creating a culture of thinking in a classroom [by] providing models or examples of good thinking, clear explanations of how, when and why to think well, interactions with other people and class assignments that require good thinking, and informative feedback about students' thinking and how it can be improved. (p. 90)

With this input from Goodrich Andrade and Perkins (1998) and the criticisms of think-aloud protocols mentioned above in mind, the following eleven steps can be implemented by writing teachers for incorporating think-aloud protocols in the writing classroom and creating a culture of thinking.

1) The teacher provides a demonstration of how to think aloud while engaged in a writing task. The demonstration should be as natural as possible so that the students see how you as a writer regulate your thinking. Keep in mind that you do want to try to weave in examples of planning, using, monitoring, orchestrating, and evaluating your work.

2) For the demonstration, create a handout divided into five sections: Planning, Using, Monitoring, Orchestrating, and Evaluating. Ask students to make notes about what strategies they see you using during the demonstration.

3) At the conclusion of the demonstration, allow the student writers to ask you questions about the regulation of your cognition. This is best done by telling the students prior to beginning the demonstration that you want them to be watching how you regulate your cognition.

4) Provide additional demonstrations as needed. One demonstration is often not sufficient to allow learners to see exactly what you want them to do.

5) Group students into pairs and ask them to work together and provide opportunities for each to regulate their cognition. One student will write while the other watches and listens to the think-aloud protocol. Then students who have acted as listeners should be given an opportunity to ask questions before switching roles.

6) While the students are in pairs, vary the activity from a focus on articulation of writing strategies to a focus on interpretation of what has been written. Sitko (1998) suggests that a partner read aloud what has been written by another student, "stopping periodically to summarize the point and make a prediction about what is likely to come next" (p. 107).

This allows the writer to verify that his/her purposes are being met in what he/she is writing.

7) A "think-aloud round robin" activity could then be conducted. Have students write silently for a few minutes with the understanding that after 3-5 minutes you will invite each to share writing strategies he/she has used.

8) A "hot seat" writing activity can be conducted. Select a student to write in front of the entire class and share what strategies she/he is using. The handout used during the teacher demonstration can be used for the "hot seat" activity also.

9) Ask the students to engage in monitoring their cognition during a writing homework assignment. Several adjustments for the homework assignment can be made. Students could divide their writing time into blocks of 10-15 minutes. One possibility would be to provide the writers with a checklist of writing strategies to check off after writing for a period of time.

10) Another possibility is to provide the students with a handout divided into three sections: planning, monitoring, and evaluating, and to record what strategies they have used during the time block. Either of these activities could easily be accomplished during homework writing assignments and help writers transfer the use of these metacognitive strategies to their personal writing settings. Table 7 provides an example of a strategies monitoring worksheet.

11) Engage writers in metacognitive activities during a writing conference. The teacher can ask metacognitive questions during the conference to get student writers to articulate strategies that they have used during planning, monitoring, and evaluating their work.

These eleven steps can be used in a variety of ways to effectively use think-aloud protocols as a pedagogical tool. The use of think-aloud protocols does not need to be time consuming. Engaging writers in a short reflective activity and sharing of strategies need not take more than 4-5 minutes of instructional time per class period. Once learners have become familiar with the purpose and format of think-aloud protocols, they are able to interact with each other in positive ways to reflect on and improve their writing skills.

Table 7. Strategies Monitoring Worksheet

Planning — Appropriate questions

1. Who is my audience?
2. Why am I writing this?
3. What do I already know?
4. How can I organize my ideas?
5. How will I know if I have achieved my goal for writing this piece?

Using — Appropriate questions

1. Whate strategies am I using to make this writing task easier?
2. Why am I using this strategy/these strategies?

Monitoring — Appropriate questions

1. Are the writing strategies I'm using helping me?
2. Are there other strategies that I could be using?

Orchestrating — Appropriate questions

1. What strategies am I combining to accomplish my task?
2. Should any one of them be changed to better orchestrate their use?

Evaluating — Appropriate questions

1. Are there additional ideas I need to add?
2. Do I need to delete something?
3. Are there grammar, spelling, or punctuation issues I need to take care of?
4. Will my audience understand?
5. Did I accomplish my purpose?

Source: The author

CONCLUSIONS

The teaching of metacognitive skills may be the most valuable use of instructional time for a writing teacher. When writers engage in reflecting upon their writing strategies, they become better prepared to make conscious decisions about what they can do to improve their writing. Strong metacognitive skills empower a writer. The empowerment results not only in improved writing but also improved learning that will transfer to other aspects of the writer's life.

References

Afflerbach, P. (1986). Outstanding dissertation monograph 1986: The influence of prior knowledge on expert readers' main idea construction processes. Newark, DE: International Reading Association.

Anderson, N. J. (1994). Developing ACTIVE readers: A pedagogical framework for the second language reading class. System, 22, 177-194.

Caine, R. N., & Caine, G. (1991). Making connections: Teaching and the human brain. New York: Addison-Wesley.

Chamot, A. U., Barnhardt, S., El-Dinary, P. B., & Robbins, J. (1999). The learning strategies handbook. White Plains, NY: Longman.

Englert, C. S., Raphael, T. E., Anderson, L. M., Anthony, H. M. & Stevens, D. D. (1991). Making strategies and self-talk visible: Writing instruction in regular and special education classrooms. American Educational Research Journal, 28, 337-372.

Ericsson, K. A., & Simon, H. A. (1980). Verbal reports as data. Psychological Review, 87, 215-251.

Evans, J. St. B. T. (2000). What could and could not be a strategy in reasoning. In W. Schaeken, G. De Vooght, A. Vandierendonck, & G. d'Ydewalle (Eds.), Deductive reasoning and strategies (pp. 1-22). Mahwah, NJ: Erlbaum.

Goodrich Andrade, H. G., & Perkins, D. N. (1998). Learnable intelligence and intelligent learning. In R. J. Sternberg & W. M. Williams (Eds.), Intelligence, instruction, and assessment. Mahwah, NJ: Erlbaum.

Olson, G. M., Duffy, S. A., & Mack, R. L. (1984). Thinking-out-loud as a method for studying real-time comprehension processes. In D. E. Kieras & M. A. Just (Eds.), New methods in reading comprehension research (pp. 253-286). Hillsdale, NJ: Erlbaum.

Prakasha, S. (1999, March 19). Market Games. Washington, D.C.: National Public Radio.

Schraw, G. (1998). Promoting general metacognitive awareness. Instructional Science, 26, 113-125.

Schriver, K. (1993). Revising for readers: Audience awareness in the writing classroom. In M. Penrose & B. M. Sitko (Eds.), Hearing ourselves think (pp. 147-169). New York: Oxford University Press.

Sitko, B. M. (1998). Know how to write: Metacognition and writing instruction. In D. J. Hacker, J. Dunlosky, & A. C. Graesser (Eds.), Metacognition in educational theory and practice (pp. 93-115). Mahwah, NJ: Erlbaum.

Smith, F. (1990). To think. New York: Teacher's College Press.

Sternberg, R. J. (1998). Metacognition, abilities, and developing expertise: What makes an expert student? Instructional Science, 26, 127-140.

Sternberg, R. J., & Spear-Swerling, L. (1996). Teaching for thinking. Washington, D. C.: American Psychological Association.

Tomlinson, B. (1984). Talking about the composing process: The limitations of retrospective accounts. Written Communication, 1, 429-445.

Whimbey, A. (1976). Intelligence can be taught. New York: Bantam.

Zimmerman, B. J., & Bandura, A. (1994). Impact of self-regulatory influences on writing course attainment. American Educational Research Journal, 31, 845-862.

Vulnerable Writers at Work

Julie Jung
Illinois State University

In "Sideshadowing Teacher Response," Nancy Welch (1998) challenges a fundamental assumption in composition classes, namely, that "the student is the writer, the teacher is the reader; the student composes, and the teacher comments" (p. 375). Instead, she argues, writing teachers need to find ways to situate their comments within an ongoing conversation, one that begins long before drafts are handed in for teacher comment. More specifically, Welch contrasts the function of teacher comments that foreshadow versus those that sideshadow. According to Welch, foreshadowing comments, due to their institutional weight, announce an inevitable future that the teacher has seen and the student has yet to glimpse. As such, these kinds of comments, while meeting the "human desire for a knowable future" (p. 383), limit the possible futures of a given draft.

For Welch, the challenge of positioning the teacher's voice as one among many thus necessitates a different narrative device, one that, unlike foreshadowing, redirects our attention away from a "predetermined future" (p. 377) and toward "the present moments, its multiple conflicts, its multiple possibilities" (p. 377). Drawing on the narrative theory of Gary Morson, Welch explains how, within the context of a composition class, sideshadowing "can multiply the stories we tell about a draft, what its reality is, what its future might be, by calling on students to initiate, to extend, a marginal conversation with their writing" (p. 377). Such an approach "disrupts the pattern of student-composes-and-teacher-comments" and "draws students into considering the competing discourses, cultural norms, conflicting intentions, and textual ideals that shape and unshape a draft" (p. 377). For Welch, sideshadowing is not limited to choosing one possible future over another; rather, it involves resisting "foreshadowing and its working to excise surplus long enough to take that surplus into fuller account" (p. 383).

Thus, in Welch's courses, students learn strategies for writing back to their own drafts in ways that encourage them to confront the competing realities that exist within them. Instead of writing margin commentary that influences students to follow a given trajectory, one that she has defined as being particularly important, Welch invites her students to stay with and explore the possibilities of the current draft by writing comments back to themselves. Her job, then, becomes one of reading these comments and using them as springboards for her own, of offering comments that refrain from identifying the one pursuable "good idea" but instead consider the implications of the ideas that challenge it, the very ideas that would, in fact, be cut if revision were defined as a process of deleting extraneous surplus for the sake of a coherent future.

Like Welch, I am interested in developing strategies that work against (re)readings that silence possible alternatives in the name of coherence or inevitability. In this essay, I explain the underlying assumptions that informed my teaching of a first-year writing course designed to help students stay with their drafts long enough to hear and learn from their multiple and uncertain realities. Specifically, I discuss the advantages of practicing a revisionary rhetoric, one committed to stepping back and granting fuller listening to possible alternatives, in a writing classroom where uncertainty and contradiction are viewed as opportunities for inquiry rather than as weaknesses to be cut. I describe ways teachers and students can engage in rigorous self-reflection that fosters connection with other writers as well as themselves. Such self-reflections, I hope to show, enable writers to speak back to texts in ways that invite those texts' authors to respond in turn. Through an ongoing process of acknowledging their partial world views, of making themselves vulnerable through the revelation of limitation, revisionary rhetors embrace disconnection, and in so doing, open the door to increased intimacy and understanding.

BACKGROUND AND CONTEXT

At the University of Arizona, English 102 is a second-semester writing course that most students take in their first year. While English 101 introduces students to rhetorical analysis, research and documentation, and argumentation, English 102 continues to develop these skills as students closely read and respond to a variety of texts. In spring 1997, I had the opportunity to teach English 102 after having done extensive research on the reading/writing connection, and I wanted very much to create a class where the hard work of reading was tied tightly to the challenge of writing responsibly. In designing the syllabus, I wanted to communicate to my students that I believe the reader/writer relationship is healthiest: that is, it permits the most growth for all, when each participant commits to the struggle of keeping the conversation going, when each person works to create a gap out of which the other can respond.

From the beginning — that is, before I had even met my students and was instead involved in the task of designing a workable syllabus — I fore-grounded what I believe to be the relational qualities of a revisionary rheto-ric, where speakers and listeners, writers and readers, are forever bound in a human struggle to communicate, to connect, and to endure conflicts with patience and nonviolence. My syllabus opens with these two epigraphs:

> [This book] operates on the miso-philanthropic assumption that getting along is one devil of a difficult task, but that, in the last analysis, we should all want to get along with people (and do want to).
> –Kenneth Burke, *Attitudes Toward History*, p. i.

> [W]hether one is constructing a self or studying a culture, one must con-front the sheer necessity for acquiring a kind of multi-vocal fluency, an ability to hear things previously shut out or ignored, to attend to matters that might otherwise be overlooked or dismissed as irrelevant, to accept, in effect, the fact that learning to speak in such a way that one gets heard is a lifelong project that involves, perhaps paradoxically, first learning how to listen better to others."
> –Richard Miller, *The Nervous System*, p. 285

Later, under the heading "Course Description," I practice revisionary rhetoric by acknowledging my partial world views, my assumptions, and make myself vulnerable by noting that my assumptions are incomplete and are, in fact, up for grabs:

> English 102 is generally defined as a course in analyzing and writing about a variety of texts (see your *Student's Guide*, p. 98, for a more complete description). In my class, I translate that general definition into the following (incomplete) set of assumptions:
> - reading and writing are recursive processes: You can only write about a text when you've read it well; you must write in order to read well;
> - reading well means reading critically; it means that you don't passively

accept the position of another but rather *that you actively work to discover and analyze hidden assumptions*; reading critically means that you abandon the idea that a published text is "good" because it's published. Instead, I argue that *all* texts — yours, the ones in the anthologies, this syllabus written by me — are a part of a larger, cultural conversation. Our job as readers and writers is to find a way to enter that conversation and contribute to it. Sometimes that "way in" will be disagreement, but not always;

- critical reading is *critical interpretation*. There are no "right" readings in the sense that any text has one, single, universal meaning. There are only *responsible* readings. (More later.);

- you can become better critical readers by learning some theories and practices of critical reading; I will teach them to you and ask you to apply them to every text we read in this class. By "apply" I mean that we'll discuss them in class and you'll use them as you write and revise your essays as well as when you critically read and respond to drafts written by your peers;

- critical readers need critical writers and vice versa. Translated: We need each other in this class. We need to find ways to listen to each other even when (*especially when?*) we disagree. Practicing critical reading can be uncomfortable.

- with my guidance and the support of your classmates, you can handle reading, writing about, and analyzing challenging (difficult!) texts and ideas;

- our culture desperately needs your generation to become better critical readers. (What do you think about this one?)

On the first day of class, I asked students to write down their goals for the course, what they need from me, each other, and themselves in order to achieve those goals, and what they fear most about writing. As they were writing, I took roll and learned their first names. I then read over the syllabus, asking them to edit incorrections with me (I had made one typo and accidentally included the wrong attendance policy). I also read over my assumptions with them, emphasizing their partial nature and encouraging them to help me revise and rethink them over the course of the term. The twenty-four students were largely European-American, between the ages of 18 and 20. One student was Japanese American; one was from South Africa; another was Deaf. Approximately 46 percent were women. Most came from middle-class urban and suburban backgrounds, but they varied widely in their educational and career goals. They had all completed one semester of composition and were enrolled in the required second-semester course.

The structure of the course was as follows: Writing assignments included eighteen response papers to assigned readings (RRs), three major out-of-class essays, with two rough drafts required for each, one midterm essay exam, and one final essay exam. For my purposes, I will focus on the last major essay assignment, the reader-response/self-reflection piece, which I will discuss later in this essay. However, it is important to recognize how the earlier writing assignments led up to the final piece. All of the response papers asked students to "critically read" (a term discussed in class and described below) the assigned text, which could be an anthologized essay, a peer's rough draft, or a classroom situation. In this way, the students applied the same critical reading strategies to all of the texts published for and by the class. Their response papers were thus the written versions of their attempts to read critically.

Classroom activities and assignments were founded on the postmodern assumption that reading is an act of interpretation, an assumption that invites students to surrender their New Critical conditioning and their belief that texts are self-contained wholes. Instead, early in the course, I asked them to claim authority as readers — as interpreters, to participate in the making of meaning rather than uncover it. As Richard Beach (1993) discusses, readers actively participate in the making of meaning by bringing their knowledge of textual conventions to all their readings. They fill in textual gaps — those spaces where a writer leaves things unsaid — based on their past experiences. Furthermore, a reader's psychological, social, and cultural subject positions also influence the ways in which she constructs meaning. Focusing on the cultural context within which reading occurs, Kathleen McCormick (1994) challenges cognitivist theories that describe the reader as an isolated individual. Such theories, she argues, lead to positivistic views of reading and interpretation: Reading becomes a universal process of acquiring a hierarchy of skills, a mental rather than a social process. Furthermore, when students are schooled to think of reading in these terms, they limit themselves to "comprehending" the text's true meaning rather than constructing it. This kind of distinction reflects an objectivist view of knowledge-making, which argues that a text has a "right" interpretation and students need to learn how to uncover it. McCormick's cultural model of reading argues instead that readers negotiate meaning with texts, that they become more critical and active readers when they realize that both texts and their responses to them are culturally constructed. Thus, when students are encouraged to view texts as things that are made rather than revealed, students can better include their voice in the ongoing conversation. According to McCormick, readers are therefore socially constructed but not without agency — they can write back.

And in their writing back, they express a multiplicity of views, a cacophony of voices that blend with, complicate, and enhance textual meaning.

A second and related assumption informing my postmodern writing classroom is that texts are cultural constructions. That is, they are products of specific, cultural contexts rather than timeless, unified wholes. To make this theory accessible to my students, I brought Legos to the second class period and asked three student volunteers to build something. Ted, an engineering major, built a complicated, detailed airplane. Melanie built a piano. And Marie built... what? I couldn't really tell. In front of my students, I picked up her construction and began taking it apart, talking aloud about my confusion and my attempts to make it mean something to me. I asked questions; I began to identify something that looked like a dog; I spoke about my love for dogs. My purpose was to get my students to see that texts — both the ones they read and the ones they write — can and in fact should be taken apart. Rather than view texts as sacred wholes, I wanted them to see how I as the reader of the thing, whatever it was, was actively drawing on my past experiences — and the inevitable biases and assumptions those experiences hold — to my interpretation.

I selected the third Lego construction, the one whose meaning was not readily available to me, because I wanted my students to see that critical reading and writing usually involve work; meaning won't simply "fall out" of the text. More radically, David Kaufer and Gary Waller (1985) argue that writing *is* reading because in a postmodern world, language flows endlessly. To get at this supplemental relationship, I assigned the introductory chapter of *Reading the Lives of Others*, in which David Bartholomae and Anthony Petrosky (1995) adopt a postmodern position, arguing that reading and writing are interactive processes and that the recursivity of these processes is what enables readers to make meaning. More specifically, they argue that readers need to write in order to read well; they need to reread a text through the lens of their own writing, their own risk at interpretation. By engaging in these recursive processes, students realize more fully that all texts, including their own, are cultural constructions: They are made, not born. Furthermore, as Bartholomae and Petrosky show, for students to feel this recursivity, to learn from it, they must be required to read long and complex texts, texts that defy easy summary and unified interpretations. Instead, the authors advocate that teachers assign challenging texts that leave the reader with some hard work to do. The challenge to work to make meaning, to fill in gaps, is what motivates students to read, write, reread, revise. The authors also link responsibility to the challenge of interpretation. That is, by assigning complex texts, teachers can foreground the feasibility of multiple interpretations without having to succumb to relativist, "anything goes" kinds of thinking. Rather, readers are more likely to accept responsibility for their interpretations when they've had to work so hard to build them. It's this kind of reader responsibility, where readers own their interpretations as their own, as well as try to understand how and why they've made them, that I tried to foster in my 102 classroom.

These two postmodern assumptions — that readers produce meaning and that readers ought to be assigned complex tasks that demand intense meaning-making — informed my postmodern reading/writing pedagogy. First, they influenced the kinds of texts I assigned to my students that semester, opting for longer, more complicated pieces — both fiction and nonfiction — than shorter and often anthologized pieces. Early in the course, I explained to my students that I wanted them to read to find a gap out of which to respond. I asked them to continue the cultural conversation by acknowledging the writer's position and then contributing a perspective that somehow enhances and complicates that position. The first half of this task demanded that my students risk interpretations of texts that could be and in fact were read in several, often competing ways. Because "right" readings were not expected, students were instead challenged to own their readings by citing the texts, explaining their interpretations, and situating their responses in relation to themselves as readers. For example, one of my students that term wrote a provocative essay in response to bell hooks' "Seduction and Betrayal." His first draft resorted to name-calling and charges of reverse racism and refused to acknowledge hooks' argument. In conference, we talked about how his strategies weren't doing much to continue the cultural conversation. "How might you respond to her in a way that she might hear?" I asked. In his first revision, this student talked about his experiences as a young white male, the ways in which he is stereotyped in different settings, and how he often feels as if he can't critique the positions of people of color because he fears being called a racist. In this revision, I saw how my student moved from a reactive, judgmental stance to a more vulnerable and situated one; he began to locate his reaction to hooks within a personal and cultural context that helps explain why he felt so strongly that she was wrong. While this student's final version still had a way to go toward recognizing hooks' position, in it he began to realize, through his own struggles with revision, that texts emerge from specific social contexts and that analyzing one or more of those contexts is a legitimate, productive way to contribute to the ongoing conversation.

In defining "critical reading strategies" for my students, I drew heavily on theories of deconstruction, which Sharon Crowley (1990) has defined as a "set of rules for reading" (p. 1), or a process of "[r]eading texts in order to rewrite them" (p. 9). This rewriting results when a text through its writer gives voice "to that which has been systematically silenced" (Crowley, 1990, p. 9), the second, nonpriveleged term in any given binary. In order to identify and interrogate binaries, James Berlin explains, students must first learn to locate key terms and place them in a meaningful context. After these hierarchies are established, students can then examine contradictions that expose the ways in which cultural codes construct the supposedly "natural" relationship between two apparently opposing terms. Furthermore, by analyzing the (dis)connections between the two terms, students can begin to understand the workings of supplementation, wherein first terms rely on their "others" for definition.

I turned to deconstruction for a number of reasons. First, I wanted to teach reading and writing not as binaries but instead as supplemental and therefore interrelated processes. I wanted to show my students how critically writing demands critical reading and vice versa. Furthermore, as Kaufer and Waller (1985) argue, teaching students deconstructive reading strategies enhances students' abilities to revise meaningfully. As the authors explain, students often see texts, including their own drafts, as outer shells, words and sentences that capture some finished interior body of knowledge. Accordingly, when asked to revise, they make only surface level changes, assuming the meaning to be already present. However, when teachers show students how everything — from ads to classroom situations to written essays — is a text that can be taken apart, students' notions of what a text is and can be are disrupted, as is their belief that certain texts are "finished" and are, therefore, incapable of being revised. Similarly, the deconstructionist belief that texts are always working with and against themselves fosters an attitude of tentativeness, one where final versions are termed "final" not because they render timeless truths but because they are due. According to McCormick (1994), this tentativeness, this resistance to closure, is necessary in a postmodern writing classroom because it opens texts up to multiple interpretations, making them available to a diverse group of readers. Furthermore, it reaffirms the notion that meaning is not derived solely from texts but is instead a cultural negotiation. And because the negotiation changes with each new reader, texts are always open to future revisions.

Because the goal of deconstructive readings is to expose binaries so that they can be interrogated (Crowley, 1990, p. 17), I began the second day of class by explaining the term *binary* and giving accessible examples, including *man/woman*, *white/black*, and *hearing/deaf*. I explained how binaries are, in fact, hierarchies, with the second term constructed as that which is *not* signified by the first. As such, second terms through the lens of binary formations are always already lacking. This confused some of my students, so I gave the example of the University of Arizona Wildcats basketball team: The men's team is simply called the Wildcats, but the women's team, by virtue of its non-privileged status, must be specially marked and termed the "Lady Wildcats." With this example I was hoping to show how first terms enjoy an invisible privilege; because they are assumed to be the norm, anything that challenges their dominance must be marked as "other." At this point, one student in the class, noting the hearing/deaf binary I had written on the board, asked, "But isn't it true that deaf people are, in fact, nonhearing people?" Before I could answer, John, a Deaf student in class, through the voicing of his sign language interpreter, explained how Deaf people are members of a cultural and linguistic minority group with its own rich history and body of tradition. As such, to identify Deaf people as people who cannot hear focuses attention on a biological absence and ignores the presence of Deaf culture, history, and language — American Sign Language.

After explaining how binaries work, I discussed specific strategies students could use as they critically read the texts of the course. These included reading for key terms (so that binary formations could be established and interrogated), repetitions, absences (what wasn't said in this context that could be considered relevant, and why not?), contradictions, and hidden assumptions. Together as a class, we practiced these reading strategies by applying them to advertisements selected by the students, and then we continued to use these same terms throughout the remainder of the course. For example, during peer review sessions, I reminded students to read for key terms, absences, binary logic, and so forth, thereby reinforcing my belief that all texts benefit from such critical readings, especially when the goal is to open them up to rereadings and revisions.

PRACTICING REVISION: THE PEER REVIEW LETTER

To illustrate how students applied these strategies to the texts they read, I include below some examples of written comments they produced for each other. For peer reviews, I required students to make copies of their rough drafts and distribute them in class for immediate feedback. Then, one student with whom the writer did not work in class took the draft home, read it critically using the strategies discussed in class, and then wrote a letter to the student, giving his or her response to the draft. Before I asked students to peer review for the first time, I reviewed their "goals, needs, and fears" sheet with them, and reminded them of what many of their classmates said they need from each other in order to achieve their goals:

- I need my readers to be extremely critical about my work (both positively and negatively). I thrive on comments or responses about my writing.
- *Real* criticism from peers.
- Criticism, but I don't work well if people tell me I'm doing terrible.
- I need my peers to absolutely tell me the truth. No comments just to be nice.
- I need the truth, no matter what, on my essays.
- I need peers to be constructive with their criticism, not to laugh at my mistakes.
- I need my peers to be blunt and honest, but give me some positive feedback.
- I need my good points to be brought out as well as what I need to change to improve.
- I need patience and gentleness from others.

Reflected in these comments are two competing voices that most writers know well: On the one hand, we want to be told what's working. We need praise, support, and encouragement. But we don't want to be lied to, so we prepare ourselves to hear what's not working. When one of these voices is missing, we question the integrity of the response. For example, when we receive negative comments only, we feel attacked and not fully heard. When all we hear is praise, the kind of "I thought it was really good" response that my students most dreaded, we worry that our writing hasn't been read carefully and that the reader is simply saying what s/he thinks we want to hear. Thus, through the language of their own needs, I discussed with my students how an effective response is one that is both supportive and critical, encouraging and suggestive. We also spent a class period discussing their past experiences with peer reviews, when they worked, when they failed. During this class, many students reiterated their desire for "real" and "honest" feedback from peers.

While in-class peer reviews gave students the opportunity to hear each other's work, the most effective feedback came in the form of the reader's letter to the writer. My students explained to me that it was easier for them to be "real" when they weren't sitting across from the writer and feeling the pressure to be critical without hurting anyone's feelings. The letter form gave readers some distance from the writer, the space to balance their responses in writing. With each draft, writers also included a cover sheet where they stated their purpose, audience, revisions made, revisions-to-be-made, acknowledgments, and three questions for their reader. In their letters, many readers used the questions as springboards for their responses. For example, in response to Marie's question, "how can I include more quotes in my essay?" Helen writes:

> I remember you were talking about your grandfather's death in class last week and you said your dad asked you if you were sitting down. I think that would be a good quote to include and a way to expand on how this experience impacted you. My grandfather died last year and I know how painful it is. Also, I am in a long-distance relationship too and I know that it is difficult to keep it going. As a reader, I would like to hear more about that.[i ii]

In her response, Helen notes the moments, both in class and in the draft, that resonated with her, those moments with which she could connect as a reader and about which she would like to hear more. She uses her own shared personal history both to support Marie — to acknowledge that her feelings are valid — and to suggest ways to improve the draft.

In a more extensive critique, Kelly responds to an analysis essay written by Nina, who explored the ways in which societal influences construct the female protagonist in Margaret Atwood's "The Man from Mars"[iii]. In her supportive opening, Kelly writes, "Overall, your essay is very clear and effective. Your thesis is supported throughout the text with your interpretations and ideas from Atwood's [story]." Kelly then follows up with a series of critical questions that encourage Nina to think through her argument more carefully. For example, Kelly asks, "I see your point that Atwood uses Christine to show how society molds individuals. My question to you is, does society create individuals, or do individuals create society? Or is it both?" Later, in response to Nina's assertion that people, especially women, are unknowingly influenced by society into becoming "uniform, submissive droids," Kelly repeats her earlier questions and writes:

> This is a very powerful statement, and I respect your risking it. It makes the reader think about his or her role in society. However, I'd challenge the

stereotype of all of society being "uniform" and "submissive." We are all different and we have a variety of ideas, styles, etc. to contribute to our society. If society was all "uniform" and "submissive" we would not see the diversity that we see. Where does the standard for the "uniform" come from? Who sets the standard? This is an absence in your essay: the influence that individuals have on society.

In this section of her response, Kelly is actively applying the deconstructive strategy of reading for absences. Following her supportive comments, Kelly restates Nina's major claim, provides a counterargument, and then asks questions to help Nina recognize an absence in her essay. That is, Kelly helps Nina identify and contend with an important binary in her argument — society vs. the individual.

In the second half of her response, Kelly offers specific suggestions for improving the draft, pointing out sections that need clarification as well as grammatical mistakes. She also gives Nina a suggestion for how she might support her interpretations more persuasively:

> I think it would be helpful if you use more of Atwood's text in support of your claim. You use a lot of single words, but I challenge you to use longer quotes. This would provide the opportunity for you to deconstruct her text to understand why Atwood says what she says. This is pretty unclear — I'll explain in class.

Here, in her attempt to offer clear advice to a peer, Kelly comes face-to-face with the messiness of language, the ways in which language slips beyond and away from an author's intent. Just as she seeks ways to help her classmate write a more persuasive argument, Kelly rereads her own words and realizes that their lack of clarity might leave her reader wondering, doubtful. In this passage, Kelly, the reader-turned-writer, has become reader again, experiencing for herself the twists and turns of deconstruction. That is, while she opens her letter by asserting that Nina's draft is "very clear" and well-supported, she ends up in the confusion that contradiction creates. Realizing that her own response inevitably lacks "perfect" clarity, Kelly does the next best thing, saying, in effect, "we'll talk again, later."

In her letter to Michael, Nina adopts a different style of response, moving through the draft paragraph by paragraph, making direct statements about what's working and what needs more. For example, in response to Michael's first paragraph, Nina writes, "Your first paragraph about revision is something interesting. You could almost change the focus of your essay to be about how revision affects your expression." Later, when discussing Michael's third paragraph, Nina writes:

> You open by admitting it is a tangent — not necessarily a good strategy. It shows that you know it is irrelevant, but you don't care enough to do anything about it. Instead, try to incorporate the concept of the reader responses [RRs] into your thesis, or make a transition from revising to RRs that makes it relevant. As I look over this paragraph again, I am realizing that it is also about revision — how you get the opportunity to revise other people's work. This would be very easy to fit in and isn't really a tangent at all — but by setting it up as one, you discredit yourself.

Like Kelly, Nina's efforts to respond to her peer force her to question and revise her original interpretation. Faced with the messiness of a draft-in-progress and the task of writing a coherent, useful response, Nina is required to read and make sense of a difficult and challenging essay, one that defies neat and easy interpretation, much like the essays in Bartholomae and Petrosky's (1995) collection. Like those published essays, their peers' unfinished drafts offered my students the chance to experience the dialectical process of reading to write in order to read again, constructing their own interpretations and claiming responsibility for them in their written letters.

Jasper Neel (1988) claims that students produce antiwriting — the "Three Reasons for Stopping X" papers where writing is a mere shell for thought — in response to their teachers' deconstructive tendencies. That is, according to Neel, students begin by attempting to write Platonically, believing before they start to write that they know certain indisputable truths about certain subjects. However, once they begin to write, their writing constantly exposes their uncertainties (hence the line, "I know what I want to say, but I can't say it"), and they begin to think they don't know enough *for sure* to continue writing. Faced with this dilemma, students turn to psophistic writing, where they "do the best they can to anticipate the arguments against their position, to adapt their own arguments to the audience at hand, and to present a closed and complete a position as possible" (Neel, 1988, p. 86). However, because they know their teachers will read deconstructively, that they will find and expose absences in their binary logic, many students avoid exposure altogether and instead produce antiwriting, thereby ensuring that their teachers have no texts to deconstruct. By playing it safe, these students retain their internal sense of security and avoid the hard struggles of getting messy with language. My students' responses to each other's drafts suggest that one way to encourage students to get messy with language is to give them messy language to make sense of.

THE LIMITATIONS OF TIDY ESSAYS

For over a decade, postmodern scholars in rhetoric and composition have been advocating that writing teachers design new kinds of essay assignments, essays that uphold rather than contradict the epistemologies of our age. In his critique of the field's overly modernist bent, Lester Faigley (1992) contends that, while we value writing *process*, we do so only as a "teleological development" toward some product (p. 14). The remnants of current-traditional rhetoric that tenaciously cling to process-oriented pedagogies support Faigley's claim. Patricia Donahue and Ellen Quandahl (1989), for example, argue that the traditional structure of the first-year student essay — a unified text with a one-sentence thesis — legitimizes "outdated" modern assumptions. That is, in its attempts to manage rather than sustain and explore ambiguity, such a structure "suppresses conflict and encourages the unconscious reproduction of social norms (self-control, for example)" (p. 14). Similarly, Lillian Bridwell-Bowles (1995), in a call for more experimental writing in the academy, argues that old patterns of argument — like the single-point thesis — run counter to social-constructionist epistemologies (p. 45). Poststructuralist ways of thinking about language and knowledge, she contends, have yet to affect the essay form — particularly the argumentative essay — we expect our students to write. Rational, reasoned arguments are viewed as being distinct from and superior to personal writing, texts with nonlinear patterns of organization, writing that contains emotion, writing that closes the gap between subject and object, and writing that does something "with" and not "to" the reader (Bridwell-Bowles, 1995, p. 47).

In a more extensive critique of current-traditional rhetoric, Sharon Crowley (1990) explores historical connections between invention and epistemology, arguing that invention, "the study of all the possible means by which arguments or proofs can be discovered and developed", translates into questions like, "what questions are worth asking?" and "what counts as knowledge (p. 2)?" When teachers rely on current-traditional rhetorics, however, they collapse invention into arrangement, thereby reducing the complex and social process of knowledge-making to a matter of selecting and fleshing out proper forms. For Crowley, this method of teaching writing is decidedly arhetorical, for it locates knowledge-making with the individual mind of a writer and ignores the social situations within which all writers must write. Thus, regardless of the rhetorical situation, students are asked to produce a generically challenged first-year college essay: one that is carefully outlined and written to a general reader (the teacher) on a topic manageable enough to be foreshadowed in a one-sentence thesis statement. For Crowley, current-traditional rhetoric is problematic for two reasons. First, and simply put, "it has very little to do with learning to write" (p. 147). Second, it promotes antiwriting.

Similarly, Jean Donovan Sanborn (1994), in an historical study of the first-year composition essay, argues that its mechanical form, which emerged circa 1900, reflects a scientistic rather than a humanistic rhetoric. More specifically, Sanborn explains how the progressive age of the 1800s ushered in the dual demand that writing be both more scientific and efficient. In such an age, Montaigne's definition of the essay — exploratory, open, conversational, with room for narrative as a way to make argument — was deemed too messy, too associative for the demands of contemporary life, and it was replaced with what Sanborn describes as a linear, hierarchical, and didactic essay. In many contemporary writing college classrooms, she argues, this latter form remains: Students are asked to write texts with one single controlling idea and a definite conclusion. Sanborn contends that as teachers, we've rationalized the absence of Montaigne's essay form in the first-year writing classroom by clinging to two contradictory beliefs: Many of us say that the looser, more associative form is too complicated for our students; others of us claim the opposite: that the form itself is not properly intellectual.

Like Neel (1988) and Crowley (1990), Sanborn explores how essay assignments founded on current-traditional assumptions hinder students' abilities to think and write critically. As she explains, "if the point of the essay is to prove a thesis, [writers] can only choose theses which are provable" (p. 133). Under such conditions, students' opportunities to write in order to discover knowledge are limited, despite teachers' adoption of process-oriented pedagogies. That is, students are less likely to revise their thinking through and in writing if they know their final product must ultimately defend a provable thesis. In addition, Sanborn critiques the didactic essay because it deems linear thinking to be natural and superior to more associative thought, and it blocks the thinking processes of students who do not adopt a linear mode as they write and revise.

Many critics of the traditional first-year essay form are careful to explain that their criticisms are not meant to be taken as a defense for intelligibility. Nor do they dismiss outright the place of more traditional forms in academic contexts. Instead, they argue, there is room for both. In my sixteen-week writing course, two of the three major essay assignments were more traditional, emphasizing clear thesis statements, analysis, and the integration of research.[ii] However, for the final essay of the course, which I titled "Self-Reflection," I designed a more experimental assignment, one that explicitly challenged prevailing notions of what should "count" as an essay in a first-year college composition course (see appendix). It also asked students to view the previous weeks and their experience of them as some of the "texts" of their lives, to reread, reflect on, and integrate those texts in order to yield fuller meaning about who they are as students, writers, and thinkers. My goals for this assignment were twofold. First, I wanted to design an assignment that invited my students to experience writing and revision as processes of getting messy with language. That is, while many of them had been reading their peers' drafts and confronting the challenges and limitations of language from the position of peer reviewer, they had not yet been able to apply those same critical reading strategies to their own writing. My essay assignment positioned the previous weeks of the semester as a draft-in-progress, and it demanded that students reread and get messy with their own life texts as they reflected on them through writing. Second, I wanted to create an essay assignment in which students' final versions enacted a revisionary rhetoric, one where the process of self-reflection creates a space for greater understanding. Rather than ask them to judge their performance in the previous weeks, I invited my students to look upon their texts with curiosity and non-judgmental awareness.

PRACTICING REVISIONARY RHETORIC: THE SELF-REFLECTIVE ESSAY

Michael: "Words Sometimes Have No Meaning"

In his self-reflective essay, Michael identifies an important binary through which he organizes and rereads his semester experiences: speech vs. writing. In his rough draft, he explains that he is "trying to discover why my written work is more effective than when I speak." Both Nina, his peer reviewer quoted earlier, and I read Michael's essay and agreed that its emerging theme dealt with the relationship between writing and revision — how the distance between writer and reader creates a space for revision that is not often possible in speech. Michael pursued this theme in his final version and used both in-class and out-of-class texts to develop it. Keeping to his same purpose, Michael begins his final version with the following:

> These past couple of months have been the most confusing and wonderful times of my life. College has been a personal growth experience for me in more ways than one. I have come to many conclusions about myself that I both fear and admire.

On the one hand, he admires how his writing has grown more confident. He attributes this to his ability to revise ideas in and through writing, to "go back and rethink thoughts." Furthermore, the permanence of writing gives it power, ensuring that there is little chance "to take back something," and its printed form allows writers to "separate themselves out from the reactions of those interpreting their work." While he is proud of his ability to use these qualities of writing to write more effective academic essays, Michael also fears the ways he has used them to hurt others. As he explains:

> In a very personal and powerful letter to my only recently ex-girlfriend, Katie, I managed to cause irreparable damage that would eventually cause our relationship to deteriorate. The beginning of the semester started with an enormous fight. We had a good relationship through the first semester, but for reasons I won't delve into, I wanted "out." In a fit of tears and emotions, I foolishly whipped out a first draft of letter that would ensure the demise of our relationship. I rewrote and rewrote until I was sure she would hate me…. Instead of verbally explaining myself to her the way I felt, I wrote. I wanted to force her to hate me so we would surely break up.

In this passage, Michael reflects on how the qualities of writing that afford it such efficacy can also be applied to achieve purposes about which we are not proud. Using writing to create a permanent record of his separation from Katie, Michael revised carefully to achieve his intended purpose: to end the relationship in a hurtful and insensitive way.

Michael returns to the theme of emotional separation later in his essay, linking his letter to Katie to the peer review letters he wrote to classmates. In both kinds of situation, he explains that we as writers

> evoke emotions in the reader, but at the same time we don't have to deal with the emotions that we stir up. Unless the author is in front of the reader, there can be no interaction between the two. After reading a text, I generally have some sort of reaction … or emotions deep down inside me. The problem is that in most cases I will never get to express these emotions to the author. This was exactly why my letter to Katie was so "effective." The letter was a way of saying

what I wanted to say without immediately having to deal with how she felt. I removed myself from the emotions that were sure to follow.

This passage interests me because in it I see the influence of Michael's shifting identity from that of writer to reader. He begins by repeating his insight that the written word simultaneously stirs a reader's emotions as it creates a safe distance from the reader's response to those emotions. However, in the next two sentences, Michael pivots to the position of reader and describes this distance not in terms of its writerly efficiency but instead as a readerly "problem." That is, while writers benefit from a distance that makes rewriting efficient and purposeful, readers aren't so lucky. They are kept out of the dialogue and are left alone with their emotions, with no writer present to hear them out.

In his final sentences, Michael returns to the position of writer; only now he has empathized with the reader and is able to re-see the limitations of efficiency through the lens of his letter to Katie. By putting "effective" in scare quotes, Michael acknowledges that he understands the irony inherent in his previous use of the term. That is, while his "effective" revision strategies might have enabled him to accomplish his purpose, he realizes that the purpose itself was in need of revision.

Terri: "You Oughta Know"

While Michael's drafting process began with a binary and concluded with a greater understanding of its limitations (is writing really more "effective" than speech?), Terri's process for writing her final essay began in class when I asked my students to bring to class all of the texts they had gathered for the semester and discuss them with a peer. Terri, who had decorated a shoebox and called it her "Spring Box," opens her essay with a scene that describes this class period, during which she shared the texts of her semester with Nina. Most of the box's contents related to Terri's relationship with her boyfriend — love letters, saved plane tickets from her trips to Boston to visit him. In her opening scene, Terri describes her anxiety over sharing these texts with Nina: "I thought she might insult me by saying I was a hopeless romantic and maybe even a little possessed with saving everything that had to do with my boyfriend." The end of the scene shifts in both tone and subject matter when Terri describes the text she shared with Nina, "the last letter clinging to the bottom of the box," a letter from her mother, that she had sent to Terri along with an angel wind chime to hang over her bed to watch over and protect her. Nervous and anxious to hear Nina's reactions, Terri asks,

"'Whatta ya think?'" and tells us that Nina answers: "'Well ...you have a lot of great friends,' she paused and twirled her small silver earring. 'And it's obvious that your mom means a lot to you'."

Nina's comment surprised Terri, who saw herself as hating her mother — an abusive alcoholic whom Terri had "gotten way from" by attending college far from home. Nina's comment helped Terri recognize and contend with an important contradiction in her final essay — that her relationship with her mother has been difficult and even violent at times due to her mother's alcoholism, *but* that her mother means a lot to her. In the body of her essay, Terri enacts this contradiction for her reader by following her opening scene, which paints a picture of a loving and protective mother, with a self-authored poem she wrote in high school. The poem, which is shaped as a bottle, opens with "clink / clink / ice falls / i shudder / i hear the bottle / i hear the poison pour / as she toasts, i wait ... / i wait for her transformation / Jekyll and Hyde after two drinks." The poem continues with descriptions of the mother's alcohol-induced fits of rage, which subside only when she passes out. Terri ends her poem with the lines: "i wait for the next evening to / rear its ugly head. Everyday / routine torture comes too soon."

The majority of Terri's essay is a prose version of her poem. She recounts episodes with her mother and reflects on them by saying that her mother's behaviors, which anger and embarrass her, make her hate her mother and have even fueled physical violence between them. Following a powerful description of one such violent episode, Terri writes: "I came to the University in order to mend the wounds, both physical and emotional, from my mother and hopefully rebuild a stronger relationship with her." This insight creates a tension with earlier claims, in which she says: "I came here [the U of A] to get away from my mother" and "I wanted more than anything to get away from her and everything she represented." In conference with Terri, I noted this tension and said something like, "It's interesting that you want to get away from your mother, and yet you're choosing to write your third essay all about her. Why is that?" In her final version, Terri responds to my question by adding the following passage:

> Sometimes I feel as if *I* am the one who has gone to the twelve-step program. I imagine myself sitting in a modest circle in a claustrophobic, smoke-filled room with recovering alcoholics, acknowledging my mother's alcoholism for her. "Hi, my name is Terri, and *my mother is an alcoholic*." She doesn't admit it, and who knows when she will. I have to do it for her. When I tell people about my mother, I feel as if I'm sharing her experiences for her. I'm the one

who's telling the horrible stories about how I wish she would quit. I'm the one who's accepted my mother's alcoholism. I'm the one who's accepted my mother's alcoholism.

Repeating this sentence, Terri signifies its importance, illustrating the connection between her choice to write about her mother even though she has traveled far from home to avoid her. That is, by telling and retelling stories about her mother, Terri is able to accept the hard truths they reveal: that her mother is an alcoholic, and she hates her for it.

In Terri's final paragraph, she transforms her essay's originating contradiction into an unresolved and sustaining paradox:

> Since I've been at the U of A, nothing has really changed between my mother and me. Not to say that we haven't grown individually, but that we haven't grown together. We still fight. I still loathe her at times. I'm still angry at her for drinking. And I still don't feel like I've gotten far enough away from her .... Nevertheless, *something* caused me to save those letters from her, and *something* causes me to keep in touch with her. I don't *have* to do those things. But I do, because regardless of how little we get along, she still means a lot to me. She means a lot to me *and* we don't get along.

The "something" to which Terri refers, of course, is the mysterious and uneasily defined bond that exists between mother and daughter, even when, or perhaps especially when, that bond is a complex weaving of love, protection, violence, and abuse. While Terri's tone justifiably recognizes that her exploration of that bond is beyond the scope of her essay, it also suggests that such an exploration is both possible and worthwhile.

Nina: "Exploring My Lack of Emotional Expression through Written Expression"

As her title reflects, Nina approached the challenges of the third essay assignment by identifying a common absence in semesterly texts — her "lack" of emotional expression in her essays and in her life. Nina attributes her resistance to expressing her emotions to societal stereotypes about people who do. As she explains early in her essay:

> The problems I have with emotional expression are linked inextricably to the negative perceptions of individuals, and especially independent women. Because society encourages harsh judgment of women who do not conform to

gender standards, my entire emotional identity is disconcerted, and the process of determining a potential solution, including the writing of this essay, has been an arduous task.

In the body of her essay, Nina begins by identifying this absence in a nonacademic scenario with which many college students can relate — her failure to confront an inconsiderate roommate. Rather than voice her anger and frustration, Nina remained an "unemotional iceberg," keeping her emotions locked inside and thereby "effectively eliminating any possibility of sorting out [their] differences." Nina eventually solved the problem by moving out, "almost sneaking away," and leaving behind a "lame" note wishing her roommate a good semester.

Nina then reports that, during that same semester, she began keeping a journal for the first time, a safe place where she could "empty out" her "pent-up frustrations, anger, and sadness." Through the process of writing in her journal, Nina explains that she began to realize how her dark emotions, when left unexpressed, "multiply and become worse." Instead of keeping them bottled up inside, she begins to explore different alternatives: "The main option I explored was becoming completely and totally open with my emotions — letting it all hang out." However, she quickly rejected this option when she realized how "emotional women" are viewed and treated by society, a realization prompted both by personal experience and by a Women's Studies course she was taking at the same time:

> I have worked very hard for as long as I can remember to not submit to the stereotypes of society, so I do not want to fake and portray a constantly happy, optimistic person that I am not. The underlying conflict of my struggle — how to become emotional without becoming either a "feminazi" or a "self-sacrificing maternal figure" — is very difficult.

It was with this awareness and struggle that Nina entered my course. More specifically, Nina reports that she entered the class feeling "animosity" toward society for "putting me, and all women" in the position of having to hide honest emotions, to fit into prescribed "boxes," and this animosity, she explains, is reflected in all the essays she wrote that term. For example, in response to Margaret Atwood's short story "The Man from Mars," Nina titled her first essay "The Brainwashing of Christine," in which she explores how class- and gender-based proscriptions about how young women should behave pressure Christine into enduring a young man's potentially danger-ous attentions without speaking her truth. Reflecting on how she came to this theme, Nina writes in her third essay:

> It is because I am acutely aware of the pressures of society that I am hav-ing so much trouble coming to a solution for my problem with emotional ex-pression. While I want to have a unique emotional identity, I do not want to suffer socially from it. The gender pressures society places on me, which have been briefly addressed in this essay, are likewise addressed in my analysis of Christine. While Christine is not aware of the different societal forces acting on her, including gender pressures, I am, and it complicates things remarkably.

Nina continues linking her personal struggle for emotional authenticity to her semester writing as she reflects on her second essay, a research paper written in response to Camus' *The Stranger*. As Nina explains, "The Prison of Society" deals with "the alienation of an individual who refuses to follow the institutions of society." However, now that theme takes on greater personal relevance, as Nina connects her own life texts to her analysis of Mersault and observes:

> My fear of becoming alienated as Mersault was, as a result of my refusal to conform to society's expectations of emotional expression, is revealed in an in-class writing, in which I state, "in order to remain a part of society, I hide my sadness." This is because society looks down on those who are unhappy, aptly referring to them as downers. Out of fear of being a downer, I hide my feelings, creating a no-win situation. I am unhappy because I let my anger and sadness grow unchecked within and I want to be able to release these emotions, but if I act how I feel, I will be alienated from society. It is a vicious game, and it will not end until I discover a balance that allows me to do both.

Although Nina states that she has not yet found this kind of balance, she does realize that she, like Mersault, is alienated from a society that upholds values to which she refuses to conform. In an attempt both to connect with and distance herself from Mersault, Nina writes:

> Upon rereading my essay I realized that so many things I said about Mer-sault are applicable to my life…. I experience isolation as he did. However, it is difficult for me to discern whether my isolation is self-inflicted as a conse-

quence of trying to avoid society's pressures, or whether it is society-imposed because I don't conform to the expectations of it. Maybe it is both. Because institutions ignore conscious individuals in favor of people who are not aware of their individuality, I am ignored and therefore isolated, but I also continue the isolation because I have little in common with other people, and therefore I do not "open up" to others. Because I do have friends, I am not completely isolated, but I still have experienced the alienation of society because I refuse to become a fake person. But knowing that my alienation is a result if my stubbornness, and is possibly reversible if I lower my personal integrity, has made it very tempting to do so in order to alleviate my loneliness. In this way, I am very different from Mersault. He was indifferent to his isolation.... But a large part of me still wants to, and needs to, have connections to society and the comfort offered in interpersonal relationships.

Nina's struggle to embrace her emotional truth within a society that devalues it becomes obvious in this passage. Her sentence constructions, from "because this" to "but that" to "however this," reflect the ongoing teetering of her intellectual seesaw, with "society's expectations" on the one end and "Nina's emotional authenticity" on the other.

In conference and in her cover sheet, Nina indicated that the paper was very difficult to write because she could not make it cohere. An accomplished student, Nina was used to having her essays come together in a more linear and traditionally clear form. The fact that this paper refused to follow that pattern worried her. In an effort to alleviate those fears and encourage Nina to get messy with her thinking and her expression, I suggested that she write about her difficulties writing, that she give voice to the hard truths of drafting and revising this essay. In response to that suggestion, Nina reiterated how her struggles to express herself emotionally are related to societal values and expectations, which she realizes are complex issues that are difficult to sort out in cause-effect terms. She then goes on to explain:

> I actually had not dealt with these complex issues until I tried to write this paper. By trying to sort out, on paper, the different reasons behind, and hindering, my expression problem, I began to realize how truly complicated the situation was. In my early attempts at writing this, I succeeded in confusing my intentions in writing the paper, my ideas about the subject of expression, and my opinions regarding the different reasons behind my problem. My state of utter bewilderment was at its greatest when my roommate and I (being the

anal-retentive perfectionists we are), trying to decide what I wanted to say and how to say it, proceeded to make a flow chart with arrows linking the topics. Unfortunately, this plan for organizing chaos failed when the chart resulted in a jumble of arrows all pointing at each other. The "never-ending" flow chart we created serves as an important illustration of this essay. It has been (and continues to be) very difficult to write about my problem, because of both my deficiencies in expression and the circular nature of my ideas. The circle is seen, I think, in the format of this paper. It seems to me as if I have been talking in circles around the issue, never really approaching it. On and on, around and around, never coming to the point.

The image of Nina's "never-ending flow chart" delights me, both because it captures her hard work dealing with complex ideas and represents a breakdown in binary thinking. No longer can she simply position social forces on one side and her own self on the other. Instead, through the lens of her chosen third term — emotional expression — Nina confronts the discursive chaos that results when writers let go of perfection and open up to struggle.

Nina concludes her essay by commenting that despite all her reflecting, she has yet to find a "cure-all solution" to her "problem." She knows she wants a balance between herself and society, but she doesn't know how to achieve it. "All I really know," she admits, "is that I need to find some niche so that I can be content with expressing myself ... and still have people look at me and respect what I have to say." She needs to find this niche, she says, in order to avoid ending up like her mother, who, at age 51, is "unable to show her sadness" and "has not yet found her 'balance'." Nina arrives at this insight after describing a recent conversation she had with her mother:

> I became upset and started crying. My mom, not knowing what was wrong, started blaming herself, asking, "What have I done to upset you?" I cowered my head and covered my eyes so my mom couldn't see my deep sadness. "Nothing," I cried back, "you didn't do this to me. Don't blame yourself." My attempt at imparting authority in my cracking voice misfired, and I only sounded desperate. Refusing to hear me, my mom asked, "How have I failed you so greatly? What can I do?" She was so helpless and powerless as she sobbed, placing her forearms over her eyes as if to conceal her humanness. I tried explaining myself, saying, "Listen to me! It's not your fault!" But she still couldn't hear me. We were both crying hysterically, both trying to hide it from each other, and both embarrassed by the outburst.

REFLECTIONS ON REFLECTIONS

Toward the end of her "Sideshadowing" essay, Nancy Welch (1998) describes writing assignments she and her students are imagining in an effort to "dramatize within a draft, including a 'final' draft, the other possible futures, forms, and readings that might have been there, that might still be" (p. 393). As I hope this essay has argued, one such assignment is the experimental essay I have described, one that when situated within the context of a course founded on principles of revisionary rhetoric helps students revise more meaningfully. As they confront and contend with the silences in their own evolving drafts, student writers generate knowledge that transforms them both intellectually and personally. For these students, the pivot from the role of writer to that of reader demanded more of them than deleting or "cleaning up" surplus passages. For Michael, the surplus in his letter to his girlfriend provided the way in to readerly empathy. For Terri, an inescapable contradiction foregrounded in competing texts resolved itself in paradox. And for Nina, the challenge of balancing intelligence and emotion, individuality and social conformity, emerged as a critique of the challenge itself, a personal/social statement that, evinced through both what it says and how it is written, refuses to go quietly. For these students, the task of rereading their semester texts, of juxtaposing them and making connections across them, created possible futures that previously did not exist. And for each, these new paths call into question the seemingly inevitable futures glimpsed in earlier versions.

YES, BUT IT'S MORE COMPLICATED THAN THAT

Tony: "True or False"

As his title indicates, Tony began his self-reflective essay by acknowledging an important binary that had been influencing him for a long time: Writing is either true or false. When I read Tony's first version, I translated this to mean that writing reflects either the writer's true feelings or it does not, in which case such writing is inauthentic and, in a way, deceitful. The fact that Tony viewed the absence of "truth" in his essays as something lacking interested me, as I'd spent quite a bit of time that semester talking about how, in a postmodern world, we're relieved of the burden of truth and can instead focus our attention on the specifics of interpretation. In an attempt to push Tony toward reconceiving of truths and lies as supplements rather than opposites, I wrote the following end comment on his first version:

This idea that your writing has a quality of falseness fascinates me. In your next version, quote your work this term to show us where and how you're being false. Maybe you could then, beneath the false passages, write some truths? I'm also intrigued by this idea that, by having to claim a position or a point of view, you feel boxed in, constrained somehow. Maybe that's why you prefer poetry to argumentative, academic essays. What do you think? If this feels right, track some of these connections in your next version, and cite more texts — the truths *and* the lies.

By asking Tony to juxtapose the two versions, I was hoping to help him contend with the contradictions of his competing texts and to generate useful knowledge about how he reads, writes, thinks, and learns, regardless of its "authenticity." In his final version, however, Tony responds to my interpretation by inserting two clarifications obviously directed toward me: "When I said that my writing has a sense of falseness attached to it, I did not mean that my essays are filled with a pack of lies. What this is saying is that I have a hard time truly expressing my feelings." And in the next paragraph, he writes: "Remember, it is not so much a sense of falseness in regards to a truth or a lie. It is more the lack of conviction and sincerity that is evident in my writing." Tony thus takes me to task for interpreting true/false as truths/lies. He also invites me to reread his essay, turning a keener ear toward hearing the subtle distinction he is trying to make.

This distinction emerges on the second page of his essay, where Tony, explaining why he has trouble truly expressing his feelings, writes: "A lot of what I am saying is what I think I *should* be saying according to the position I have taken." He later connects this insight to the realities of evaluation, explaining, "The problem that I have is also related to the fact that these papers and essays are all assigned and handed in for a grade. Therefore, I feel boxed in and restrained because I am worried more about turning in the paper than I am about what it says." As an example of how assigned readings and essays box him in, Tony refers to Sam Hamill's essay "The Necessity to Speak," which I had assigned in the first unit and about which Tony decided to write his first essay. Describing the challenges of the drafting critical analyses, Tony writes:

> Not only do I have to pick a point of view, I [also] have to back up my statements. It is very hard to back up what you're saying when you yourself don't believe it. For example, ... in the paper I describe a few things that Hamill said and then I go on to say, "In other words, he sounds very condescending

and as a reader that makes me angry." This statement is one-hundred percent false. I have since gone back and read parts of that essay over again and Hamill sounds nothing like the way I describe him. However, because I stated that I was going to challenge him I felt the need to belittle him to those reading my paper. Furthermore, even if Hamill did sound condescending that wouldn't bother me in the least. It certainly wouldn't make me angry. Finally, at the end of the paper I use a classic strategy of finishing a paper without having to back up claims. In the conclusion, I stated, "In this particular essay Hamill's bias allows for a lot to be questioned." Well, what does he leave to question? Better yet, what are his biases? I have tried to say what I think the readers want to hear, not what I want to say or really believe for that matter.

This passage interests me on a number of levels. First, there are the assumptions Tony makes about his readers, or more likely, the reader who is grading him — me (and the academic audience I represent). He assumes that a persuasive challenge to a text necessitates the belittling of its author. And then later, in his "classic" conclusion, Tony assumes his readers prefer it to the answers suggested by the critical questions that follow it. Indeed, most composition teachers *want* students to ask and explore such questions. Why does Tony believe I would prefer otherwise?

Second, there is the fact that Tony went back to reread Hamill's essay, thus discovering through the lens of his first essay that he manufactured a feeling in order to write persuasively. I began to realize how he feels forced to manufacture conviction in response to an essay, and that it is this feeling which grants him the authority to write. As he explains, "There are times when I get really into something, some issue, and it is those times that I truly feel my writing is powerful." Clearly, his response to Hamill's essay wasn't one of those times. As a teacher, I feel this passage encourages me to explore with my students ways to generate intellectual curiosity that don't necessitate complete support for or disagreement with a text's thesis. In fact, Tony's essay seems to speak to the limitations of pro/con essay assignments, where students are expected to take a clear-cut stand and then defend it. Such assignments legitimize binary thinking and, as Tony describes, box students in, forcing them to choose black or white, and leaving them no room for the grays of indifference and ambivalence. These assignments also send a clear message concerning what we as teachers believe about writing: It is true (good, powerful, persuasive) when it springs from deep conviction; it is false when it originates in indifference.

I'm tempted to end my analysis of Tony's essay here, but I feel nervous, so I know there is more to be said. And what needs to be said is this: How do I know Tony isn't doing the very same thing in this essay — manufacturing a feeling that he believes his reader wants to hear? I read "[t]his statement is one-hundred percent false" and "that wouldn't bother me in the least," and the conviction of such totalities prompts me to ask, "Really? Is that *true?*"

Notes

i. The student writing reproduced in this essay appears with each author's permission. I've changed their names for confidentiality.

ii. A few other contextualizing "texts" studied that semester are worthy of mention here. On the second day of class, one student (Tony) discussed the Dylan Thomas poem, "Do Not Go Gentle," which he had recently seen recited by Rodney Dangerfield in a movie called *Back to School*. This student, who was very vocal all semester, said he liked the line, "rage, rage against the dying of the light." I can't remember now how we got onto the subject of that poem, but I admitted that I'd never read it, and then, because my student's energy around the poem was so contagious, I found it and photocopied it for the rest of the class. The following class period, I passed it out, and that same student read it aloud. We talked about the poem, why it appealed to so many students in the room, and how Dangerfield's recitation of it in a major Hollywood film is one example of intertextuality. That poem and the phrase "rage against the dying of the light" were mentioned often throughout the semester — it became a kind of inside joke that we referenced whenever one of us used the term "intertextuality."

In the second unit of the course, a student-run text selection committee proposed five or six possible texts, one of which the entire class would read for the second major essay assignment. Some of these texts included: *Gone with the Wind* (the movie), *Calvin and Hobbes* (collected strips), *The Simpsons*, Machiavelli's *The Prince*, and Camus' *The Stranger*. For two class periods, students discussed which text they wanted to read and why, and the debates were heated and emotional. The most conventionally "good" students were very upset by the notion of writing a college research paper based on a TV show or a comic strip. They worried about finding persuasive research in the library and connecting it in a way that produced an A paper. Other students were excited about the idea of researching a nonconventional text, and argued that because TV has such influence in contemporary culture, it would be useful for them to learn strategies for researching and analyzing it. At the end of the second class, we held a vote, and Camus' *The Stranger* won by one.

The students' debates generated several more class periods in which we discussed, "what counts as a research-worthy text, and why?" For the midterm, I assigned David H. Richter's essay, "Falling into Theory," which builds on this question and asks students to consider what, how, and why they read. I asked my students to reflect on their semester-in-progress, analyzing what they've been reading, how, and why, and asking them to consider how the course has both supported and challenged dominant literary paradigms. For many of my students, this midterm essay assignment served as an early rough draft for their third essay, the self-reflection.

Finally, I can't conclude this note without mentioning that it was during the spring 1997 semester that the University of Arizona's men's basketball team won the NCAA championship. Underdogs throughout most of the tournament, the team, led by two juniors and no seniors, beat powerhouses like Kansas and Kentucky in nail-biting games that went into overtime. Three of my students attended the final four in Indianapolis. One student was in the pep band. On the day the team returned to Tucson, the school held a huge "welcome home" pep rally in the football stadium. I went to it, but had to leave early to meet my composition class on time. Many of my students were late. We spent the majority of that class period discussing the final games — pivotal plays, where we watched them, with whom, and what we did afterwards. It all had very little to do with writing and a great deal to do with feeling connected by a common thread that felt stronger and more magical than us all.

iii.   Margaret Atwood's story is about a young woman named Christine and her efforts both to connect with and separate herself out from the attentions of a visiting foreign student. Atwood's telling of the story is intentionally ambiguous: Is the foreign student simply unaware of cultural norms, or is he stalking and threatening Christine? The story's ambiguity generated wonderful classroom discussions about the process of creating an "other" and how class- and gender-based values influence that process. For example, many of the women believed Christine to be the victim of a stalker; many of the men believed that Christine was simply the unfortunate recipient of an overly enthusiastic admirer.

Appendix
Unit Three: Reader-Response
Essay #3: Self-Reflection

The final essay assignment in English 102 is typically termed a "Reader Response" essay. This is the language your *Student's Guide* uses. As your *SG* explains, a reader response approach demands that readers critically reflect on how their own life experiences, biases, assumptions, and values inevitably influence how they read and interpret a text. More specifically, when you write a reader response essay, you analyze how and why you — as the person you are — make meaning as you do. In a way, the reader response approach is another kind of text-in-context essay. But instead of going to the library to find contextual sources, *you mine your own memories and life experiences and select specifics that demonstrate why you interpret a text as you do.* You've already done of a bit of reader response work this term. For example, I asked those of you who read and responded to the hooks essay to examine why and how — given who you are in relation to her — you might have felt angry and/or threatened by her style and her content. I believe strongly in the reader response approach. I believe that, when we acknowledge who we are and why we interpret as we do, we write more responsible analyses. We contribute to the ongoing cultural conversation in such a way that acknowledges our views *as our own*, but we also open up a space for those who disagree with us to do the same. This is the fundamental question that shapes my reasons for teaching writing, why I believe learning how to write responsibly is so important: how can we as readers and writers create a gap out of which others might feel able to respond? In short, how can we keep the conversation going?

In units one and two of this course, you learned critical reading and writing strategies that helped you closely read, interpret, and respond to a variety of texts (shorts stories, creative nonfiction, and a novel). <u>Your job in your third and final out-of-class essay this term is to apply these strategies to a reading of yet another kind of text: your own life.</u> Specifically, I want you to reflect on how you've been reading, writing, thinking, changing, growing, learning as a student, a thinker, a writer — a human being — this semester. I want you to gather your research-in-progress and remember — or "reread" — everything you've done this term — in this class, your other classes, and your life outside of school (here is where your journal will come in handy). How have you revised yourself this term? What has changed for you? What have you learned about yourself and the person that you are?

What I'm looking for, specifically… An essay of about 5-7 pages wherein you do the following:

> <u>bring together some of the "texts" you've read and written this term</u>. Remember that in this class we've been challenging the idea of what a text is. We can argue, if we choose to, that movies, conversations, drawings, photographs, and memories are all texts. When I say "bring together," I mean I want you *to quote or carefully paraphrase from these texts specifically.* If it's more appropriate, perhaps you can attach the text(s) or incorporate them into your essay in some creative way. You'll probably quote yourself as your reread and reflect on your own writing thus far this term; <u>analyze (reflect on) the significance of these reread-</u>

ings. Don't simply give us a chronology of your work this term ... "And then I read "The Man of Mars" and wrote about that and then I read *The Stranger* etc." Instead, *explain why and how you read, wrote, and thought as you did and do.* Why do you interpret as you do? What life experiences, values, assumptions inform your meaning making? get creative in both your content and your form. Who you are as a person — the contexts of your life — should shape both your ideas and the form you use to express them. Do you identify as a student, a writer, an artist, a photographer, a filmmaker, a musician, a poet? How do these identities shape your making and communicating of meaning? How does the medium convey the message? Because this is a writing class, I'll need to see writing, but you can experiment with the kinds of writing you include as well as the form you use to communicate your meaning.

In short, this essay assignment is experimental; as a teacher I'm assigning it because I want to shatter some literary paradigms by asking the following questions: What is a text? What is an essay? Why should students write essays? What is proper essay "form"? I hope you'll join me in a spirit of serious play as we take on the challenges of this unit.
Audience: You'll be writing your essay to the people in this class — me and your classmates.

Evaluative Criteria
See the "Grading" section in your *Student's Guide* for a description of general grading criteria. I follow these standards closely as I evaluate your essays. For this particular assignment, I will be impressed by an "essay" that demonstrates your ability to analyze creatively. I'm looking for something called "analytic passion." Can you show me what it looks like? I want descriptive, full-bodied moments from the texts in your lives accompanied by wickedly intelligent analyses of their significance.

References

Atwood, M. (1996). The man from mars. In B. Alvarado & B. Cully (Eds.), Writing as re-vision: A student's anthology. Needham Heights, MA: Simon and Schuster.

Metter, A., with Dangerfield, R. & Kellerman, S. (1986). Back to school. London: Orion.

Bartholomae, D. & Petrosky, A. (Eds.). (1997). Reading the lives of others: A sequence for writers. Boston: Bedford.

Beach, R. (1993). A teacher's introduction to reader-response theories. Urbana, IL: NCTE.

Berlin, J. (1996). Rhetorics, poetics, and cultures: Refiguring college English studies. Urbana, IL: NCTE.

Bridwell-Bowles, L. (1995). Experimental writing within the academy. In L. Wetherbee Phelps & J. Emig (Eds.), Feminine principles and women's experience in American composition and rhetoric (pp. 43-66). Pittsburgh: University of Pittsburgh Press.

Burke, K. (1998). Attitudes toward history (3rd ed.). Berkeley: University of California Press.

Camus, A. (1998). The stranger. New York: Random House.

Crowley, S. (1990). The methodical memory: Invention in current-traditional rhetoric. Carbondale: Southern Illinois University Press.

A teacher's introduction to deconstruction. (1989). Urbana, IL: NCTE.

Donahue, P. & Quandahl, E. (Eds.). (1989). Reclaiming pedagogy: The rhetoric of the classroom. Carbondale: Southern Illinois University Press.

Faigley, L. (1992). Fragments of rationality: Postmodernity and the subject of composition. Pittsburgh: University of Pittsburgh Press.

Hamill, S. (1996). The necessity to speak. In B. Alvarado & B. Cully (Eds.), Writing as re-vision: A student's anthology (pp. 457-464). Needham Heights, MA: Simon and Schuster.

Kaufer, D. & Waller, G. (1985). To write is to read is to write, right? In G. Atkins Douglas & M. L. Johnson (Eds.), Writing and reading differently: Deconstruction and the teaching of composition and literature (pp. 66-92). Lawrence, KN: University Press of Kansas.

McCormick, K. (1994). The culture of reading and the teaching of English. Urbana, IL: NCTE.

Miller, R. (1996). The nervous system. College English, 58, 265-286.

Neel, J. (1988). Plato, Derrida, and writing. Carbondale: Southern Illinois University Press.

Richter, D. H. (1996). Introduction: Falling into theory." In B. Alvarado & B. Cully (Eds.), Writing as re-vision: A student's anthology (pp. 4-14). Needham Heights, MA: Simon and Schuster.

Sanborn, J. D. (1994). The essay dies in the academy, circa 1900. In P. Sullivan & D. Qualley (Eds.), Pedagogy in the age of politics: Reading and writing (in) the academy (pp. 121-138). Urbana, IL: NCTE.

Thomas, D. (1953). The collected poems of Dylan Thomas. New York: New Directions.

Welch, N. (1998). Sideshadowing teacher response. College English, 60, 374-395.

"Since the Dawn of Time...":
Thinking/Writing in the Gaps

Andrew Stubbs and Michael Whitehead
University of Regina

> To write.
> I can't.
> No one can.
> We have to admit: we cannot.
> And yet we write.
>
> Marguerite Duras, *Writing*, p. 32.
>
> I am a pour righter.
>
> Student Self-Evaluation.

"Since the dawn of time... " is the opening of a student paper in a first-year English class one of us encountered a few years ago, one that marks the depth of its writer's fixation on the totalizing conception, the fixed viewpoint. The paper goes on to say that, from the origin of life, human beings have feared the dark, and Shakespeare's excellent novel *Macbeth* is no exception. The truth or falsehood of the claim seems less interesting to us now than what it symptomatizes, i.e., reveals indirectly about the student's expectations of the text, the course, and the instructor. The statement invokes, nostalgically, an authorized body of knowledge and/or values, in terms of which its writer might be judged once and for all, finally, for good or ill. Guiltily, we wonder how this desire might have been inculcated, unconsciously if not consciously, by the instructor, by the nature of the teaching-learning situation itself.

The wrong reaction to the student's claim would, we think, have been to correct it, even if it turns out *Macbeth* isn't a novel. In fact, there's a lot of surface truth here: it's natural to fear the dark, and terrible things do happen in the play. The problem appears to be that the union of darkness and fear isn't very surprising. What we object to, then, is a too-simple or too-direct link between (general) precept and (concrete) instance. We'd prefer this connection to be problematic, challenging: we like friction between ideas. In this way, *Macbeth* might be seen as creatively ambivalent, paradoxical. This in turn might open a research path, raise a question about, say, the attractions of evil. Joining desire and evil, if not exactly earth-shattering, at least captures a tension. How can we be seduced by what we should abhor?

Our point is that the student's rather ordinary initial remark *could* be taken not as a sign of mediocre thinking but of his high (too high?) valuation of the import, mystique, and status of the subject. This, needless to say, is the attitude one would want, as a literature teacher, to nurture; and obviously it's promoted by the institution of literature teaching itself. After all, the student was simply trying to carry out, in what he assumed would be compliance with his instructor's wish, Northrop Frye's (1957) "first postulate," namely, "the assumption of total coherence" (p. 16). Here, however, the "inductive leap" (Frye, p. 16) proves counter-productive because it leads the student away from what we like to think of as the play's complexity — and humility. The writer's desire is aimed at producing a statement that's so true it can't be contested, which of course cancels the need for interpretation at all.

What we wish to examine here is the role of monolithic — as opposed to critical — thinking in determining, i.e., promoting or undermining, student ideas of success, especially in first year. The puzzle is that, especially in the writing class, the weakest student productions may result from an *over*-estimation of the classroom regime — as if failure is a function of trying to succeed. Our conspiratorial linking of confrontational terms (failure/success) ties in with Marguerite Duras' (1998) observation about writing: to begin writing one must accept the impossibility of writing. Obviously we won't get far without acknowledging student perspective as a conditioning, or indeed pre-emptive factor. As David Bartholomae (1989) has pointed out in a well-known essay, students are continuously constructing their learning environment: "Every time a student sits down to write for us, he has to invent the university for the occasion — invent the university, that is, or a branch of it ..." (p. 134). Thus, students are positioned rhetorically, adopting various masks for various audiences, which makes them the ideal carriers of the burden of diversity, and so (apparently) the ones best situated to understand the contingencies, uncertainties of academic practice:

He has to learn to speak our language, to speak as we do, to try on the peculiar ways of knowing, selecting, evaluating, reporting, concluding, and arguing that define the discourse of our community. Or perhaps I should say the *various* discourses of our community, since it is the nature of a liberal arts education that a student… must learn to try on a variety of voices and interpretive schemes — to write, for example, as a literary critic one day and an experimental psychologist the next, to work within fields where the rules … are both distinct and, even to a professional, mysterious. (Bartholomae, 1985, p. 134)

Our claim is that the "peculiar" and variable aspects of academic discourse impinge on students in a threatening way, provoking writing performances that are either too much of something or not enough of something. This confusion may simply herald students' not having noticed, or found a language to represent, their real, latent experience of diversity. Alternatively, their omniscient declarations, their univalent writing performances, may be signs of their attempt to deny the abhorrent asymmetry that otherwise distinguishes the institution's way of thinking. The student must be willing to read what Joseph Harris (1989) calls the "polyglot" text of the academy, where "competing beliefs and practices intersect with and confront one another" (p. 20). This will well may define actual learning (ability); the thing is, finding the hidden link between fields is not just finding unity in multiplicity: it's a way of uncovering contradiction, and so of "embracing contraries" in Peter Elbow's (1986) illustrative phrase. No doubt, detecting the *hiddenness* of the hidden connection is a transgressive act, involving departure from norms, and so is full of risk, so learning means breaking into knowledge areas that the institution as institution might prefer to keep shrouded, "mysterious."

The problem is how to begin. Let's take as an instance of writing that starts from consciousness of confusion, doubt, contrariness bell hooks' admission in her introduction to *Teaching to Transgress*:

In the weeks before the English Department at Oberlin College was about to decide whether or not I would be granted tenure, I was haunted by dreams of running away — of disappearing — yes, even of dying. These dreams were not a response to fear that I would not be granted tenure. They were a response to the reality that I would be granted tenure. I was afraid that I would be trapped in the academy forever. (p. 1)

This is an opening paragraph. Witness the initial paradox, the author's feeling of conflict, of doubled emotions (attraction and resistance, desire and fear) towards a single object: the academy.

Along similar lines, students entering university face divided expectations, due in part to the volatility of the first-year experience itself. First year — under the best conditions — is about transition: one is no longer "there," not quite "here." Note that the feeling of vertigo is expressed as a double negative. At the risk of pathologizing first year, let's observe the downside of this neither/nor dialectic. Life in the gap, for a sizeable number of students, is *naturally* anxiety-breeding. So, university as (con)text, *as an experience*, impacts students' levels, even chances, of survival negatively.

Let's say for now that "the gap" is a deficit condition, in that it reduces the amount of perceived (i.e., by the student) contact between student and institution. By contact we mean not only students' proximity to support services, learning resources, technology, etc. We mean, as well, the awareness students develop of the institution itself as a learning environment. It was to promote such awareness that, twelve years ago, the University of Regina developed a course now known as University 100: Introduction to University. University 100, formerly the Entrance Program Seminar (the title changed in 1997 when the course, over fairly strenuous faculty opposition, was awarded credit status), was required for mature students (students over 21 who did not have a high school diploma), who were admitted to the University through its open admissions policy. Students had to take the course to transfer to their major, were allowed to take it once only, and were graded on a Pass-Fail basis. The course reflected a trend at Canadian universities towards student services curriculum development (the Universities of Prince Edward Island, Guelph, and Winnipeg, for example, evolved programs in this field). The gains are in the areas of student retention, success, skill acquisition. All these trace their ancestry to the Freshman Year Experience program at the University of South Carolina (Gilbert, Chapman, Dietsche, Grayson, & Gardner, 1997).

One goal of University 100 was, as its title implies, to smooth the entrance to university. This would be done by introducing students to various academic resources, networks, protocols, etc. It aimed to close the distance between the learner and the site of learning. Notice we say "close the distance": the apparent aim was to enclose, fill up, and so mediate the encounter with university, thus making transition palatable. From a student viewpoint, this is how to reduce/eliminate the angst of transition. It turns the contact zone into a comfort zone, inculcating a sense of belonging, of community.

Ironically, closure is exactly what we wanted the course — a course purporting to *open* the ways and means of university life to students — to avoid. Learning, we told ourselves, involves (like transition) acceptance of unknowns. This could be taken as self-evident, but worth saying because it seemed to apply across fields. The course designers found themselves bound, however, by student perceptions — and prescriptions. "Give us," they said, "basics" or "the basics." (Translation: a complete, self-explaining set of skills that can be repeated blindly in all learning sites.)

This sketches the perceptual problem that University 100 — a course that was itself on the margins of the academy — encountered with students. Transition, they hoped, would be dealt with by being effaced, not confronted and possibly normalized as a function of learning. What's curious is that students, under these safer conditions, enter into communication with the university with a view to extending a deficit condition. But the desire to end the problem — so thoroughly as to make it seem there never was a problem — is itself problematic. There's an overlap here between students' denial of complexity and a condition in therapeutic practice. This situation is outlined by Michael White and David Epston in *Narrative Means to Therapeutic Ends*, which examines clinical applications of client writing:

> In regard to family therapy — which has been our area of special interest — the interpretive method, rather than proposing that some underlying structure or dysfunction in the family determines the behavior and interactions of family members, would propose that it is the meaning that members attribute to events that determines their behavior. Thus, for some considerable time I have been interested in how persons organize their lives around specific meanings and how, in so doing, they inadvertently contribute to the "survival" of, as well as the "career" of the problem. And, in contrast to some family therapy theorists, rather than considering the problem as being required in any way by persons or by the "system," I have been interested in the requirements of the problem for its survival and in the effect of those requirements on the lives and relationships of persons. I have proposed that the family members' cooperative but inadvertent responses to the problem's requirements, taken together, constitute the problem's life support system. (p. 3)

Students who cling to a desire to perpetuate faulty learning practices have, in effect, rationalized — normalized — failure. A symptom of this personalization of under-achievement is a compensatory overdetermination of the status and power of the university. This may manifest itself as an uncritical taking for granted of institutional practices, controls, not to mention professors' knowledge. But at the same time it's fostered by the entire affect of organization, from calendars, program prerequisites, and course syllabi to library information, deadlines, and professors' office hours. The "problem" is also "advanced" by the language of win-lose. This is a polarized language, a language that implicates the university in the whole range of student performances, both best and worst — a dynamic, if fraught, situation.

To go back to hooks's dilemma: note how her insertion of personal perspective creates an opening to the social politics of the academic milieu. The personal, then, is an object of knowledge and, at the same time, a *way* of knowing, a window into the space — the classroom — where knowing takes place. For hooks this is an inclusive act, where knower and known infiltrate one another. This constructed intimacy de-stabilizes the object of knowledge, pointing beyond this to a site where paradigms collide and healthy chaos reigns: "I celebrate teaching that enables transgressions — a movement against and beyond boundaries" (hooks, 1995 p. 12). As an opening move in the writing game, the overlapping of conventional and antithetical produces exactly the thought condition that T.S. Kuhn (1962, 1996) writes of: "Like artists, creative scientists must occasionally be able to live in a world out of joint — elsewhere I have described that necessity as 'the essential tension' implicit in scientific research" (p. 79).

> There is no such thing as research without counterinstances. For what is it that differentiates normal science from science in a crisis state? Not, surely, that the former confronts no counterinstances. On the contrary, what we previously called the puzzles that constitute normal science exist only because no paradigm that provides a basis for scientific research ever completely solves all its problems. The very few that ever seemed to do so (e.g., geometric optics) have shortly ceased to yield research problems at all and have instead become tools for engineering. (Kuhn, 1996, p. 79)

Claiming the personal has epistemic value outside the special genres of personal writing itself poses a threat to formalist instruction. In particular, raising contradictions disrupts the standard, univocal, thesis-support method of teaching composition — recall Paul Heilker's (1994) manifesto: "Thesis statement. Topic sentences. Supporting details. The unholy trinity of composition instruction" (p. 1). Allowing for combat between instance and counterinstance suggests a means of negotiation between contraries, as we see in the dialogical rhythm linking the parts of Kuhn's text. In the Kuhn passage, statements are nuanced by acknowledgement of reader reaction at each stage, a progressive anticipation and forestalling of reader demands, queries, resistances. These are overt signs of a negotiation process. The process involves question and answer, concession, self-revision, which are made explicit in mediating devices: "For … ; "Not, surely …"; "On the contrary…."

University 100 underwent significant development over time, a pivotal change being its switch in titles in 1997, which, again, reflected its new credit status and, as was thought, enhancement of its overall credibility in the eyes of students and faculty. Also in 1997, University 100 was partnered with a new course, University 110: Writing for Academic Success (the planned title, felt to be too esoteric to attract student interest, was "University Discourse"). University 110 — also offered for credit — enabled both courses to broaden their horizons, to take in issues of, say, the politics of human interaction at university. However over-the-top this phrasing may sound, it expressed an intention that the courses do more — and be seen as doing more — than merely find a cure for what ails you. In evolving their mandate in this direction, the course designers sought to give the courses a self-consciously interdisciplinary edge. This involved identifying more mobile thinking strategies and attitudes, ones that students could, it was hoped, carry from course to course, year-level to year-level. We'll bypass various obstacles to implementation that were faced and move to the real question: what are transferable thinking-as-writing skills and how does one decide when students have acquired them?

We started by saying the first year of university can be a negative experience because it reduces contact between student and university. Placing the gap results in the institution's becoming increasingly invisible to the student. This, we're arguing, leads to an overdetermination, by the student, of the authority of the institution and a concomitant underestimation of one's chances of success — again, extremes meet. Notice we're claiming a general pattern here: all students, from the up-scale to the at-risk learner, are vulnerable to this situational angst. Indeed, the one who seems initially positioned for success may turn out to be most prone to underachievement, while the so-called at-risk candidate, tortoise-like, closes in on the finish line. The university is a crossroads, a point of collision and transformation, which gives full force to the idea that the university — as an environment — powerfully yet subtly influences one's learning curve. This influence is radical in the sense that it's potentially downward or upward and, so, impacts on students seeking to read the institution — as bell hooks reads Oberlin College — as double. We'll examine the nature and import of this perceived duplicity in a moment, but let's first be clear about what we're not saying. We're not claiming that the stresses of transition affect one incoming student population more than another, or that failure or success can be predicted with any exactness for one group or another. Nor are we arguing that such stressors should or can be reduced or eliminated through add-on courses or support services. We're in fact suggesting an epistemological crisis of sorts: we're allowing for a maximum degree of ambiguity about the causes, symptoms, outcomes, and methods of treating academic stress. We're saying this tension is characteristic of the relationship between students and particular learning environments. It is, in Thomas B Farrell's (1993) terms, a "norm" of the "rhetorical culture."

Certainly it's a presence that students are particularly sensitive to, without necessarily being in a position to articulate, possibly because few courses focussed on providing content require students to analyze a subject that seems so beyond the pale. To rephrase Stanley Fish (1980), this is the *non*-text in any class. Yet, from the depths as it were, this stress — this silence that silences (it's both agent and action, noun and verb) — puts pressure on students to adopt a set of fairly specialized behaviors. These behaviors, which tend to surface in the interstitial realm of the composition class, we're characterizing as both counter-productive and, paradoxically, conventional. So, by a kind of Catch-22, failure is one of the things a university *expects* you to produce as a sign of having arrived. Under such conditions, success at university may no longer be a matter of mastering the overt rules of the place but of constructively misreading or finding substitutes for them. If angst is a normal marker of institutional life, then to be aware of the angst factor *may* lead to insight — if this isn't too grand a leap — into the way a university thinks. In other words, the university can become a subject of inquiry or, more specifically, a signifier capable of being deciphered, translated, questioned, recycled—in theory by anyone, at any layer of the hierarchy, from the vantage point of any discipline, within the university community.

What we're aiming for here is an understanding of the university as a perception, as an appearance in the mind of the student. But this is nothing other than to denote the university as a rhetorical formation, one marked by what Farrell (1993) calls "the tension that Aristotle captures with his rhetorical mood of *contingency*" (p. 27). It's also to construct the university as a site of unrest, "wherein differences are crystallized in opposed directions which may be resolved one way or the other" (Farrell, 1993, p. 27).

Our readings of ethical and aesthetic norms of rhetorical culture depend strongly on the critical importance of contingency for propitious conduct and judgment. But what is already clear is that the very meaning of rhetoric's materials — the probable or contingent, what may be one way or the other

— derives from rhetoric's characteristic approach to appearances. (Farrell, 1993, pp. 27-28)

It's the *rhetoricity* of the university's demand that, we're claiming, the student is not *prima facie* equipped to deal with. Yet this demand is crafted by the student, inadvertently we might say, through immersion in the daily routines of university life, which brings the lived and felt aspect of the university as text to the fore. This text is continuously evolving, which is to say being written, which raises the question, how does one become aware of this text — how does one become aware it *is* a text?

One answer might be that if we see this text as a student-institution collaboration, then what we need to show students are ways of uncovering the self-reflexive, in effect self-narrated element of it; certainly this was the aim of University 100 and University 110. What instructors ran into was a student mind-set resistant to reflection in favour of a primary identification, outward, with the surface language of instruction. Some time ago, Gregory S. Jay (1987) named this identification in Lacanian terms as the student's demand for "a subject who is supposed to know (sujet supposé savoir), a demand every teacher has felt in the classroom (a space in fact constituted by this demand)" (p. 785).

> It is the most exacting and intractable imposition that teaching and its institutions make upon an instructor, and the one which must be analyzed and resisted if education is to be something more than socialization or consumption. This demand is the essence of the "transference" that structures the classroom experience, in which the teacher is called to assume the authorized position of the one who is supposed to know, thus relieving the student of any responsibility for the production or effects of knowledge. (Jay, 1987, p. 785)

Merging with the totalizing fabric of knowledge is a primary symptom of the whole discourse of incapacity, which can be detected in students' flawed replication of instructor desire, a failure that routinely draws them to the writing class as a means of cure — the faint hope clause. In other academic areas, aptitude — say an ear for music, a passion for numbers — is a reason to enter a program; whereas ability to write is normally a reason to stay out of a writing course. So, we find many times the very technical language of composition as a discipline (sentence fragment, run-on, agreement problem) perpetuates dysfunction.

This is very situation Kenneth J. Gergen (1990) describes in "Therapeutic Professions and the Diffusion of Deficit": "How do I fault thee? Let me count the ways... Impulsive personality, Malingering, Reactive depression, Anorexia, Hysteria..." (p. 353 [107]). The construction of deficit, Gergen tells us, depends on a myth of an objective, impartial frame of reference, which indicates how invested deficit is in the neutral measurement of student outcomes. For Gergen, the quantitative language of the therapeutic professions carries a subtext of negativity through the very genre of taxonomy (of diseases); so, the act of naming is always reductive:

> Whether in the therapeutic context or daily life, the presumption that the language of the mind reflects, depicts or refers to actual states may be termed *reificationist*. That is, such an orientation treats as real (as ontological existants) that to which the language seems to refer. As otherwise put, it is to engage in the *fallacy of misplaced concreteness*, treating as concrete the putative object rather than the sign. (p. 354 [108])

Students who express misgivings about their chances of success, thus cooperating with the program's "official" language of reification, validate — in fact re-institute, or "re-conserve" — a norm, one that asserts, in J.L. Austin's (1975) terms, phatic over rhetic (pp. 92-93). They are auditioning for full immersion in a discourse community by dressing up, as it were, adopting its outward signs: posing "be" (to borrow a line from Wallace Stevens' "The Emperor of Ice Cream") as "the finale of seem." Thus, one University 110 student, having been asked in his first University 100 class to describe himself as a writer, produced: "I am a pour righter."

Here is an instance of effacement of the writer's agency at the same time that the writerly role merges with that of the institution as Mosaic lawgiver. Even allowing for ironic intention, there's a strange confluence of impersonal and personal. Impersonal becomes an attribute of the personal, as desire is directed to a stable situation where the sign, as cultural product, is commensurate with the real. Apparently we need to foreground the student writer's agency in the construction of text. Along with this we must allow for the exigencies of occasion — the setting of writing — to play a role in the construction. This would be a way of re-introducing the personal factor as a point of mediation with the learning site. It would also celebrate the virtues of duplicity, dialogue, open-endedness as these are furnished by student writers in their various written productions. What works against this is the normal handbook mode of instruction (e.g., *The Broadview Book of Common Errors in English* ([1995]). The formal model, with its "uncritically and automatically invoked template" (Heilker, p. 3), endures.

Giving primacy to critical thinking, as this is involved with the dynamics of the learning site, and with the conflicts of institutional life, would mean turning the mirror of discourse around, so in the midst of recording outward perceptions one also captures inward transformations — a history of learning. Under optimum conditions, such writing (as we were hoping to achieve in University 100 and University 110) becomes an entry point to other types of university writing and, indeed, to academic discourse. The stresses to which students are exposed — the gaps in their consciousness of what a university is — are exactly *what* students need to learn. The next question is, what prompts students to recognize, or not, such omissions as features of the "interface" with the institution, and therefore as potentially instructive?

This question becomes pivotal in light of issues of success-failure and how, rather than defining mutually exclusive domains, these terms may originate from one melting pot. We might even think of them as each other's source, which would be to alter radically students' estimations of what a university education is, what it is for, and how best to attain it. Again, that contradictory terms blend in some way suggests an anomalous, even non-rational situation, but the blending is significant: it means that success and failure are figures of speech. Our adaptation to the problematic of university survival must involve rhetorical analysis, because our subject is trope. Reflect for a moment on Michael Bernard-Donals' treatment of Platonic rhetoric, his observations on how Plato's crucial rhetorical dialogues circle, return to themselves:

> It is complex — if not altogether impossible — because rhetoric is inevitably bound up with other ways of knowing — it borders them, or it includes them, or it mediates them — but can never finally be separated from them, and as much as Plato wishes to carve out a rhetoric that is purely refutative, or that is purely figurative, or that allows the rhetor to occupy a place that is somehow outside or at some remove from the objects of investigation (which will always include the rhetor himself), then that rhetoric will inevitably circle back to reiterate the rhetor. (p. 37)

Students enter a rhetorical situation, and a rhetorical practice, when they realize their relationship to the institution is mediated by the "otherness," the strangeness, of knowledge. Their obligation then, presumably, is to study the factor of mediation, what we're calling rhetoric, or discourse, rather than seek direct access to knowledge as "object." Specifically, students as rhetors should try to discover or create opening, search for and maintain uncertainty rather than close this abyssal presence off. Whatever detachment from knowledge objects they may try to sustain, this stance is defeated when they understand that, and how, their rhetoric reveals *them*. It shows that their outsider status is really a symptom of their immersion in the place of learning, their alienation, ironically, a sign of intimate connection with, or adaptation to, its structures.

Meanwhile, the communicative power they arrive at, under the best circumstances, remains a function of failure. The position of alienation is compromised by rhetoric's return to the rhetor: "So, while it is true that the *Phaedrus* and the *Gorgias* enact what they claim to enact — they do, in fact, show what the rhetoric defined by Socrates looks like — it is enacted by its failure to work" (Bernard-Donals, p. 37). So by speaking/writing one inscribes oneself in the institution's history of instability.

We've said that students see a gap as something to be filled: in effect, they seek, in the end, plenitude. The way to fill a gap is through an identification — in fact over-identification — with what students' project as the university. One puts oneself in the place of the other, to see oneself (like Blake's Albion) from outside. This conjunction is metaphorical. But keep in mind that the student as rhetor is really taking two positions, namely writer and reader. The student sends messages while being an audience for messages delivered by the university. Meanwhile, the first-year student in particular fulfills a classic condition of the audience to a rhetorical performance by being a non-specialist. We come back to our opening paradox: the student as both member and non-member of a specialized discourse community, one whose specialization alone gives it authority. Borrowing terms set out by Ian Angus and Lenore Langsdorf (1993), we might say a student adopts, or is assigned, the stance of "beginner" or "generalist": "The beginner and the generalist do not have to wait; they can be assured of prompt, piecemeal gratification of their epistemic and ethical needs to know" (p. 7). It is not that the student is operating with incomplete knowledge, which is not in itself a fault. For a rhetorical stance — as we know from Aristotle — is occupied with probability (enthymeme) not certainty. In other words, it's concerned with the possibility of action when full knowledge is not in view. The problem is that the student may act upon incomplete knowledge as if it were full. The interval gap between author and reader ceases to be problematic. Subsequently, the gap goes underground, becomes an *indirect* influence, a ghost in the machine.

What are we to make, ultimately, of this factor of identification; and, indeed, is this a question of theoretical understanding or practical use? We've been characterizing identification as disaster and, so, calling for a writing that extricates students from a naïve, overtly literal acceptance of the author-ity/authenticity of their surroundings, thinking that this move will foster critical thinking. The flip side of this would be to nurture identification, even if it is excess — or, indeed, *because* it is excess.

The fool who persists in his folly becomes wise, Blake says. Accepting the necessity, even heroism, of the identifying movement leads to drama-tism. This is the whole performative aspect of rhetoric as devised by Ken-neth Burke. We can't forget that, unlike most disciplines, writing involves performance. One doesn't just *know* writing; one *does* writing: one is judged by the action (symbolic) that one produces. Ideally, identification indicates a displacement of self outward. It is movement into a field of text occupied — dominated — by another. Crucially, for Burke, identification necessarily entails transformation. Indeed, transformation implies a kind of metaphori-cal drama whereby things become their opposites:

> Distinctions, we might say, arise out of a great central moltenness, where all is merged. They have been thrown from a liquid center to the surface, where they have congealed. Let one of these crusted distinctions return to its source, and in this alchemic center it may be remade, again becoming molten liquid, and may enter into new combinations, whereat it may be again thrown forth as a new crust, a different distinction. So that A may become non-A. But not merely by a leap from one state to another. Rather, we must take A back into the ground of its existence, the logical substance that is its causal ancestor, and on to a point where it is consubstantial with non-A; then we may return, this time emerging with non-A instead. (Burke, 1969, p. xix)

A and non-A — terms positioned in a binary. For Burke these can, in the molten liquid of their source — to which they can return at any time — trade places. By the same token, as a matter of definition, one can identify oneself as what one is not. One produces the written statement, "I am not a writer." Or one can say, "I am a pour righter," which both denotes "I" as failure and acts out this failure in front of an audience. Such a self-absenting move her-alds a Burkean return to origin as potential self-exchange. Clearly, self-efface-ment under these circumstances is a kind of paranoia. It is a belated attempt at personal re-integration. It is a defensive move designed to overcome, or at least allay, uncertainty.

It's possible to think of the double move we've sketched above as violent, or an expression of students' sense of the violence of their predicament. It may also be a kind of nostalgia for the fullness of the blank page. We might say, oxymoronically, it's passively aggressive. It's a stage where inaction and action articulate one another, by mutual substitution. Here Burke's ratios overlap with Harold Bloom's (1973), where contraries engage in a struggle for (temporal) priority. The question is, how can a declaration of non-power be a means of gaining power? The answer may lie in the neither/nor dialectic, encapsulated in the ratio Bloom names "kenosis":

> ...a breaking device similar to the defense mechanisms our psyches employ against repetition compulsions; *kenosis* then is a movement towards discontinuity with the precursor. I take the term from St. Paul, where it means the humbling or emptying out of Jesus by himself, when he accepts reduction from divine to human status. The later poet, apparently emptying himself of his own afflatus, his imaginative godhood, seems to humble himself as though he were ceasing to be a poet, but this ebbing is so performed in relation to a precursor's poem-of-ebbing that the precursor is emptied out also, and so the later poem of deflation is not as absolute as it seems. (pp. 14-5)

This gives us a more specialized means of characterizing the situational angst felt by the student, namely as a version of Bloom's anxiety of influence. A student is in a relationship of consubstantiality — which includes opposition — with the academy. So, one means of gaining strength/knowledge would be to trade places with the institution. We see the student as ephebe (the one initially in a position of lesser authority). But the student so inscribed performs a self-emptying action. This is intended to influence the university-as-precursor to engage in a similar act of self-humbling. The pressing of one lack against another causes energy to flow from the prior to the belated text.

Notice, though, the structure of the binary survives intact: only the parties to the relation have moved, reversed positions. The relation itself, since it is not subject to change, functions like Burke's "great central moltenness." Hierarchy is reinstated as if it had never been in question. Conflict becomes a conserving move, a longing for source. It becomes, at the extreme, an impersonation of the other leading to appropriation of the other. Rhetorical ratios — Burke's and Bloom's — entail the very style of gap thinking we've been pursuing. In fact, they consolidate it. And, inevitably, they mark the writing lesson as the practice of — to name another oxymoron — negative capability. Let's look further at this consolidation of the binary. We're saying that binary thought is the main mechanism of institutional thought. Struggle, uncertainty — these are simply expressions of the university's daily conversation with itself, which students struggle to overhear.

Think again of the minus and plus sides of the student's situation. One of the more pervasive messages sent by the university to new students is that university is a place of diversity and specialization. It is both at once — two institutional fabrics in one, implying two value schemes. Students, incidentally, encounter diversity as they survey program and course options. They "live" this diversity on a day-to-day basis as they move between courses, fields, and year-levels. As we've said, the student is a primary carrier of the transdisciplinary ambience of the university, and the one most touched by the fractures between disciplines. Now, as a student, one is encouraged to adopt an attitude of risk: to explore. Diversity puts a premium on the open-ended formation, which supposedly pays dividends for life-long learning. This in turn is reproduced as the ability to mount inquiry, conduct research. The downside is that this learning model often has no official weight. Admittedly, it may be seen positively as a means to an end, as facilitating certain kinds of measurable result, but whether it's valued in itself — as an end in itself — remains up in the air. For the open-ended model, if pressed to the edge, alters one's overall perception of what learning is, and may produce few clear signifiers that learning has actually taken place. And we need to gaze on such markers. We feel a need, at some level, to guarantee that academic practices have applications in, say, the post-university job-world. Consequently, students — attitudinally — opt for a more and more specialized language of knowing. This, of course, they do anyway as they advance to upper years. This journey is in line with each discipline's particular expectations: success results from a process of inculcation, of acceptance of the methodologies, jargons, of one's subject area. Carried to an extreme, the process ends in one's becoming a professor, in charge of a limited area of knowledge. "Limited" implies shrinking, reduction, the miniature: the homunculus version of an academic discipline/code. The tiny, basic, perfect man lurking inside a subject who, by synecdoche, contains it exhaustively.

Needless to say, specialization fulfills a much more prestigious institutional agenda than mere cross-disciplinary models of thought. Of course, it's the space between disciplines that, presumably, writing inhabits. The crux of the issue is the transferability of knowledge from one locality to another. Or, how does one make one degree or type of knowledge a foundation for another? One clue is that, as we've seen, oppositions are unstable, terms in a binary trade places. If we apply the rule of kenosis, even diversity and specialization can be reversed. So the distinction lies not between polar terms but in the institution itself. That is, disciplinary autonomy and pluralism are the same phenomenon viewed from two angles. The goal should be to find ways of foregrounding the distinction. Doing so, one articulates the university to its public and to itself. The place to create, by the way, is within — the interior of rhetoric, marked by recurrence and inclusion.

The act of making or uncovering the distinction is a rhetorical act, from which it follows that discerning the point of contact and slippage implies a recognition of the university as an interactive but unstable environment. Rhetoric is implicated in a double messaging wherein both the interdisciplinary and the specialized are equally — ambivalently — fictions. Ever duplicitous in its management of opposition, or relationship, ever threatening to affirm or falsify its objects, rhetoric as messenger god plays to both teams on the field. The alternative to accepting the rhetorical factor in all this is repudiating rhetoric in the interest of solidifying formalist, solitary, exclusivist methods of knowing. Think of Oscar Wilde's denial, from prison, of the rhetoricity of his claims: "I am not speaking in terms of rhetorical exaggeration but in terms of absolute truth to actual fact..." (1987, p. 99). Such a pronouncement does not make rhetoric disappear; it merely advances a new rhetoric — the rhetoric that there is no rhetoric here, that one means everything one says.

Let's return to University 100 and 110 and examine the types of writing practice situated here. The following compositions appear in the *University 110 Course Manual*. The first, "Going Home," was in fact written several years ago in a first-year writing course at a Southern Ontario university and was used in the pilot edition of University 110. The others were produced in different University 110 classes taught by different instructors over several years. All are samples of "personal" writing.

> I really do want to go home. Whenever Christmas comes around, I start preparing for the trip weeks in advance. It sounds silly, maybe, but when I haven't been home for months, I really miss the place. But when I'm packing, there's always this knot in my stomach that isn't excitement or anticipation but something else — something not so nice.
>
> Everyone else I know goes home every second weekend. That's something I could never do. It's just too far away. By the time I got there, I'd have to come right back. Or at least that's what I tell others. When it comes to convincing myself, though, I know that as much as I miss the place, I wouldn't go home that often if I could. Not that I don't want to. I just wouldn't. (Elaine Hudson)

The subject is, initially, the writer's home town, Pembroke Ontario, to-wards which she harbours contradictory impulses. She wants/doesn't want to go home. The contradiction is not just in the subject, i.e., "out there" (in the town), but also *within* herself — it's a matter of desiring and/or imagining. And the contradiction is simply presented, not resolved, in these first paragraphs.

But declaring the unknown, harbouring duplicity, opens the author into her text: confusion, therefore, is functional. Take the first sentence: "I really do want to go home." We might anticipate a follow-up reader response along the lines of, "What makes you so sure?" Elaine's next sentence gives a concrete reaction to this query: "Whenever Christmas comes around...". By the third sentence, she has further anticipated the reader's skepticism, and replies: "It sounds silly... ". At each stage, the text is linked by the writer's projection of reader feedback. The dialogue supplies a sequence to thought. The sequence, meanwhile, is constituted by interruption, discontinuity. The result is a text that's more collaborative, interactive. Admittedly, the dialogue is a construction, not, say, a transcript of actual conversation. So the writer takes some control of what feedback is given. At the same time, though, the reader's response is not known until the sentence is uttered. So, a projected spontaneity is maintained. In fact, the writer must be sensitive to potential swerves called up by her own assertions. This suggests that she's really in conversation with her own text, playing double roles of writer and reader. The writing happens in an invented interval, where subject and dialogue merge. The third paragraph begins: "But don't get me wrong. I love my hometown...."

How does this process get translated into University 110 writing? Here are three opening moves:

1. *To My Darling Jim*: My eagle; my inspiration; my friend; my hero. I love you. You know that. Recently this love took a nasty turn because I was afraid that you were going to die. I was scared, scared right to the centre of my being. I hung on. Just like a pitbull. You and I both; we dealt with each day as it came. Point blank; no questions asked.

    I am happy that this trial is over. I am glad we can smile again and feel genuine joy about even the smallest stuff we do together, but I am also plagued by questions, frustrations, anxiety, and ANGER. Lots of anger. Why? How dare life! Will the brain tumor come back again? Will this fear be repeated again? (Lori Read)

2. *A Trip to Jerusalem*: Mom! The day has arrived. This day that I have dreamt about most of my life. I can remember all the talks we used

to have when I was a kid about the Holy Land. We would talk about all the different locations, like Bethlehem and Jerusalem, and how we would try and imagine what they looked like and how it would feel to be there. Today I arrived in Jerusalem. The anticipation is almost unbearable. I realized that I had placed many expectations on my visit to this great city. The descent into Jerusalem is very hot, dry, and dusty. I am remembering stories from the Bible that you read to me as a child as we are entering the city. Even though I am excited and have a lot of anticipation, at the same time I have an uneasy feeling. I am fascinated by what I am seeing and yet the sight of some things causes me to be a little baffled and discouraged, even a little angry. (Chris Griffin)

3. *My Kitchen Clock*: The clock in my kitchen hangs alone on an otherwise bare wall. I don't recall anyone complimenting me on the clock, just questioning where it came from. I understand very well because it is not a work of art, it is not in style with its surroundings, and if it were not for the emotional value, I wold take it down and pack it away.

   It is square in shape, the background is white and the numbers are cross-stitched in blue with blue flowers around a pink heart in the center. Over the top, my name is stitched and along the sides the names of my two children. (Beverly Bachorick)

   In "Going Home," we isolated two qualities of "successful" writing: one, the foregrounding of the uncertainty; the other, dialogue.

   In the three University 110 papers, we encounter the same provocative initial disharmony. Lori admits to love *and* fear in her relationship with "Jim," her reader. Chris admits the disparity between a dreamed Jerusalem and a real Jerusalem. Beverly admits attachment to an object that seems too trivial to bear any emotional weight. In each instance the subject is doubled, breached.

   The results of this breaking are diverse. In the first two cases, an outreach to a specific reader is immediately created, as if indeterminacy leads to the projection of a collaborator, as if the writer is unable to assume sole responsibility for writing. Lori relies on metaphor, a sequence of ecstatic affirmations of "love" that are undermined by fear of its loss — as if the words somehow fail to name the feeling she's pursuing. Chris calls up the past in anecdotes, shared story-incidents, which get woven into the fabric of his unfolding narrative. Beverly's reader is more generalized: it's any person, not an individuated "you," who may have seen her kitchen, may have seen the clock, may have asked why it hangs there. In each case, the text invites a reader *in*. The writing process takes us from a present perception of the need to write, a sense of the currency of the occasion of writing, backwards into the history of the subject.

Consciousness that one is communicating with an audience that is, more or less, here/now increasingly compels these writers to become aware of their language *as* they write. This accentuates the rhetoricity of the textual performance, which gives it a reflexive dimension that makes possible a tentative resolution of the initial problematic. According to the terms of the assignment, writers had to arrive (back) at a memory: a concrete event in the past that could be a turning point in their understanding of their task. In other words, awareness that this *is* a text, based in a particular occasion, turns out to have been a pre-condition for the writing and its meaning: again, timing — the role of occasion — becomes crucial. The writer asks, not "what do I want to say?" but "why am I writing now?" "Going Home" provides a paradigmatic instance of such a hinge moment. Here's how it ends:

> I used to think that the changes in the town were what bothered me. Maybe I wanted to go home but was afraid of what I'd find (or not find) there. I used to think my worries were all about going home and not seeing what I expected to see. Maybe the familiar faces would be gone or my favourite places would be torn down for new development. I thought I wanted everything to stay the same.
>
> But on my last trip home, I realized I had thought wrong. Last May, when the bus pulled away from the Pembroke depot and drove through the town, I had the urge to look out the window, to look back. And that feeling of apprehension returned. I didn't want to leave. Not because I didn't want to come back to Waterloo. I just didn't want to leave. And I realized then that I wasn't worried about the town changing. It could never change enough that it wouldn't be the same.
>
> It wasn't the town that I was afraid would change. It was me that I *knew* would change. It's me that *has* changed. I realize now that every time I return home I am a different person. It doesn't matter if the town changes or not — I can never see it the same because I'm not the same. I've seen too much and been through too much to ever be the same girl that left home three years ago....
> (Elaine Hudson)

The ending of "Going Home" evolves from the text as a process: it's not tacked on, not premeditated, but appears to have been between the lines all along, though not noticed until a certain point. In a way it's not an ending at all so much as a new opening, a new vantage point from which to observe the same subject again. The writer has refigured the initial problem: it's no longer the town that's her subject but herself; in fact it's not just herself but the act of composing. Her earlier, fraught awareness of loving her home town while fearing it will change has been replaced by a combined acceptance of/resistance to change in herself. The new idea takes place as she looks back on the town through the window of a bus as she leaves.

If her writing has been a meditation on the past, a looking back, then looking out the bus window as she leaves the town is nothing other than a reenactment, an instituting, of the *form* of her writing as a physical detail inside the writing. The form, what we're calling the occasion of writing, has now been inscribed as a juncture, a point, a seam in the narrative. How have the University 110 writers managed this process?

So, what was the purpose of all this fear and anxiety and then joy and elation? I don't know. Part of me just wants to jump back into life and live it more intensely and without restrictions. The flip side of this story is that I'm afraid that this is not the last we'll see or hear from "Eddy" [i.e., the tumour]. I'm scared that this was only the beginning. Do we need to visit this place again — but, then again, if we never visited this place again, would we be this much alive? (Lori Read)

The last place I am visiting is up on the hill outside the city walls. It is the garden of Gethsemane. Jesus spent his last hours in the garden of Gethsemane, which was his place of solace to be alone with his father. Yes, there is a church here also, but strangely enough it is the "Church Of All Nations," which is a church that belongs to everyone and is not controlled by any particular Christian sect. Right beside the church is part of the original garden. All the trees are staggered with paths passing beneath them, and as I look upon this place things begin to come back into perspective for me. Before I came here I felt that each one of the Christian sites in Jerusalem would be protected and untouched by this world. Instead, seeing Christians and other religions exploit this place causes me to confront all I believe in. But, as I stand in this garden, I discover my place of solace was with me all the time. Peace is not a place. It is a faith. It is not affected by where you are or who you are. Even though many things about Jerusalem have been nothing that I would have expected, I am glad that I came because I discovered what my faith really means to me through the experience. (Chris Griffin)

Harry has passed away since he gave me the clock and even though the thought of taking the clock down has crossed my mind, I end up with the same conclusion. I will only take the clock down if it stops working and cannot be repaired. I will not likely be able to throw it away, and it will be packed away carefully in a special place on a shelf. The emotional attachment to the clock will always be there to help me forgive the physical appearance that prevents it from blending in with its surroundings. (Beverly Bachorick)

Each ending features a dialectic between permanence and change, which is staged in a specific framed scene in a certain place, such as Chris's Jerusalem, so timing plays a role in the evolution, suggesting methodology. That is, each stage of the writing develops, and is seen to develop, from an earlier stage into the next stage. Each moment of text is an unfinished experiment.

To reflect on the permanence/change relation: Lori's ending, for instance, doesn't really change anything. It's more an acceptance of how love and fear are entangled, how love is dependent on, intensified by fear. But she began by knowing about this entanglement, even while interrogating it. Self-consciousness, by the end, born of reflection on her own process, involves active acceptance of a life-irony. Meanwhile, by walking in the footsteps of "Jesus," Chris revises his relationship with his faith. Once it involved the tangible: the (imagined) physical experience of place. Now it's a perception of place as virtual. Place has become thought: it has gone inside, become portable, something he can carry with him — between places. Beverly visualizes the clock not just as memory but a symbol of memory. It will be kept not simply for itself but for what it contains — a portmanteau. It will be on display or in a secret place, just as memory both preserves and is preserved. She has created a secret space within her composition where some final decision will be made, maybe, at an undisclosed future time, in another writing.

The arrival at awareness of mutability, coupled with the deferral of final decision, involves rigorous attention to the textual process leading up to the ending, not just the ending itself. The logic of process is, then, a logic of reinstatement: process re-places or restores what has gone before; conclusion: writing acts are — intensively, recursively — self-reading acts.

This, of course, is precisely the condition we're in as rhetors as we move from considerations of content and form to considerations of readership — as we move from issues of how to structure information to awareness of the non sequiturs of readerly response, which includes the complexities of instrumentation (technology) as well as the vagaries of marketing. It may well be that "successful" writing entails a stringent conservatism, in the sense of a return to what has gone before. But it's important for students to recognize the double messages that writing, which is always already an institutional practice, and always local, yields up, and how this doubling arises only in part from what is said, or acted out: it also emerges from the silences within a text, captures and restores these silences, these placements, which one needs to acquire multiple ways of reading.

References

Angus, I. & Langsdorf, L. (1993). Unsettled borders: Envisioning critique at the postmodern site. In I. Angus & L. Langsdorf (Eds.), The critical turn: Rhetoric and philosophy in postmodern discourse (pp. 1-19). Carbondale: Southern Illinois University Press.

Austin, J.L. (1975). How to do things with words (2nd ed.). Cambridge: Harvard University Press.

Bartholomae, D. (1985). Inventing the university. In M. Rose (Ed.), When a writer can't write: Studies in writer's block and other composing problems (pp. 134-65). New York: Guilford.

Bernard-Donals, M. (1998). The practice of theory: Rhetoric, knowledge, and pedagogy in the academy. Cambridge: Cambridge University Press.

Bloom, H. (1973). The anxiety of influence: A theory of poetry. London, Oxford, New York: Oxford University Press.

Burke, K. (1969). A grammar of motives. Berkeley, Los Angeles, London: University of California Press.

Chapman, J., Stubbs, A., Whitehead, M., Leonard, R., McLeod, G., & Hengen, S. (Eds.). (2000). University 110 course manual 2000-2001: Writing for academic success. Regina: University of Regina, First-year Services.

Duras, M. (1998). Writing. M. Polizzotti (Trans.). Cambridge: Lumen.

Elbow, P. (1986). Embracing contraries: Explorations in learning and teaching. New York: Oxford University Press.

Farrell, T.B. (1993). Norms of rhetorical culture. New Haven and London: Yale University Press.

Frye, N. (1957). Anatomy of criticism: Four essays. Princeton: Princeton University Press.

Gergen, K.J. (1990). Therapeutic professions and the diffusion of deficit. The Journal of Mind and Behaviour, II (3, 4), 353 [107]-367 [121].

Gilbert, S., Chapman, J., Dietsche, P., Grayson, P. & Gardner, J.N., (1997). From best intentions to best practices: The first-year experience in Canadian universities. Columbia, SC: University of South Carolina.

Heilker, P. (1994). The essay: Theory and practice for an active form. Urbana, IL: NCTE.

hooks, b. (1994). Teaching to transgress: Education as the practice of freedom. New York and London: Routledge.

Jay, G.S. (1987). The subject of pedagogy: Lessons in psychoanalysis and politics. College English, 49, 785-800.

Kuhn, T.S. (1996). The structure of scientific revolutions (3rd ed.). Chicago and London: University of Chicago Press.

LePan, D. (1995). The Broadview book of common errors (2nd ed.). Peterborough: Broadview.

Stevens, W. (1981). The emperor of ice-cream. The collected poems of Wallace Stevens. New York: Knopf.

White, M. & Epston, D. (1990). Narrative means to therapeutic ends. New York and London: Norton.

Wilde, O. (1987). De profundis and other writings. Harmondsworth: Penguin.

Uncertainty and the Acquisition of Academic Writing: A Pedagogy of Genre Destabilization

Randall Popken
Tarleton State University

n trying to describe the situation that students find themselves in when they begin college, discourse theorists often depict students metaphorically seeking "membership" in the academic community (e.g., Bizzell, 1986). Such work often emphasizes the role of written discourse in college students' success or failure at becoming a part of academia. One way of looking at students' entry into the academic community through their writing appears in the work of a number of genre theorists[i] (Berkenkotter & Huckin, 1995; Bishop & Ostrom, 1994; Cope & Kalantzsis, 1993; Freedman & Medway, 1994a, 1994b; Johns, 1997; Reid, 1987; Swales, 1990). Work by some of these theorists investigates the features of academic genres (Bazerman, 1981) and the principles governing how writers acquire and develop their abilities with these genres (Freedman, 1993; Freedman & Adam, 1996).

However, an especially troublesome and largely unexplored aspect of understanding written genre acquisition has been what we might call its linearity — the processes by which writers progress from learning one genre or sub-genre[ii] to learning another and another and so on (Popken, 1999b). One of the few scholars attempting to discuss how developing writers move from genre to genre through a set of tasks in an academic setting is Prince (1989), whose work involves what he calls the "mediation" among genres. Prince bases his theory on the notion that students come to college already knowing some culturally important genres such as the letter and the written dialogue. Then, what Prince offers is a syllabus that utilizes these genres as a point of mediation between students' pre-academic and their academic lives. [iii] In other words, the letter and the dialogue serve as points of mediation between students' pre-college discursive lives and the genres of the academic context.

Specifically, Prince's syllabus looks like this: The semester begins with three incremental assignment sets, all involving the first mediating genre, the letter. The first writing assignment, which entails three different letters written to classmates, begins with a "letter of biographical introduction to a classmate"; it also includes a letter asking for more information about the classmate to whom the letter has been written and then a follow-up letter asking further about the significance of the information. The second writing set, which also consists of three letters, begins with one that "describes an important event or experience to someone who was not present initially" (p. 745) and includes two others in response to another student's letters. Writing three involves two letters, an "imaginary letter of advice from Theo Van Gogh to his brother, Vincent" and a letter of advice to a friend (pp. 745-746). By the fourth writing of the term, Prince moves his students into his second mediating genre, the dialogue. Students begin with "a dialogue on the problem of success" and then revise it into an essay "developing a thesis about the problem of success" (p. 746). Writing five has three stages, involving three genres: it begins with a summary of two articles and then requires an imaginary dialogue between the writers of the two articles. Then, in the third stage of writing five, students are asked to produce "an analytical essay developing a specific thesis" (p. 746). Finally, the sixth assignment begins with "a summary of two difficult articles on the question of affirmative action" followed by "an argumentative essay favoring or opposing affirmative action" (p. 746)

Prince's theories are anchored in the eighteenth century, where he believes genre mediation began. The whole idea, he says, is based on egalitarian goals of Scottish and English moral philosophers who saw genre mediation as a solution to the problem of culturally important knowledge only being accessible to people familiar with "elite intellectual genres" (the treatise and school syllogism). Because such a discursive gap existed between these genres and the conversational genres of most people, a high percentage of the populace was shut out of the educational process (p. 742). However, utilizing more "accessible" genres such as the letter, the dialogue, and the periodical essay could help mediate between familiar conversational genres and "more difficult institutional forms" (p. 742), thus bringing new ideas to a larger number of citizens. Prince likens this situation of the average citizen in eighteenth-century England and Scotland to the situation of a typical first-year college student in North America, who also faces a "gap between the modes of social interaction with which he or she is familiar and the kinds of writing endorsed by educational institutions" (p. 742).

Although Prince claims that one of his goals in genre mediation is to "disrupt" versions of the "standard essay" which his students bring with them to college (p. 744), in fact his system mostly attempts to stabilize discourse in order to increase his students' chances of acquiring academic genres. That is, he assumes that writers can best acquire new academic genres in a controlled pedagogical environment where (through mediation) the curriculum does most of the work of closing gaps between the genres that students bring to college and the ones academia calls on them to learn and use. Prince's syllabus carefully scaffolds his students' genre development: the letter leads them to the dialogue; the dialogue to the summary; and the dialogue also to the essay.

In contrast to Prince's proposal for a stable, scaffolded syllabus for students entering the genres of academic life, I prefer the exact opposite: to destabilize students' discursive experience. That is, whereas Prince's model is based on assumptions of discursive certainty, I argue for the necessity of discursive uncertainty. Furthermore, whereas Prince's syllabus is scaffolded, mine is intentionally unscaffolded so as not to fill the gaps between the students' genre repertoires and the genres I introduce to them in class.

In this paper, I begin by mapping out my theoretical rationale for a pedagogy of genre destabilization as it involves students' acquisition of the genres of academia. As I will argue in the first part of this paper, a critical part of work in a genre-based course is that students begin to experience the unsettling condition of acquiring an unfamiliar genre — so that they can come to the point of relying on their own genre acquisition strategies. I conclude this paper by offering some samples of how I intentionally destabilize the discourse experiences of writers in beginning writing classes.

INSTABILITY AND THE INTERGENRE STATE

First, it seems to me that destabilization is necessary for students acquiring academic genres because it reproduces the natural "interlanguage" situation of written language acquisition. Interlanguage, a concept which originated in second language learning theory (Selinker, 1969), is a complex psycholinguistic state in which language learners are suspended between their first (L_1) and second (L_2) languages while they are trying to learn L_2. Because it consists of forms from both L_1 and L_2 (Selinker, 1969, p. 71) the interlanguage state is "highly structured" (Selinker, 1969, p. 71). However, because it is temporary and transitional, interlanguage is also highly unstable; i.e., in constantly-evolving ways, fossilized forms from L_1 and hypercorrect versions of L_2 coexist with appropriately used forms from L_2 (Selinker, 1977).

In explaining how interlanguage applies to writing development, Kutz (1986) illustrates how writers ping-pong between what they have written in the past and what they are trying to learn, all the time "constructing and testing hypotheses about the new language" (p. 393). For instance, she shows how "[c]onvoluted syntax and malformed or misused words" are likely to appear (p. 392). Sometimes there can be "a return to abandoned features when the learner encounters new or stressful discourse demands" (p. 393), and there may even be times during which a writer's text may contain "features that do not occur in either the first or the target language" (p. 392).

The concept of the interlanguage state can also be applied to the acquisition of academic genres, which involves a special kind of interlanguage: writers are suspended between the genres that make up their personal repertoires (Bakhtin, 1986; Lucas, 1988; Ivanic, 1998; Popken, 1996) and the genres of power in academic life — in short, between familiar genres (G_1) and unfamiliar ones (G_2)[iv]. Ultimately, in this interlanguage state (perhaps more accurately the "intergenre" state), writers come to grips with the norms for G_2 established by the academic community (and various smaller communities within academia) and how those norms translate into genre forms.

An excellent illustration of the instability of the intergenre state appears in Berkenkotter, Huckin, and Ackerman's (1988) study of "Nate," a doctoral student in rhetorical studies. Earlier in his career, Nate had received an M.Ed. and taught in an English Department at a small college in the U.S. Thus, his Ph.D. studies in rhetoric placed him between two fairly distinct academic communities: the "teaching and expressive writing communities he had belonged to for many years" and "the more research-oriented community of rhetoricians and composition theorists he was trying to enter" (p. 39). Nate's writing before he entered the Ph.D. program had been influenced by "literary journalistic prose style" (p. 16), so he found enormous problems trying to acquire genres of rhetorical scholarship; in fact, much of Berkenkottter, Huckin, and Ackerman's study shows the anguished condition Nate is in during this intergenre period. For instance, he "struggled to... reconcile a familiar, informal style with what he thought were the appropriate conventions of formal discourse" (p. 19). We also see him going through "months of confusion during which his writing suffered from numerous stylistic problems" (p. 19), including "hypercorrect, over-inflated diction" (p. 22), inappropriate foregrounding of self (p. 24), and a register that often misses contextual appropriateness (p. 25).

I think it is likely that developing writers at all levels experience this intergenre state when they move into G_2^v; thus, experiencing the intergenre state is important for students trying to acquire academic genres. Getting students to experience the intergenre state, it seems to me, is where the destabilized genre pedagogy comes in — because it has to do with the means by which writers acquire new genres. The importance of the means of learning genres has recently been observed by Freedman and Adam (1996), who argue that college graduates "not only need to learn new genres... but they also need to learn new ways to learn such genres" (p. 395, emphasis mine). Freedman and Adam go on to show the means of genre acquisition in workplace contexts where (in contrast to scaffolding such as in Prince's model, discussed above) acquisition is aided by the social interaction between newcomers and their co-workers; writers acquire genres largely as a natural by-product of actually doing the task which calls for the discourse in the first place.

Therefore, if (as I believe it should) writing instruction intends to prepare students to be self-reliant and able to acquire G_2 on their own (in ensuing classroom contexts and elsewhere), then we need to replicate the acquisition situation by creating an intergenre state for students to experience. By experiencing the uncertainties of intergenre, students can begin to learn how to cope with it; in short, destabilization forces writers into the intergenre state, where they can put genre acquisition processes into practice. Let me now turn to some of these processes.

INSTABILITY AND INTERDISCURSIVE LINKING

Current theory deriving from work by Bakhtin (1986) maintains that the process of acquiring G_2 is essentially interdiscursive. That is, as Prince also acknowledges, a major means of genre acquisition is for writers to draw on genres they have previously experienced as speakers, hearers, and writers and then to apply them in some way to the unfamiliar genre (Lucas, 1986; Ivanic, 1998). Two such "interdiscursive linking" processes used by writers for negotiating the gaps between G_1 and G_2 are genre transfer and genre transliteration (Popken, 1992; 1996; 1999a). In both of these processes, developing writers search for places of potential connection between the familiar and the unfamiliar (new) genres; then, they use the unfamiliar as points of extrapolation to the familiar. Though there has been debate about the issue (Williams & Columb, 1993; Fahnestock, 1993), it seems likely that, for many developing college writers at least, these processes are largely unconscious, inextricably tied to the discourse's context of use (Freedman, 1993; Freedman & Adam, 1996; Wertsch, 1991).

In the first of these interdiscursive linking processes, genre transfer, writers fill gaps between G_1 and G_2 by taking structural features from the former and reproducing them in the latter (Popken, 1992). For instance, a student who has written technical documents might utilize special formatting such as bullets, numbering systems, or headings on papers in college courses; or, more noticeably, the student may attempt to incorporate short, topic sentence-less paragraphs, much the way they are used in professional letters and some business documents.

On the other hand, the second kind of interdiscursive linking process, genre transliteration,[vi] is a more complex and less easily understood socio-cognitive phenomenon that goes far beyond the one-to-one structural reproduction going on in transfer. In transliteration, writers take features (formal or nonformal) from G_1, and they bend, reshape, and transform them — often beyond the recognition of an outside observer — in order to fit their renditions of G_2. In other words, they use transliteration as a special entryway into the territory of the unfamiliar such as academic genres.

For instance, consider a hypothetical example of transliteration in a task I commonly use in a first-year writing class. The assignment is for an "overview" paper, a kind of review-of-the-literature that covers three or four articles. One of the important textual features of this paper is what Bakhtin (1981) calls "double-voicing." That is, drawing directly from the articles, the text has to reproduce (as well as compare/contrast) ideas on the issue(s) involved: Smith says x; on the other hand, Jones says y; Garcia says z, and so on. Although most of them aren't conscious of it, many students in my class already have a G_1 from their non-academic lives that they could transliterate to the overview paper: the oral reported-speech monologue. I heard a student using this genre just last week as she recreated for a friend an argument between herself and another woman:

> So, I was, like, "You've got to be kidding me!" And then she goes, "You're wrong! It's true! Marcia did go see him, three times." And then I go, "I don't believe you." And then she goes, "Well, it started during Spring Break last year when Angie was in South Padre." Then I was, like, "You're wrong. Angie didn't go to South Padre, she worked at home that whole week." And then she was all, "Whatever."

Of course, this passage serves a very different illocution than would a passage from an overview paper. Nevertheless, it includes globally both a script and a persona that resemble what I expect of my students — that is, it shuttles back and forth from speaker one to speaker two, detaching itself from their remarks, and reporting them as spoken. Of course, a writer who would transliterate double-voicing from this genre to the overview paper will have to do much transforming and reformulating superstructurally, stylistically, and semantically.

However, the passage above illustrates just a fraction of the potential for transliteration going on at any moment in any one student. Each student in a class might have hundreds or maybe even thousands of potential interdiscursive links either to transfer or to transliterate into G_2. Some of the most interesting links are ones that the instructor could never have imagined. For example, one student whom I studied for a recent project found a link between the G_2 of the academic essay examination (which she had to write in her introductory American history course) and the G_1 of the business letter (particularly the kind she had been writing for years in the professional world), two genres that, to the observer, have little similarity (Popken, 1996, 1999a). The writer seems to have seen that, like the letter, the essay examination (a) has to be written rapidly, (b) is often read quickly, and (c) has only short concluding sections. Coming at the essay exam in this way appears to have helped this developing writer find a superstructure for her essay exams and even to find a style that would help the text be read more quickly and easily. Another student appears to have found a link between persuasive academic papers he was assigned to write in first-year composition and an oral genre he often used in order to break up fights at a youth rehabilitation center where he worked (Popken, 1999a).

However, though both transfer and transliteration are powerful processes in written genre acquisition, they are also so unpredictable that they don't lend themselves to much pedagogical control. That is, even though, in the case of the double-voiced monologue cited above, developing writers might potentially transliterate from G_1 to G_2, we can't automatically assume that they will. Mitigating against pedagogical control of transliteration in particular is the fact that it is individualized and largely invisible to teachers; as I have commented elsewhere, genres in students' own G_1 repertoires (especially the film review, the tourist brochure, and the newspaper article) can override attempts to teach them genres of academic life (Popken, 1998; 1999b).

To return, then, to the issue of destabilized genre pedagogy, a scaffolded syllabus such as Prince's attempts to manufacture interdiscursive links for students: it assumes that students will follow its implied links from one genre to another en route to acquiring G_2. But, since we can't control interdiscursive linking, it seems to me that we need to take a different stance. Rather than trying to control it, we ought to liberate it through the destabilized genre pedagogy. In other words, we need a course syllabus that allows transfer and transliteration to take place naturally in an intergenre state; in such a syllabus, writers are forced to use their own G_1 in constructing their renditions of G_2, their own "idiogenres" (Popken, 2000).

INSTABILITY AND ACADEMIC GENRES: A PEDAGOGICAL CONCLUSION

For courses whose goal is to integrate students into the academic community through writing, instructors have several adjustments to make in incorporating a destabilized genre pedagogy. For one thing, they absolutely must be patient with errors and evaluate writers on the potential of their discourse performance. That is, as might be expected, texts produced by students in destabilized classes often feel shaky, the result of the fact that the writers are groping about through unfamiliar territory. What this means is that one has to look more globally at student writing as genre acquisition in process. For example, I am favorably inclined toward a paper that, though it be syntactically rough or cohesively vacant, shows signs of actually coming to grips with the new genre; by contrast, I normally give a much lower grade to a paper which, though it may be mechanically perfect and syntactically easy to read, misses the global intention of the genre.

Furthermore, destabilized genre pedagogy works best if instruction is carried out inductively (Lewis, 1901). In other words, instead of trying to describe aspects of a G_2 to students, I prefer to sketch it out generally and then try to get students to figure its features out for themselves by producing exploratory drafts (Popken, 2000). Then, from working on these drafts, students normally have a number of questions about the G_2; in response to these drafts, I usually open the class up for a question-and-dialogue period where I respond to areas of the students' uncertainty by discussing options for how their own texts might be.

Also, it is important to offset the destabilizing of genres in such a class with stabilities of other sorts.[vii] In particular, it has been my experience that genre acquisition is not well supported when students are confused over the subject matter they are writing about. Therefore, if the course does not already have a pre-determined course subject, I strongly suggest a single course topic for the semester's work; most recently, I did a course called Generations in America, and my next one will be called Work in America. Thus, even though tasks may involve different genres and sub-genres, there will be a continuous subject matter for students to draw upon, making them more able to concentrate on the discursive aspects rather than the semantic ones.

In Figure 1, I offer a sample set of assignments that could be used for an academic writing course or adapted for a non-writing course. The order of the assignments is by no means absolute (Popken, 1999b), and other genres or sub-genres could substitute for the ones here.

Figure 1: A Sample Set of Genres for a Writing Course

Writing #1:   Empirical paper
Writing #2:   Theoretical paper ("argument")
Writing #3:   Hour essay exam
Writing #4:   Overview ("review-of-the-literature") paper
Writing #5:   Evaluation ("critique-of-article") paper
Writing #6:   Final essay exam

If I want to destabilize my students' genre experience from the beginning of the term, I start with an empirical paper assignment.[viii] My experience has been that, wherever in the sequence one places an empirical paper assignment, it will be a hard one to write for most students, especially first-year students. Unlike papers they may have written before, the empirical paper typically has a purpose statement (rather than a thesis), it foregrounds methodology, and it separates findings from a discussion of those findings. Normally my empirical paper assignments involve students in doing a formal "study" of some sort: perhaps interviewing one or two people in a case study or even doing a formal campus-wide survey conducted jointly by the entire class.

The second task in the sequence in Figure 1 takes students in a very different direction than the first one does. What I mean here by "theory paper" is that students develop their own theses about an issue through a body of four or five readings. Many students find this to be a hard task as well, especially since I ask them to draw specific textual examples from these article sources and use them to support their own theories. After the empirical study and the theory paper, I throw the students another change-up, shifting now to the genre of the essay "hour exam." I examine students over the contents of three or four readings in an attempt to replicate the curricular essay exam situation. Students have to adjust, of course, to the special time and structural constraints of the essay exam genre (Popken, 1989; Pace, 2000). The fourth assignment is another abrupt turn: this time students summarize the major contents of articles. This "overview" or review-of-the-literature paper is difficult for many students since they often don't see the virtue (from a reader's standpoint) of reading such a genre. The fifth assignment asks students to address specific premises made by an article writer; the difficulty here comes in identifying major premises of an argument and, secondly, in being able to evaluate the legitimacy of those points. And, the final exam, though somewhat similar to the hour exam, is longer and more complex.

Through the twists and turns of a set of assignments such as these six, most students will receive quite a rhetorical workout. Ultimately, I hope that such a destabilized pedagogy can help my students achieve some of the lofty genre goals established by Bazerman (1995):

> The best way to learn the power of writing is to write and become engaged in a compelling discourse. Then you learn that the hard work of writing well is worth it. The best way to learn flexibility in writing is to become engaged in a second discourse, and perhaps a third. When you experience the rewards of writing well in one domain, you are likely to demand of yourself that same high level of participation in any discourse you will engage in the further. The lesson that it is worth working hard at writing is perhaps the most important lesson, and it is the one most transferable. The lesson only goes wrong if you cannot differentiate the nature of the second discourse and keep trying to reassert the strategies of the first. More integrations, more fully, into more discursive systems is the answer, not fewer. (p. 257).

Notes

i.   This paper assumes non-formal definitions of genre such as those of Devitt (1993), Miller (1984), and Swales (1990).

ii. A "sub-genre" is a specific version of a genre, often one referred to in popular use by its global illocutionary speech act. For instance, the application letter, the thank you letter, and the inquiry letter are among the many sub-genres of the business letter. Similarly, the academic paper (a genre I refer to in this paper) has sub-genres such as the empirical paper, the review paper, and the theoretical-argument paper.

iii.   I find a little inconsistency in Prince's discussion about the end point of his pedagogy. He seems to denigrate the genre I refer to as the *academic paper* (his term for it is the *treatise*), preferring instead the genre of the *essay*. In fact, he says that as a teacher of college writing his job is "to teach the essay" (p. 740). Ultimately, though, his assignment on affirmative action (which he calls an *argumentative essay*) is much more like what I call a *paper* than it is an essay, at least an essay in the Montaignian tradition. (See here Popken, 1994.)

iv.   As I use the terms G_1 and G_2, I don't necessarily mean single genres; i.e., a writer's G_1 may consist of a repertoire of hundreds of past genres. Similarly, I will use G_2 to represent any new genres that a writer is attempting to acquire.

v.   By the way, by "developing" here I simply mean anyone who is entering a new genre. This happens to professionals in many fields with some regularity. For instance, in the last five years, I have struggled to acquire these genres: an accreditation self-study section report; an encomium upon the retirement of one of my mentors; a eulogy upon the death of a graduate student.

vi.   I have adapted a term from classical composition pedagogy. According to work by Murphy (1990) on the early teaching of writing, in transliteration exercises students were expected to take the content of a text in one genre and recast it into an entirely different genre: an epic becomes an oration; a deliberative speech becomes an epideictic one; and so on (pp 50-51).

vii.   My own is taught in a computer classroom; it has a web-page environment that creates a context for publishing writing; students share their writing in peer commenting sessions; and student sample papers from the past serve as a means of *imitatio*.

viii.   By an empirical paper, I mean "data-driven" discourse (Peck MacDonald, 1989) based on a formal investigation. Although such writing is rarely discussed in composition textbooks, it is, of course, the genre of choice in many disciplines in the sciences and social sciences. What I am assuming here, then, is that, though they aren't identical, curricular genres ought to resemble genres used by scholars. That is, as is suggested in work by Lave & Wenger (1991), students are discursive apprentices to teacher-scholars.

References

Bakhtin, M.M. (1981). The dialogic imagination. M. Holquist (Ed.). C. Everson & M. Holquist (Trans.). Austin: University of Texas Press.

————. (1986). The problem of speech genres. In C. Everson & M. Holquist (Eds.), V. McGee (Trans.), Speech genres and other late essays (pp. 60-102). Austin: University of Texas Press.

Bazerman, C. (1981). What written discourse does: Three examples of academic discourse. Philosophy of the Social Sciences, 11, 361-387.

———————. (1995). Response: Curricular responsibilities and professional definition. In J. Petraglia (Ed.), Reconceiving writing, rethinking writing instruction (pp. 249-260). Mahwah: Erlbaum.

Berkenkotter, C. & Huckin, T. (1995). Genre knowledge in disciplinary communication: Cognition/culture/power. Hillsdale, NJ: Erlbaum.

Berkenkotter, C., Huckin, T., & Ackerman, J. (1988). Conventions, conversations, and the writer: Case study of a student in a rhetoric Ph.D. program. Research in the Teaching of English, 22(1), 9-44.

Bishop, W., & Ostrom, H. (1994). Genre and writing: Issues, arguments, alternatives. Portsmouth, N.H.: Boynton/Cook.

Bizzell, P. (1986). What happens when basic writers come to college? College Composition and Communication, 37, 294-301.

Cope, B. & Kalantzis, M. (1993). The powers of literacy: A genre approach to teaching writing. Pittsburgh: University of Pittsburgh Press.

Devitt, A. (1993). Generalizing about genre: New conceptions of an old concept. College Composition and Communication, 44, 573-586.

Fahnestock, J. (1993). Genre and rhetorical craft. Research in the Teaching of English, 27, 265-271.

Freedman, A. (1993). Show and tell? The role of explicit teaching in the learning of new genres. Research in the teaching of English, 27, 222-251.

Freedman, A. & Adam, C. (1996). Learning to write professionally. Journal of Business and Technical Communication, 10(4), 395-407.

Freedman, A., & Medway, P. (Eds.). (1994). Genre and the new rhetoric. Bristol, PA: Taylor and Francis.

———————. (Eds.). (1994). Learning and teaching genre. Portsmouth, NH: Boynton/ Cook.

Ivanic, R. (1998). Writing and identity: The discoursal construction of identity in academic writing. Amsterdam: John Benjamins.

Johns, A. (1997). Text, role, and context: Developing academic literacies. Cambridge: Cambridge University Press.

Kutz, E. (1986). Between students' language and academic discourse: Interlanguage as middle ground. College English, 48, 385-396.

Lave, J., & Wenger, E. (1991). Situated learning: Legitimate peripheral participation. Cambridge: Cambridge University Press.

Lewis, E. (1901). Inductive lessons in rhetoric. Boston: D.C. Heath.

Lucas, T. (1988). Beyond language and culture: Individual variation in students' engagement with a written genre. ERIC document. ED 304 005.

Miller, C. (1984). Genre as social action. Quarterly Journal of Speech, 70, 151-167.

Murphy, J. (Ed.). (1990). Roman writing instruction as described by Quintilian. A short history of writing instruction: From ancient Greece to twentieth-century America. (pp. 19-76). Davis, CA: Hermagoras Press.

Pace, S. (2000). An examination of the curricular essay exam as a genre with special emphasis on an empirical study concerning sophomore literature essay exams. Unpublished Master of Arts thesis, Tarleton State University, Stephenville, Texas.

Peck MacDonald, S. (1989). Data-driven and conceptually-driven academic discourse. Written Communication, 6, 411-423.

Popken, R. (1989). Essay exams and papers: A contextual comparison. Journal of Teaching Writing, 8, 51- 65.

—————. (1992). Genre transfer in developing adult writers. Focuses, 5, 3-17.

—————. (1994). Discourse types in writing courses. In C. Russell & R. McDonald (Eds.), Sites of contention: Teaching composition in the 1990s (pp. 119-134). New York: Harper.

—————. (1996). A study of the genre repertoires of adult writers. The Writing Instructor, 15(2), 85-94.

—————. (1998). Genre mixing, popular media, and the evolution of the academic paper: One writing teacher's response. Writing on the Edge, 10(1), 67-84.

—————. (1999a). Adult writers and academic survival: The interdiscursive linking strategy. In M. Kells & V. Balester (Eds.), Attending the margins (pp. 56-73). Portsmouth, N.H.: Boynton/Cook.

—————. (1999b). Writing assignment sequencing: Some insight from genre studies. CCTE Studies, 64, 1-10.

—————. (2000). Hypothesis formation and testing in written genre acquisition: Induction and the teaching of writing. Unpublished manuscript.

Prince, M. (1989). Literacy and genre: Towards a pedagogy of mediation. College English, 51, 730-749.

Reid, I. (1987). The place of genre in learning: Current debates. Deakin, Australia: Deakin University Press.

Selinker, L. (1969). Language transfer. General Linguistics, 9, 67-92.

—————. (1977). Interlanguage. In J. Richards (Ed.), Error analysis: Perspectives on second language acquisition (pp. 31-54). London: Longman.

Swales, J. (1990). Genre analysis: English in academic and research settings. Cambridge: Cambridge University Press.

Wertsch, J. (1991). Voices of the mind: A sociocultural approach to mediated action. Cambridge: Harvard University Press.

Williams, J., & Columb, G. (1993). The case for explicit teaching: Why what you don't know won't help you. Research in the Teaching of English, 27, 252-264.

Process Report://computing.interactive.classrooms

Robert Luke
University of Toronto

> But there is will. "Future" is inherently plural.
>   - William Gibson. *All Tomorrow's Parties*, p. 107.

THE HOLOTROPE: COMPUTER ASSISTED LEARNING AND INTERACTIVE PEDAGOGY

The emergent field of Computer Assisted Learning (CAL) is character-ized by a pedagogical approach that combines old practices with new technologies to create a *holotropic pedagogy*. This entails curriculum and cultural identity negotiation within a "whole time" continuum, allowing for an adaptive pedagogy that is continually contemporary. The transforma-tive possibilities inherent to education mediated by CAL construct a self-re-flective educational space, negotiated via an interactive pedagogy. Academic institutions can maintain core material while enabling culturally relevant curricula to surface. This lets institutions adapt and grow with the changing needs of the communities they serve, on or off campus.

Within computer-mediated learning environments, students are em-powered to participate in the construction of curricula. Students are pre-sented with the opportunity to critically examine and more directly inform the educational process by interacting with the course material as it is, and as it may be taught in the future. The student participates in the process of learning by contributing to course Bulletin Boards and to web pages as part of the learning architecture, or even just by advising the instructor or course programmer of dead links. But an instructor who uses computer-based re-sources must teach critical media literacy, and acknowledge the very real possibility that information may not always be available at a given site, or "cite" of reference. Since Internet sites can be adjusted at will, educators have a responsibility to ensure that their links are updated, and that students can be taught to access relevant and timely information. While this problem is not as evident within courseware that is maintained at the host institution, increasingly, universities are collaborating over the World Wide Web (WWW), sharing information and resource databases in a textual web. This facilitates unprecedented access to the information and experience(s) which construct knowledge.

PROJECT: LOOKING AHEAD OVER THE PAST

```
qsilver1% cd www/janus/
/export/home/humanities/6ral/www/janus
qsilver1% whoami
6ral
qsilver1%
```

%whoami

This paper focuses on my own experience as both student and teacher within the university, as well as a researcher and designer of CAL tools since 1994. I draw on my experience at the University of Northern BC, where I began exploring the pedagogical aspects of online media through Independent Study projects as part of undergraduate course work. In 1996, I was part of a design team that researched, designed, and implemented four UNBC English courses (all of them fourth year/graduate courses) that are currently being taught via the WWW. [Access the UNBC Course Online Project at http://quarles.unbc.ca/english/adindex.html].

Our team at UNBC examined the potential pedagogical ramifications of computers and online media, and how these new technologies can best enable a university like UNBC to serve a community spread over a vast geographic area. While nothing can compare to face-to-face interaction, online learning networks can at least serve as information banks that students can access at their discretion from remote locations. The courses we designed consisted of a basic template that the instructor then tailored to individual tastes. Students enrolled in the courses are then familiarized with a basic schema that allows for easy adaptation to the differences in each front end — the interface used as the "virtual classroom." Each course consists of a weekly lecture, assignments that are submitted electronically, a readings list (including some online readings), and a chat area where students can converge in a virtual environment to discuss course concerns. Software written by Professor Stan Beeler at UNBC incorporates a search engine with user tracking routines, enabling instructors to follow usage patterns of the students. Students can then be graded on how well they have engaged the material. This reinforces the pedagogy that underlies active learning as process and allows a modicum of individualized context and culturally or community relevant curricula to be realized. An important feature of UNBC's Distance Education mandate is that it offers the communities it serves a curriculum that can be relevant to living in the North.

Later, as a Teaching Assistant for English 211: Medieval Literature at Queen's University, I had the opportunity to use an HTML version of Chaucer's *Troilus and Criseyde* as a learning tool with my students. The database reference tool was used in the class to demonstrate how close readings are gleaned from textual data. Students are presented with the primary text alongside critical interpolations that are then linked to an essay example. Here, the students are shown how to integrate textual quotation within their writing. As this database is itself always under development, I was able to learn from the experience of using it in the class, gathering feedback from my students in order to retool the site to the specific requirements of each class that will use it in the future. These learners were engaged in writing the course requirements as well as participating in the larger scheme of the course's development. As such, they became active participants in the learning process, helping to produce a constantly retooled learning environment in order to meet the needs of the changing community utilizing the database in the future. The courseware can be adjusted as per students' suggestions; this encouraged students to be active in the learning process. It also generated input — and output — into and from the community at large, be this local, national, or global.

As both a teacher and learner in this process, I am able to realize my own goals of teaching the students the primary text as well as how to integrate it within their own critical essays and responses. The students and I share a responsibility to engage the course material, and with this particular classroom technology I also try to teach them a response ability: to the text, and to writing the university itself. Students participating in this ongoing project are allowed an avenue of expression on par with the course material as I will teach it. They become "the text" by actively engaging the course material and in helping to keep it current. My paper thus presents a self-reflective argument that will critically examine how technology can and is deployed within the university institution based on my own experience of designing HT tools since 1994, and in particular the project with *The Chaucer Janus*. Access the site at http://qsilver.queensu.ca/~6ral/janus/index.html and explore the links found in this paper. Engaging the reading process in conjunction with the learning tool itself will help foster an interactivity within this frame of reference and participate within a holotropic pedagogy.

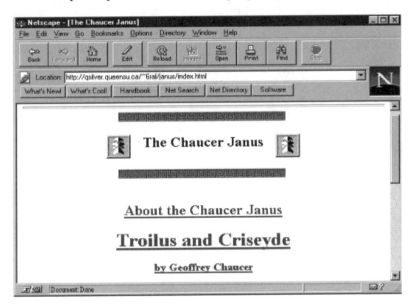

Process Report://computing.interactive.classrooms/thought/ computerMediuMclassroom

The Chaucer Janus was originally conceived as part of course work for my Master's Degree in English Language and Literature at Queen's University in the summer of 1997. My idea was to construct a CAL tool that could be used as a corollary to the book. I developed the project in consultation with Professor Phil Rogers, Department of English, Queen's University, who was then my instructor in Medieval Literature. The theme statement I appended to the index page outlines my intentions for the project:

> This etext version of Chaucer's poem represents a transition between old and new forms of scholarship. It is not intended to replace reading a book. Rather, it is meant to be used in conjunction with a book for scholarly purposes as a gateway through which new avenues and ways of looking at the poem may be explored.
>
> janus/janus.html

I had not done much work on the project for some time when, as a Teaching Assistant for English 211, I was given the opportunity to lecture on *Troilus and Criseyde*, and so use the *Janus* to explore my own needs as a teacher and the needs of my students as learners of literature and writing.

The design is simple, relying mainly on text with a minimum of graphics in order to project a "clean" and uncluttered environment. This foregrounds the text itself, as well as enabling fast downloads. This is an important feature that provides a simple and easy-to-use interface. The text is accessed via a search engine — "Search for sonnets.cgi" — designed by Professor Stan Beeler of UNBC; it uses perl programming language to find words or phrases within documents of text. To modify the search engine the Chaucer Janus, I worked with Troy Kay of Information Technology Services at Queen's University. The search engine makes possible a "virtual pagination," whereby the text is downloaded into small chunks, or virtual pages that match the pages in *The Riverside Chaucer*. The "Navigation Explanation" explains the virtual pagination system developed to make the etext correspond to the book pages, thereby making citations exact, even when viewing the etext with different browsers that may download the pages differently.

> From the search results menu page, you can follow the links to the page(s) with your search query. Your search term(s) will be converted to upper case letters, and will be in bold script (depending on your browser). Your search query will also appear in parentheses at the top of each page.
>
> From the search engine, each page will be downloaded separately. You can navigate through the article by following the ◄ (Page Back) and the ► (Page Forward) links, or you can start a new search by following the **Search for new terms** ? link.
>
> Moving forward and back through the database will not maintain the bold/ uppercase search term(s). You must return to the search results menu page using your browser's "Back" button, and follow each link that appears there to allow the search engine to make your query term(s) stand out.

[From the search engine, each page will be downloaded separately. You can navigate through the article by following the (Page Back) and the (Page Forward) links, or you can start a new search by following the Search for new terms link.]

From the search results menu page, you can follow the links to the page(s) with your search query. Your search term(s) will be converted to upper case letters, and will be in bold script (depending on your browser). Your search query will also appear in parentheses at the top of each page.

The primary text is presented alongside textual explication and secondary source material (see Figure below). This is to provide a visual mnemonic cue to the actual textual explication; the student can see the primary text at the same time as the critical reading of it, which aids in the teaching of critical reading skills. This method also helps keep the myriad of critical linking grounded in the text itself, as the student can always see, and so remember, what part of the primary text started a particular stream of thought or link exploration.

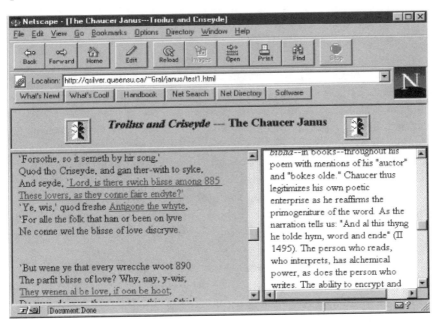

One of the drawbacks to this method is that the user must be familiar with the intricacies of navigation on the Net, specifically, how to move back and forward within frames. While this is accomplished with right mouse button clicks and is relatively straightforward, instructions are provided in the "Navigation Explanation" page.

My primary objectives in using this tool were as follows:

1. To teach my undergraduate class some themes in *Troilus and Criseyde*, as per my duties and responsibilities as a Teaching Assistant.

2. To show, and tell, how textual explication functions as a part of literary criticism.

3. To demonstrate how these explications and primary text quotations can be integrated into essay writing.

4. To test and obtain feedback from my class as to the use of this particular CAL tool currently under development.

The timing of the class could not have been better as the students were getting ready to submit their second and final formal writing assignment. While grading the first batch of essays, I noticed that many students were having difficulty with integrating quotations within the body of their writing. Literature departments are not required to teach writing skills per se; rather, they focus solely on the literature being studied. This leaves it up to individual students to seek out help from university writing centres. However, not all students seek out writing centre help. Those who do still wonder how to write according to "what the professor/grader is looking for," an indication of the writing standard deviation even within the same university department. Simply hoping that students will take the initiative to seek out the knowledge they require to succeed at university writing is somewhat defeatist, in that it fails to meet the pedagogic responsibility of ensuring that students have the skills necessary to their success in the classroom. This *laissez faire* approach to education — with administrative mandates restricting what is taught during class time — will only maintain the status quo and the perception of falling writing standards. Some of my students had expressed a desire to have writing tutorials on how to write critical essays on literature, and I was presented with a problem of facilitating this request while adhering to my responsibility to teach the course material, not writing.

Using *The Chaucer Janus* seemed a perfect solution to this dilemma. It would provide me with an opportunity to do both of these jobs at the same time: demonstrate critical writing skills while simultaneously teaching some of the major themes present in Chaucer. Moreover, I was also afforded the opportunity to test and debug the *Janus*, and to obtain feedback directly from my students as to the efficacy of this exploration of CAL tools in general.

Process Report://computing.interactive.classrooms/thought/action/

The Virtual Reality Realized

2 March 1998

The lab setup was very user friendly. It came equipped with an NEC Video/Data Projector with a standard personal computer interface. The projector shows on a screen what is being run on the computer, and both Windows and Macintosh computers were available for use. There is a live feed to the Internet, but I did nonetheless bring backup files on floppy disks in case the network were to go down during my presentation.

I began the class by stating the objectives of the day. We were going to explore some themes from Chaucer's *Troilus and Criseyde* while simultaneously paying attention to the structure of writing a critical literary essay. We were to learn about the text and some of its meanings, as well as how to communicate these meanings in written assignments. The students in the class write two essays — one per term — as well as translation tests and quizzes. Many of the students did poorly on the first essay, and many exhibited the same problems with textual explication and the integration of quotations in the body of their writing. I was able to construct and retool *The Chaucer Janus* to meet the pedagogical demands of this classroom.

I explained that the class was to be part of my action research into CAL tool classroom use and integration, and that this was the first time I had used this tool in a class. This particular class was to be a Writing Tutorial and a Lecture at the same time. In order to get the most of the experience, I asked for class participation and subsequent feedback, as this would be essential to understanding what was to happen that day. I made the class aware of their participation in my learning process, just as I was in theirs. Education at that moment was Interactive, and I brought this to the attention of the class because I wanted to underscore their role in the educative experience. Our experience was to mirror the interactive capability of the technology we were using. I felt that by making them aware of the status of the technology as a tool we were all going to use and learn from that day, I would better be able to smoothly integrate the technology, to normalize its usage amongst all of the class participants. This did indeed have the intended effect. I noted, however, that their role was to be somewhat passive, as it was only I who was to actually interact with the technology proper, but that this was in keeping with my responsibility as their teacher to direct the classroom activities. I had the responsibility to interact with the hardware myself, while we all interacted with the software.

THE ELECTRONIC TEXT, THE COMPUTER TERMINAL, AND THE LOCUS OF AUTHOR-ITY

@text

In the lecture I used a metaphor — "Literary Alchemy" — to discuss the cultural power of the Word, as used by Chaucer, in combination with classical notions of poetry and epic conventions. This creates a literary alchemy based on the present or presence of narrative enunciation: the actual speaking of the poem itself. I argued that this narrative *event* seeks to attain a kind of mythic immortality. To underscore this, I reminded the class of the fact that they were studying this text 600 years after it was written; so Chaucer, his poetic characters, and the mythic/historical events of the Trojan War had indeed attained some semblance of immortality: in the currency of remembrance at least. I used classical notions of poetry and the epic conventions of contemporary movies that are common currency in the pop market iconosphere we share. This had the effect of demystifying the terminology and the patterns of its principles. I used linked HTML files outlining terms, epic and classical poetry conventions as visual aids for support, and as an introduction to the focus on the screen. The class was able to listen to what I was saying as they read the basic principles I was expanding on in the oral lecture, thereby making distinct correlations between spoken and written argumentation. The lecture was also there for them to return to if they desired.

Only 3 of the 31 students in attendance had read beforehand the files that I had asked them to read the week before. It was unclear how many students had reread the passage we were to subject to a close reading that day. This was a problem because it meant that I had to go over some basic principles that formed part of the foundation to understanding the deployment of my literary alchemy metaphor, and how it was to function as a re-presentation of what we were to study in the text and in the writing tutorial.

I found that the way the technology was set up in the classroom itself required me to turn my back to the class to use the computer, something I noted at the time as perhaps distracting, albeit necessary. Also, I was essentially tied to the terminal; it literally became a stopping place for me, although I did frequently walk across the front of the room in the first part of the class in order to engage the entire room.

The first part of class consisted of 45 minutes of textual explication, with me essentially reading my lecture from the right side screen that contained the linked textual explications, and expanding on these themes in the conversation with the class. This demonstrated how my lecture was grounded in the text, and how I was using the text to put forth my ideas, now read to the class. After a break, we spent the remaining time (approximately 35 minutes) reading over an essay (see Figure on facing page) I had prepared for the occasion. I read each paragraph in turn and asked the class to critique it.

After lecturing about the power of the word and those charged with its dissemination — including foregrounding my role in this process with reference to the present classroom experience — I then held up my writing as both an example for emulation and object of critique, negotiating the interstice of both teacher and student simultaneously. The students debated what was good, acceptable, or in need of correction. I defended my writing while at the same time criticizing it, at once positioning myself as both student and teacher. This went a long way to demonstrating my understanding of their position: I was both marked by, and marker of the university writing experience.

NOWNOTES OR, "DO YOU SEE WHAT I MEAN?"

I used *The Chaucer Janus* to show the text with my interpolations and criticisms alongside it. With the primary text displayed alongside my lecture notes, the class was able to see the effect of writing in the margins of the book. This particular presentation equalizes my writing with that of the primary text, promoting an equal engagement of ideas, illustrating the importance of ideas written next to the text; each note is linked to the primary text it is intended to explicate.

The students were presented with the primary text as an object equal in appearance to what they see on the Internet and on word processors. All students hand in essays produced on word processors. This demystification applied also to my lecture, as they were able to see both my meaning, and how what I was attempting to articulate was literally joined to the text. I marked the text according to my lecture, my ideas and my metaphor of literary alchemy, which I then deployed in the essay example the class critiqued. As I suspected, most of the students jumped at the chance to criticize their TA's writing; I am the marker of their papers, and even though this power dynamic must be acknowledged, I was able to demonstrate that I was also marked by them. Their participation in this activity showed them how their own writing is evaluated, at the same time as demonstrating how to effectively build primary textual quotations into the logic and structure of writing in general.

There were several queries along the lines of "Is this what our writing should be like?" and "Is this how you want us to write?" reproducing the climate of the university writing and reading experience in general. Student concerns over finding the exact "how" reflect the demands of achieving a grade standard, as well as betraying a perception that there is indeed a single standard I could illustrate for them. I responded that they were free to be creative in their interpretation of the texts we study, but that successful literary writing will deal with language and text in a very explicit way, and that in order to communicate effectively what we want to say, we must be able to articulate our thoughts and theories within the works we study. The free reign I allowed the class over my writing — as an object for critique — showed them that their grader was subject to the same rules that apply to them, rules *in*scribed in and by the university (as text).

READING MYSELF ALOUD (AS TEXT)

I felt an initial awkwardness in reading aloud my lecture; I felt I needed a screen in front of me so that I could maintain eye contact with the class. Accustomed as I am to lecturing from very sparse point-form notes, it was somewhat disconcerting at first to read aloud the textual explications that constituted my lecture material. I found myself reading the script only, versus my normal practice of talking about points relevant to the lecture theme. One of the student responses returned to me said that this combination was effective for both kinds of learners — aural and visual. There was also some initial awkwardness integrating the lecture — what I was teaching them about the text — with the writing tutorial and the focus on writing and quotation integration.

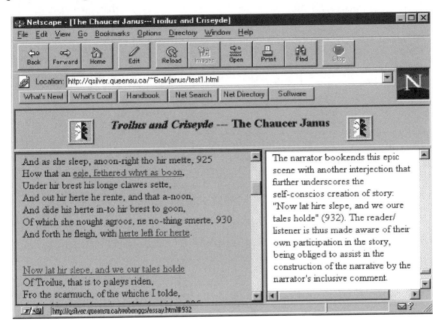

The university as text was my writing as object for study and critique. My students must trust me to teach them things they need to know and which are sanctioned by the instructor in charge of the class, Professor John Finlayson. By drawing attention to the power of the word as deployed in Chaucer, I was able to underscore the metaphor I was using to talk about Chaucer's poem *Troilus and Criseyde*. I spoke of a textual *mise en abîme* — the disappearance point created by two mirrors facing each other — effecting a kind of transcendence and perpetual present via the presence of narrative enunciation. I likened this to the event of poetry, to which the narrator of the poem makes constant reference. Within the poem, a character named Pandarus essentially creates the love union of Troilus and Criseyde, which in turn is created as the narrator speaks of the written work he reads as he tells the story. The narrator, drawing attention to both the speech act and the written source being read, also refers to other "bokes old" that the author of the poem has read, inferring that if the members of the audience could read, they would see for themselves that what was being read — after having been written — was true. Thus, the written word was foregrounded as a source of power, a locus of author-ity. Writing-as-figure was displayed as writing-as-ground, echoing McLuhan's premise that the medium is the message. That is, the use of writing in literature as well as an institutional "technology of reason" (Trifonas, 2000) became the focus of analysis. Writing-as-figure — the actual poetry of Chaucer in this instance — led us into an examination of the cultural apparatus of power associated with writing.

My lecture was a mirror of a mirror of words and written discourse, reflected on a monitor projected before the class. My lecture was reflective of my position as both student and teacher with/in the university writing experience. By holding up my own writing as an object for both study and critique, I was able to illustrate for my students how learning and writing are inextricably linked in university literary education, and how this learning is constituted by text and textuality.

Process Report://computing.interactive.classrooms/thought/action/ reflection/

Cultivating a Critical Friendship with my Classroom: "I had fun learning today"
It was a challenge for me to hold up my writing as both example and object of critique. At times I was defensive of my argument, but I learned from the class, and was able to tell them that some of the criticism they were leveling at my writing I had heard before. I felt that this critique of my writing led to an effective communication with the class and a mutually improved understanding of the nature of writing literary papers. Several students mentioned having problems with understanding my writing, saying it was too complex; these remarks echoed comments relating to clarity and diction in writing that I had written on their essays. By showing them an example of my writing I was able to work within the power relationship of teacher/ student interactivity and promote a process of learning in which we could all engage together.

I was able to use the resources available to me to achieve the double objective of teaching the course material and writing essays on this material, to help the students understand their role as writers in the university institution and the importance of writing clearly and concisely with close regard for source material and argumentation. Although I was to an extent tied to the terminal as operator — the computer terminal was literally a stopping point for me — I was still able to facilitate this articulation with the text we study and the writing experience itself. This means being aware of oneself as participant within the larger experience of the university as text. The textual environment of the university institution was foregrounded as the axis of this ideology, and access of text and language in this instance was afforded by computer technology. Holding up my written work thus enabled me to hold up my use of technology, my academic work as well as my pedagogic work; the technology of language became the language of technology, as students were encouraged to see that they too can engage in re-writing the texts studied as part of literary education. I was able to demonstrate this re-vision, to show a different way of (de)constructing text — in this case Hypertext — that is a more direct engagement with the writing experience, and which therefore demystifies the writing experience: "hypertext blurs the boundaries between writer and reader and therefore instantiates ... Barthes's distinction between readerly and writerly texts" (Landow, 1997, pp. 45). The reader is not just a passive consumer of texts but a producer of meaning from the writing/reading experience. Encouraging active engagement with textual space, at its most basic level, lets students see their part in this production of textual space, in the text of the university, and the university's texts.

RE-PRESENTING WRITING FOR CRITIQUE: RESPONSE ABILITY

My responsibility to teach the students something about the text we studied that day interacted with my response ability to the task of teaching them something about writing as well; I responded to their need for direction in writing essays. I was able to use my skills as a programmer and teacher to develop and retool the technology available to me in order to construct the writing experience as displayed to the class. The students engaged their responsibility to learn the course material, as well as an ability to respond to the lecture and writing tutorial. Their role in the pedagogic process was equal to mine, as each of us in the classroom that day engaged the writing process. Implicit in the lecture and the tutorial was the questioning of the underlying structures of writing and its many malleable meanings. I encouraged the students to see that writing — even the canonized writing they study as "texts" — can be contextualized within the same medium, in this case a web browser, underscoring an aspect of the democratizing potential of computer and hyptertextual technologies.

The students and I shared a response ability: theirs was the ability to respond to the texts we study and how "we" are studying it and re-presenting it in written work, and mine was the ability to teach writing skills and encourage the written exploration of literature while being conscious of writing as cultural capital. We all exercised the ability to interact in the teaching/

learning process with technology, and we all used it to our mutual advantage. I ended the lecture with general questions and by asking the class for their feedback on a questionnaire I had distributed at the beginning of class. This underscored the fact that their participation in my research was to be extremely helpful in my future work designing and using CAL tools. The *process* of education was thus actualized, as I made them aware of our shared identity as students and active learners in the university writing experience.

PRINT: A PEDAGOGY OF PERMANENCE

Many students say that once something is written on their word processor they are reluctant to change it because it has a sense — I would say an illusion — of permanence. This sense of permanence was undermined by my lecture theme, which encouraged questioning the ideology behind writing and examining the associative power relations at work in print culture, an examination at work (and play) within Chaucer's poetry as well. Another problem associated with writing on a word processor is some students' difficulty in beginning the process of writing itself.

Had I opened a word processing platform for the class to see and started rewriting the essay under scrutiny according to their critique, we would have further demonstrated how writing itself could be part of a collaborative process, as informed by reading. While their own individual writing is just that — their own — this would have had the effect of reinforcing the notion that once something is written it can be changed; it can be *subject* to further revision. A common problem among these students was reworking what they have already written. This bespeaks a general reluctance to delete what appears on their computer screen because of the perception of permanence ascribed to the cultural apparatus of the written word.

While there was not enough time in the class to undertake this kind of real-time collaborative writing, the lecture's thematic focus on the implicit power of written text coupled with the writing tutorial that deconstructed my writing (the marked marker) went a long way toward showing not just the malleability of meanings inherent in language and poetry, but also the malleability of my own, and by extension their own writing, based on the primary text under study. Also, the awkward management of the technology — the fact that I had to turn my back on the class in order to interact with the computer — meant that it was not very practical to undertake revision with the class. Besides being confident that my writing could be held as an example of textual integration for my class, rewriting in real time would have taken too much time in this instance. As I am required to focus my lectures on thematic aspects of texts under study, and as this was my primary concern for the lecture that day, it was not practical for me to devote more time than I did to the mechanics of writing.

Of course, repeating the multi-dimensionality of this experience is problematised by the difficulty of finding a primary text that replicates Chaucer's concern over poetic enterprise, language, and written work in general. However, with the aid of scanners and coding ability, the experiment and lesson can be replayed with any text, in that any text can be used as an example for writing exercises.

THE CHANGING PROGRAMME OF CLASS

I was revising parts of my lecture aids until fifteen minutes before the class. This included the simple adding of links between the various documents I was using, as well as checking all the links to ensure they were working properly. I had a backup disk on hand in the event of server glitches, as well as my copy of *The Riverside Chaucer*, which contained the poem with my notes written in the margins of the text. This marginalia is the writing of the read text, and, as Landow (1997) points out, hypertext can allow much more marginalia. This in turn allows for much more information to be both explicated and referenced. Underlined text in my copy corresponded to the hyperlinks in the primary text onscreen, and I was able to use the hyperlinked documents to offer reference to my textual explications that the students could, if necessary, revisit.

My students participated with me in the process of learning, and also helped shape my future use of CAL tools in the classroom. They actively engaged the course material and the writing experience as mediated by the transformative capabilities brought about by the use of this technology. Just as I taught about texts and the process of writing itself, so too did my students help write the curriculum. The curriculum that day was written specifically for them, and they helped articulate the future of CAL as I will learn from the experience. This represents an interactive pedagogy.

STUDENT RESPONSE: USER INPUT

I let the students know that their participation in the process of learning was not going to be limited to the class; they would inform part of my writing on the experience. The questionnaire I distributed contained the following four questions:

1. Do you feel you have learned anything about the text, and about writing? Has the writing tutorial been effective in demonstrating textual explication and quotation integration?
2. Was the use of the computer overhead effective? How could it have been
   better designed to suit your needs, or the needs of the class in general?
3. What is the effect of this kind of "interactive" teaching tool? How did
   you respond to it?
4. Any other comments or suggestions?

The questionnaire provided my email address for direct feedback, and
confidentiality was assured.

I received 24 responses to my questionnaire. All respondents reported
that the technology interface was effective in demonstrating explication beside the primary text. There was general approval of the split screen, as it
gave a good idea of how to glean ideas from the text under study. As noted
above, one person said my reading of the overhead was effective for both
aural and visual learners, while another said that this reading detracted from
the learning experience. This person said the tool was "effective" and "It
was exciting to have something new introduced but I find it difficult to decide whether I should pay attention to you or what's on the screen." Since in
most instances what was on the screen was the same as what I was saying,
this student's comment illustrated the "permanence of print" and its effect
on both students and the learning environment. One student reported, "My
admiration for putting your own writing on the board and saying 'what's
wrong'," underscoring the interstice of student/teacher which this process
bridged. Judging by the number of students who participated in critiquing
my writing during the class, I would say that this was a shared feeling. By
showing the students that I am subject to the same kind of criticism they are,
I was able to reflect writing as *process*, as even my "finished product" served
for consumption was susceptible to revision according to what the writing
community — the class — felt was appropriate.

Process Report://computing.interactive.classrooms
/thought/action/reflection/thought/

Affirming a Future Framework: Some Possibilities
With the aid of various Markup Languages (HTML, SGML, SHTML,
XML, etc.), perl script, cgi, and other coding languages, online learning
environments allow for the subversion of traditional linear and autocratic

teaching practices. In keeping with recent trends in pedagogy, the learner becomes, at least potentially, an active participant within the course material, as opposed to just a note-taker in a lecture hall. This has the effect of enhancing the educative experience, and making it truly "interactive." The student engages the course material — under the guidance and direction of the instructor — but is encouraged to chart her or his own way, following intuitive links through the mass of educational material the student is charged with learning. The student thus literally writes "self" into the text of the university. S/he is encouraged to explore the "democratizing" potential of the computer medium by engaging with the course material and writing personal homepages that can be used as part of the class experience, both for distance and face-to-face education. This has many benefits for those engaged in distance learning, and facilitates the creation of community learning networks that can work together despite geographical barriers.

Recognizing the problem of traditional product-centred education and acknowledging education as a continual process that always, and all ways, involves the communities it serves represents an important step towards re-defining pedagogy in Canada. "The significance of 'end-oriented thinking' to the development of the modern university cannot be underestimated," and moving away from and questioning the "technologies of reason" that have established the notion of education as product entails a radical rethinking of the ends of education itself (Trifonas, 2000, p.123). "Educational hyper-text redefines the role of instructors by transferring some of their power and authority to students. This technology has the potential to make the teacher more a coach than a lecturer, and more an older, more experienced partner in a collaboration than an authenticated leader" (Landow, 1997, p.222), a revo-lutionary pedagogy that Landow acknowledges will not be embraced by all within the formal structures of learning. The move towards lifelong learn-ing principles and the production of virtual learning communities can help to enhance the sense of a shared space. Communities dispersed over large geographic areas can interact with and have continuous access to resources for qualitative educational development: the construction of spaces of pos-sibility as responsible transformative pedagogy. Education as process thus becomes a fully participatory — and shared — experience.

The virtual community can help with the construction of new pro-grams, offering an avenue of support to remote areas in virtual or real time. This helps decentre educational policy-making as it acknowledges the impor-tance of community input. Multi-Site Authoring tools and dedicated Course-ware environments made possible by CAL create a "cite" of reference that all participants can post to, reporting not on progress but on process. This reaffirms a holotropic pedagogy that is collaborative and interactive, both between student and teacher and within the general academic and teaching communities, as well as within the larger space of the community in general. The notion of online space as a place for learning is entirely predicated upon creating a textual architecture. "Computer conferences should be thought of as spaces that can be shaped by topical structuring and sequencing to form an educational environment" (Harasim, Starr, Teles, & Turoff, 1995, p.139), and this idea of space is inherently textual, wherein worlds are constructed in words within a text-based medium. Cultivating information literacy "involves gaining the skills and knowledge to read and interpret the text of the world and to navigate and negotiate successfully its challenges, conflicts, and crises" (Kellner, 2000, p. 197). Learning to learn with online technologies requires learning to use text to construct the learning self, to participate in creating the textual space where the interaction takes place in an open, active learning environment. By encouraging this kind of critical information or media literacy, and by using these technologies in learning situations, this technology is rendered transparent by virtue of the fact that it becomes just another medium for information delivery in the pursuit of knowledge.

The proliferation of computers and the advent of the World Wide Web have seen computers functioning as innovative educative tools. Accordingly, "we need to develop new literacies to meet the challenge of the new technologies, and literacies of diverse sorts — including an even more fundamental importance for print literacy — are of crucial importance in restructuring education for a high-tech and multicultural society" (Kellner, 2000, pp. 196-7). "Although the latest generation of Internet software has stressed multimedia applications, the public conversations and personal encounters that characterize the non-commercial culture of the Internet remain almost exclusively text-based" (Porter, 1996, p. xv), and this is especially applicable to academic uses of the Internet as well. It is thus imperative to be able to use the technology and to be able to write self into this textual and technological environment.

Providing access to innovative uses of learning technologies reinforces the idea that "students should learn new forms of computer literacy that involve both how to use computer culture to do research and gather information, as well as learning to perceive the computer as a cultural terrain which contains texts, spectacles, games, and new interactive multimedia requiring new modes of literacy" (Kellner, 2000, p. 206). The online cultural terrain is a textual one, and as the university as text is reconstituted in cyberspace for critical examination and reflection, it becomes even more important to encourage multiple critical literacies. The incidental skills that students acquire through exposure to and use of hyptertext learning tools break down the textual barrier that constitutes the university experience, democratizing the reading and writing experience. It is therefore important that "genuine computer literacy involves not just technical knowledge and skills, but refined reading, writing, research, and communicating ability that involves heightened capabilities for critically accessing, analyzing, interpreting, and processing print, image, sound, and multimedia material" (Kellner, 2000, p. 206).

While still relatively young, the Internet has become a medium that transcends geographical and cultural margins. It provides archiving features with hypertext linkage to an enormous potential database. A recent study of the amount and accessibility of information on the WWW indicates that only "About 6% of web servers have scientific/ educational content (defined here as university, college and research lab servers)," and the "estimate of the number of servers on the publicly indexable web as of February 1999 is 2.8 million" (Lawrence & Giles, 1999, p.107). With this in mind, it is important for educators to realize they have a responsibility to ensure that their students are shown where and how to find appropriate and relevant information. Using the WWW and the Internet within educational settings requires much more work than might be expected. Pedagogical issues such as teacher/student interaction, resource availability, and technological and access problems are just some of the issues that need to be explored in this area.

The transformative possibilities of a continual dialogue mediated by CAL can help people in remote areas to access, design, and implement educational programmes. This will teach the skills necessary for living in the global economy, while maintaining educational directives that are locally relevant. While this analysis is somewhat problematised by the economics of access — only those who can afford the technology can log on — the bias of print culture is subverted: anyone can publish on the WWW. And, even though there exists the very real danger of an information elite and a growing digital divide, this same elite is forced to renegotiate its own citation fixation regarding what can constitute an authority. Traditional hierarchies of power are subverted, and in their place is implemented a community-centred and experiential discourse that can collaborate with other communities. While this is a kind of utopia, the potentialities of Computer Assisted Learning and community learning networks can be used to open the educative conversation to all voices in the community, provided the community is given access to the technology. The sharing of resources, both informational and technological, will further reinforce the coherence of the larger community that constitutes the connected intelligences of the virtual collective. The shared experience of the virtual thus informs the real, providing a framework for the construction and maintenance of a global community that shares itself, in itself, creating a discourse that begins where it ends: as textual transmission.

Process Report://computing.interactive.classrooms
                    /thought/action/reflection/thought/post.script

After Words, Writing

Writing this paper has been an educational experience for me, especially since it has differed from what I "normally" write in the course of academic research into literature. This in itself is interesting in view of the construction of the university writing experience. It underscores some of the variance in writing effected within the institutional parameters of the university as text. I have been experimenting with CAL tools since 1994, and this action research project has led me through the thought/action/reflection/thought process that has further enhanced my use and design of using computer and online learning technologies in the classroom.

I have been aided by a critical community in my research, and it is the construction of this critical community that has created and fostered a continual awareness of the need to listen to all aspects of and participants in the educational experience. I am most indebted to Professor Stan Beeler of UNBC for programming help and expertise, and pedagogical advice. Several colleagues have been crucial to the actual writing process and the pedagogic implications of CAL. Sandra Neill, professor of English at George Brown College in Toronto, has provided invaluable pedagogical advice and editorial assistance. Jason Vacheresse, Faculty of Education, Queen's University, provided pedagogical advice and assistance. Informing my dialogue are numerous other people, not the least of whom are the students of English 211 (1997-98) and Professor John Finlayson. Of particular importance in mediating Medieval scholarship and CAL is Professor Phil Rogers for his help in the initial construction of *The Chaucer Janus*, as well as Professor John Pierce, Department of English, Queen's University, and Troy Kay for technical advice. Also important is the community at UNBC for sparking my initial interest in this area, especially Professor David Dowling and Professor Dee Horne for guidance and supervision during my first CAL projects.

All parts of my critical community have come together to provide commentary and feedback on my position as a writer of the university text. Overall, and most importantly, it has been the *process* of designing and exploring CAL that has helped inform me about the process of writing and learning in general. The feedback and commentary from various members of my critical community has enabled me to both share my research findings with the communities in which I live and work and to continue the conversation around Computer Assisted Learning with both teachers and students within the university writing experience.

A reflection on writing is necessarily a reflection on the critical community that I write in and out of, and it is the construction of these critical communities that creates the writing experience that constitute the university itself. The university experience is the textual intersection and interaction between communities. If the university *is* text, then the communities it serves are the all-important marginalia that seeks to both interpolate the text and explicate, or understand it. The transformative possibilities of CAL allow for this centre/margin dichotomy to be broken down somewhat, allowing all users of the text the potential to participate with parity within the larger construction of the textual environment that dominates the university economy and print culture in general. While the economics of access still maintain a hegemonic force over who can access this environment, increased awareness and public participation within the educative conversation will allow for the construction of a community-centred curricula that can constantly interact with the local, national, and global community, as mediated within the textual space of computer technology.

References

Gibson, W. (1999). All tomorrow's parties. New York: Berkley.

Harasim, L., Hiltz, S.R., Teles, L., & Turoff, M. (1995). Learning networks: A field guide to teaching and learning online. Cambridge, MA and London: MIT Press.

Kellner, D. (2000). Multiple literacies and critical pedagogies: New paradigms. In P. P. Trifonas (Ed.), Revolutionary pedagogies: Cultural politics, instituting education, and the discourse of theory (pp. 196-221). New York and London: Routledge.

Landow, G. (1997). Hypertext 2.0. Baltimore and London: Johns Hopkins University Press.

Lawrence, S. & Giles, C.L. (1999). Accessibility of information on the web. Nature, 400, 107-109.

Luke, R. The Chaucer Janus. http://qsilver.queensu.ca/~6ral/janus/

McLuhan, M. (1964). Understanding media: The extensions of man. New York: Signet.

Porter, D. (Ed.). (1996). Introduction. Internet culture. New York and London: Routledge.

Trifonas, P.P. (Ed.). (2000). Technologies of reason: Toward a regrounding of academic responsibility. Revolutionary pedagogies: Cultural politics, instituting education, and the discourse of theory (pp. 113-139). New York and London: Routledge.

Learning Journals at Lakehead: Four Pedagogical Perspectives

Bill Heath, Kim Fedderson, Frederick Holmes, and Jeanette Lynes
Lakehead University

INTRODUCTION

Although Lakehead's English 1100 is primarily a literature — as opposed to composition — course, some instructors at Lakehead sought ways to incorporate more writing into their 1100 syllabi.[i] This endeavour proved to be challenging, given the large class sizes. The four instructors who offer accounts of their classroom experience developed "learning journals" as a way of including more writing in their undergraduate literature classes. These instructors worked collaboratively on the learning journal experiment, in that: they shared a commitment to increased writing activity as a means of enhancing first-year students' learning experiences in English 1100; they saw learning journals as a means of breaking down the anonymity of large classes; they frequently exchanged assignment material and writing "prompts" pertaining to learning journals; they often compared notes on how the journals experiment was progressing, and, in some instances, attended instructional development study groups on writing; they attempted, as much as possible, to involve graduate teaching assistants in the journal component of their courses; and they found it necessary to re-evaluate the effectiveness of learning journals at regular intervals and, inevitably, to "fine-tune" or even re-conceptualize journal-writing in substantive ways as a learning tool.

In the following discussion, the four Lakehead instructors featured interrogate their own pedagogies with respect to the use of learning journals in undergraduate courses: specifically, the "Major British Authors" survey and, in Bill Heath's case, the third-year American poetry class. These accounts focus on how each instructor envisioned journal writing as a means of facilitating student writing and learning. Although the philosophies informing the use of journals vary in certain respects from one instructor to another, as the following accounts reveal, the common thread running through these discussions documents what Kim Fedderson calls the "shifts in pedagogy" that accompanied the use of journals for each instructor as he or she confronted, over several years, which aspects of journal writing "worked" and which didn't. Thus, the discussions focus, to a large extent, on learning journals as evolving practice. All four accounts remind us of how we are constantly revising our own pedagogies within the context of the changing discursive communities around us and those that we and our students inhabit.

I. BILL HEATH: "WHY USE LEARNING JOURNALS?"

Why use learning journals in the classroom? That was the question I posed to a dozen colleagues from different departments several years ago when I chaired a study group on the use of student learning journals. We identified a variety of reasons for assigning journals: to stimulate critical thinking; to reinforce the nature of learning as a process of discovery; to give students an opportunity to write in a more personal, self-expressive way than is the case with traditional writing assignments; to open a dialogue between student and teacher on course-related subjects; and to break down the anonymity of the classroom by helping the teacher and the student to experience one another not just as types or role-players but as really existing people. In essence, these benefits can be grouped under three main headings: thinking, writing, and sharing. In this article, I will argue that learning journals facilitate each of these activities, filtering my comments through my own experience working with learning journals in literature courses.

Because the process of thinking is inseparable from the process of writing, I will consider them together. When I first began assigning journals, I thought of them as a place where students could record their learning experiences while working through the materials of the course. Thus conceived, the journal would be a "reading log," a record of the discoveries, impressions, insights, and questions that occur to students as they read, or afterwards. Such insights cannot be forced or summoned at will; they are often involuntary and unexpected, but no less valuable for being so. However, unless they are recorded while they are fresh, they can easily be lost. These kinds of insights are more important and longer-lasting than lecture notes, and in a very real sense they form the crux of any person's education.

I still believe in the value of a journal as a reading log, but I no longer consider that to be its most important function. Working with journals in actual practice in the classroom has helped my thinking about them to evolve. The danger inherent in the idea of a reading log is that the journal will be viewed as something static and passive, a mere repository of thoughts, rather than a place where thinking occurs. Students benefit when they see that the *process* of thinking is more important than arrived-at thoughts. It is axiomatic that "writing is discovery." E.B. White once observed that the easiest way to have thoughts is to start writing them down. Or, as Mihalyi Csikszentmihalyi (1991) explains in *Flow: The Psychology of Optimal Experience*:

> If the only point to writing were to *transmit* information, then it would deserve to become obsolete. But the point of writing is to *create* information, not simply to pass it along. In the past, educated persons used journals and personal correspondence to put their experiences into words, which allowed them to reflect on what had happened during the day. The prodigiously detailed letters so many Victorians wrote are an example of how people created patterns of order out of the mainly random events impinging on their consciousness. The kind of material we write in diaries and letters does not exist before it is written down. It is the slow, organically growing process of thought involved in writing that lets the ideas emerge in the first place. (p. 131)

Traditional essay assignments, which sometimes attach a greater importance to research than to reflective thought, do not facilitate these "patterns of order" the way a journal can, whether it be one's personal journal or a student learning journal. Emerson said that experience is what a person thinks about all day, and in that word day, or *jour*, lies the root of the journalizing habit, the connection between having thoughts and writing them down.

What is thinking? Wittgenstein described it as "seeing connections" (Monk, 1991, p. 308). Robert Frost (1995) implied as much when he said that all thinking is essentially metaphorical: "[Thinking] is just putting this and that together, it is just saying one thing in terms of another" (p. 723). That is what I encourage my students to do in their journals — to "see connections" between the writers we study, to put "this and that [writer] together" — with the emphasis on the act of "seeing" more than on the connections seen. Some of the best journal entries I have read were based on recognitions of links and affinities between writers that occurred to students *as they wrote*. In a class in American poetry, one student devoted a journal entry to his experience of reading Emily Dickinson and Elizabeth Bishop, whom he cleverly called

"Sisters of Paradox." The entry began by noting that although the two poets seemed very different: "they evoke a similar experience in me. *My goal is to find out why*" (Knutsen, p. 12; emphasis added). That last sentence sounds the authentic note of the learning journal: not just a place to report the results one's reading, but a place where one "finds out why" something is the way it is.

Connections between writers are not the only kind of connections students make in their journals. I welcome connections students make between writers and themselves. I agree with Gold (1992) that "the value of literature lies in its energy to extend the limits of the reader's personal experience either by offering 'new' information, 'new' arrangements of 'old' information, or confirmation and reinforcement of existing information, along with the pleasure attendant upon those recognitions" (p. 7). As an illustration of this premise, consider the imaginative and creative student, from the same class mentioned above, who wrote her journal on Elizabeth Bishop in the form of a close, line-by-line poetic imitation of Bishop's poem, "Arrival At Santos." She called her imitation "Arrival at Elizabeth Bishop" and paralleled Bishop's somewhat disillusioning experience of arriving in Brazil for the first time with her (the student's) own difficult first encounter with the poetic "landscape" of Elizabeth Bishop herself. The student's version of an Elizabeth Bishop poem was clever, but more important to me was the student's discovery of the very Keatsean analogy between reading and travelling, which *the act of writing the poem* helped her to make.

The third major benefit I have discovered from using learning journals is in the way they facilitate sharing between student and teacher. The main premise I start from as a teacher is that the teaching and learning experience is not just a shared process but, literally, a process of sharing. The goal of this process is to create in the classroom what Gold (1992) calls "a network of shared responses" (p. 15), one that sees the teacher and the student as co-participants. "Each class member is a source of information for all other class members. The teacher is one of the class members" (Gold, 1992, p. 2). Needless to say, this reciprocal model is a goal or an ideal, not a classroom "given." It must be prompted and cultivated. The learning journal activity facilitates this "network of shared responses" when it functions as a conversation or dialogue between the student and the instructor. Sometimes this can almost literally be the case. After he got back his journal entry on the "Sisters of Paradox" and read the comments that had been written about it, the student mentioned above wrote the following comment back: "Just wanted to thank you for your kind comments and helpful hints. You help to make this a *learn-*

ing journal! I've really enjoyed writing these so far... it's such a different assignment in that I can explore with a free rein. The best part is that I can have fun with them. And, they make me think — lots! What I like best is the fact that the poets become important for *me* and approachable for *me*." If, as Gold (1992) claims, "The important thing now... is to restore some pleasure, purpose, and credibility to the study of literature and also to the experience of reading" (p. 5), then dialoguing and sharing such as this suggest that learning journals have a definite place in the classroom.

II. KIM FEDDERSON: ACCOMMODATION AND RESISTANCE IN ENGLISH 1100

I have always admired that passage in *The Philosophy of Literary Form* in which Kenneth Burke likens critical exchanges within cultural communities to those interminable conversations that take place late at night at a party. The conversation is in full swing before we arrive. We listen for a while to get our bearings. Tentatively, we join in. Finding a voice, we state a position. Someone responds with another. Someone else responds to that position. And so it goes until we have to leave, the conversation continuing long after we have left. Burke's analogy goes to the heart of what I do as one of the teachers of English 1100. Indeed, it makes me think about the abilities students require if they are going to participate in this conversation and what role my class plays in their acquiring those abilities.

Initially, I thought that the best preparation that they could get would come from writing designed to help them find their own voices. I was very concerned that those voices be "genuine," "authentic," and that they not merely ape the styles and concerns that have over time come to dominate the discipline. As I learned more about my students and the abilities they were developing in my class, I discovered that my concern with their finding a voice often entailed their failing to find an audience. In what follows I try to trace how and why I shifted the focus of my teaching of writing away from the needs of individual writers towards the needs of writers embedded within communities.

I had read about learning journals, and I thought they could be used to create a space within which students could express themselves in relation to the works we were studying. Given the size of the class (usually 80 to 100 students), the students spent most of their time listening to what I had to say about the history of English literature or reading what critics had to say about it. I thought that they might find the course more engaging and decidedly less oppressive if they had the opportunity to express what they felt about the subject. Unlike the formal essay and the two examinations the course also required, the journals were what some might call a counter-hegemonic strategy, a place for individual expression outside of, or just to the side of, disciplinary constraints. Following Cooper and Selfe's (1990) distinction, I conceived of them as a place for individual resistance within an academy that requires accommodation.

I provided two kinds of topics: self-directed and instructor-driven. And as I was concerned that some of the students would be puzzled about self-directed writing, I provided a list of possible topics. Students, however, were free to invent their own topics as long as they were connected to what I called "the concerns of the course," a phrase as vague now as it was then. During the term, I also handed out instructor-driven prompts related to specific works discussed in class. By the end of the year, students were expected to have written an equal number of entries of both kinds. They were required to respond frequently (once every two weeks). My reason for this is that I wanted their writing to record their experience as readers moving through an historically oriented survey course. I also wanted them to improve as writers, and I saw the journal entries as the discursive equivalent of laps: non-competitive opportunities for practice. I told them the writing could be informal because I was interested in their personal responses. And because the writing was expressive — of and for them rather than for me — I told them I would not grade the work. I would merely record that it was done and those who did all the entries would receive 30 percent of the course grade. I did, however, comment on the writing as I saw fit and as I had time, praising the students who were doing well and coaching students who were having a harder time of it.

While this experiment was not without its benefits — no doubt some students found that frequent writing practice and coaching had developed their abilities as writers — on the whole I discovered that the goal of having students find their individual voices was rather ill-conceived. The structure of rewards was such that students could and did express themselves all year on the works. What was missing was any discernible development in their voices. I found that providing students with opportunities to express themselves for the most part simply served to reinforce the idioms, strategies, and repertoires they brought with them on the first day of classes. All of these have value within the discursive communities that the students came from and belonged to outside of class, but I began to question their value within the community that their registration forms indicated they had a desire to join. Returning to Burke, their voices, while capable of certain melodies, were still largely untuned for the music I had in mind. Rather than developing voices able to carry on the conversation, they continued to use their voices to signify their distance from and awkwardness within that conversation.

I began to think that the class should not under the guise of empowering individual student voices within a hegemonic disciplinary community simply leave the students as it found them, nor should it leave the students' voices at the end of the year as unmodulated by the standards of the disciplinary community as they had been at the outset. Rather, the goal of empowering students might paradoxically be served by a more normative approach designed to assist students in situating their voices within the discipline. I began to reshape the journal exercises so they would focus on the disciplinary community and the ways in which language is used in that community. Exercises in self-expression became exercises in adaptation. And where the journals had previously not been evaluated, now they would be graded on the basis of the students' success in developing a voice that worked within the community of the classroom. As before, there was a combination of self-directed and teacher-driven prompts; however, the ratio was changed to favour the latter. A typical exercise would require a student to read a few excerpts from some critical articles placed on reserve in the library and to develop an argument from these (e.g., the knight in Chaucer's "General Prologue" is a literary not an historically accurate depiction of this medieval military estate). These arguments, written in the form of two-page drafts, would then be brought to class, and the students, divided into small groups, would read each other's work. After reading, the students would have some general discussion on the topic, and we might conclude the session with a full-class discussion. One week later, the draft papers would be revised in light of the in-class discussions and then handed in for evaluation. As before, I would respond to the papers as time permitted, but I would also add a grade to tell the students how well they had adapted their writing to meet the expectations of the community in the classroom.

This change in approach to the journals changed the act of writing. First off, writing became public, and thus became visible to the community. Students began to see their writing in relation to other students' writing. They saw what persuaded, what didn't, what amused, what irritated, what stimulated, what bored. A series of expectations and a community standard began to emerge. Second, as students' writing frequently followed their having read published critical writing, there was a sense that the community that emerged in the class extended beyond the class, and contained writers of widely varying ability and notoriety. Thirdly, the writing that students did was both process and product. Writing was used to clarify a student's initial thinking on the topic and then in the small groups to stimulate others, thinking on the topic. Eventually, the writing became a finished piece of work. And lastly, this finished product was seen as having been shaped by a collaborative process in which a community of fellow readers and writers had the opportunity to influence other writers' work.

It might be argued that the shift in pedagogy recorded here reflects that same sorry transformation that we see in the work of Neil Postman whose *Teaching as a Subversive Activity* (1979), written in collaboration with Charles Weingartner, gives way to one of the earliest reactionary salvos in the culture wars, *Teaching as a Conserving Activity* (1979b). Blake puts it best: the revolutionary Orc eventually becomes the tyrannical Urizen; the indulgent narcissism of youth gives way to the stale conformity of age. I don't think this is the case.

Adhering to the same Frankfurt school line implicit in Cooper and Selfe's (1990) distinction between accommodation and resistance, I began the journal project arguing for a pedagogy which created a space for resistance rather than one that required accommodation. What I failed to recognize was the dialectical play between resistance and accommodation. Resistance is made possible by being situated within a community: it is the very strictures of the community — its codes, rules and conventions — that create the objects of resistance. Despite its rhetorical perils, hockey can serve as an apt metaphor. Gretzky's ability to resist the attack of an opposition forward is predicated upon his being in the game. If he is not in the game, resistance isn't an option. Outside the game, he's either not participating at all or he is participating only as a spectator. In the absence of the strictures that one can resist or accommodate, one is simply an Other that stands outside the community. And while, as Said teaches, respect for the Other's autonomy outside of our potentially coercive gaze is essential if we are to avoid the pitfalls of Orientalism, such respect can be overplayed if our goal is to build a community of Others joined in a common project.

Creating a community of readers requires what Althusser calls interpellation. Our students need to be called into the game and need to recognize themselves as members of the community. Creating a community of readers also requires accommodation. Students need to adapt their discursive behaviour to the rules of behaviour expected within the community. There is, of course, a danger here for those of us who believe that a liberal education should be liberating. Our acts of interpellation and requests for accommodation may be so forceful that all future resistance is precluded. Our pedagogy may simply habituate our students to the norms of the discipline and so turn them into unthinking conformist pawns within the game of literary studies. Such fears, I think, dramatically overestimate the power of the classroom and the power of our teaching. Our students come to us already situated in a variety of communities. They are "always simultaneously a part of several discourses, of several communities ... [are] already committed to a number of conflicting practices" (Harris, 1989, p. 19). They already possess a variety of discursive strategies and repertories developed within those communities. And as they take a place within our classroom community of readers, they are not dipped, as Plato would have it, in a river of forgetfulness. The communities within which they have previously defined themselves attend them as they come into the classroom. And following their encounter with the discourse of the classroom, they begin the complex process of negotiating the place that the discursive moves required in this new community will have, if any, within their already complex repertoire available to them. The space necessary for resistance was secure before they entered the class and will in all likelihood remain with them after they leave. What's needed in the classroom is a space where they can become acquainted with the discursive moves that define that community, and on the basis of their knowledge of those moves decide if and how they wish to play the game.

III. FREDERICK M. HOLMES: "FROM LEARNING JOURNAL TO CRITICAL NOTEBOOK"

In the 1991-92 academic year, I and my colleagues who are collaborating with me in this project launched a pedagogical experiment in tandem with one another: we all required the students in our respective sections of English 1100: Major British Writers to write learning journals. In my part of this chapter, I want to explain some of the problems which I encountered during that year and the solution which I devised, the transformation of the journal into an assignment that I dubbed the critical notebook. I will conclude with some theoretical ruminations about the significance of this shift in relation to how we conceive of the learning situation faced by first-year university students.

What were the benefits which my colleagues and I hoped that our students would derive from keeping journals? We intended to promote active learning by providing them with frequent occasions to think and write about the literature on our reading lists. We all believed that the students would not only improve as writers through regular practice but would in the process also learn to respond more thoughtfully and subtly to issues arising from the literature.

Many of the characteristics of the assignment followed from the analogy between the learning journal and the private journals and diaries of ordinary life. Like those documents, the learning journals were designed to occasion and record the development of individuals over a substantial period of time. This goal necessitated that students write frequently; accordingly, I required a minimum of twelve separate entries of approximately one page each. Students were invited to take a personal approach to their subject matter in these entries, just as they would in private journals. In order to make it easy for them to write, I did not impose the usual formal requirements that govern the critical essay and that often intimidate first-year students.

Of course, the learning journals were different from private journals in two important respects: the educational focus of the entries and the audience for which they were intended. Although they could adopt a personal focus and voice, the students were required to write on subjects relevant to their studies in English 1100. Half of the topics were selected by the students from a group designed by me, and the other half were created by the students themselves. A further limitation of the freedom enjoyed by writers of private journals was the fact that the learning journals were not private. Diarists may imagine a variety of readers looking over their shoulders, but most write for an actual audience of one. My students, however, knew that their entries would be read by two relative strangers, me and my teaching assistant. And those entries were mandatory; my students, unlike the writers of private journals, did not have the option not to write at all.

The learning journal was thus a hybrid — neither an entirely private document in which students could express themselves freely on whatever subject and in whatever way they chose nor an assignment which imposed the scholarly detachment and formal conventions usually expected in academic writing. This blend created a problem for which there was no satisfactory solution: how to ensure that students would actually compose the entries. Although I did not wish to evaluate the journals, I did decide to allot term marks to them (twenty percent of the final mark) in order to ensure that students would actually do the work required. It did not seem appropriate or feasible, however, to grade such personal, expressive writing as one would essays, tests, and examinations. I reasoned that, although I would read the journals, they would be written by the students primarily to and for themselves. It seemed fitting, therefore, to restrict my evaluation of the entries to determining whether or not the students had completed the work and made a real attempt to grapple with issues pertinent to the course. Moreover, the large class size of around eighty students and the large number of assignments (two essays and two examinations in addition to the twelve journal entries) meant that I did not have the time to comment extensively on the journals. Consequently, I employed a pass-fail system in which any entry that was deemed to be a minimally acceptable effort was awarded a grade of pass. Students who handed in twelve acceptable entries when they were due received the full twenty percent of the term marks allocated to the journals.

After experimenting with the learning journals for a year, I was dissatisfied with the result. While a tiny minority of students used the journals superbly to enhance their learning in the course, most wrote the entries in a perfunctory, uninspired fashion. It is true that this criticism could be made of most conventional first-year essays, but at least these assignments require students to address significant critical issues, to do scholarly research, and to practise the analytical and rhetorical skills which we would like them to master. Many of my students' journal entries seemed mechanical, unfocused, and lacking in direction. The licence which they had to express their subjective reactions had not enabled them to write anything very stimulating about either themselves or the works that they were reading.

Furthermore, because they had no need to strive to produce work of high quality in order to earn high marks, a surprisingly large number of students treated the exercise rather cynically, concocting unproductive topics and doing the bare minimum to qualify for a grade of pass. After tallying the final marks in April, I concluded that they were inflated relative to how little effort the majority of students had put into the journals and how little benefit they had as a consequence derived from them. I had increased the volume of writing done by my students in English 1100, but I had not, apparently, thereby enhanced their ability to think creatively and critically about the literature that they had read.

In the following academic year, I changed the emphasis of the learning journal and renamed it the critical notebook. It now consisted of a few short writing assignments (about half as many as did the learning journal) on topics assigned by me that arose from class lectures and discussions. Whereas formerly students would typically write on their likes and dislikes or on the difficulties which they were encountering in trying to understand Shakespeare or Donne, I no longer invited them to keep an evolving, expressive record of their personal development in the course. The expectation now was that the entries would be more objective, scholarly efforts to apply ideas and methods current in the discipline of English. My teaching assistant and I now allotted to the assignments the full range of grades from A to F, and we made what we hoped were constructive comments on each entry.

Some of the assignments — a standard new critical reading of a Shakespeare sonnet, for example — required no secondary reading, while others did entail some research in the library. One such entry focused on Chaucer's use of social and literary conventions in creating the portrait of one of the pilgrims from the "General Prologue" to *The Canterbury Tales* that we had not studied in class. A couple of the entries (an outline and a progress report) were stages in the completion of longer assignments, and they were the basis of students' participation in small-group workshops conducted in class. Very few students were absent from these sessions because those who did not participate in them were not eligible to hand in the critical notebook entries coordinated with them.

I have been very satisfied with the results of the critical notebook. Predictably, the entries span the full qualitative range from excellent to poor, but it seems to me generally that the students are attending to the assignments with more seriousness and learning more from them. The small-group workshops have proved to be good occasions for collaborative learning. I have been impressed with the extent to which they encourage students to take a proprietorial interest in the texts on which they have written and to become responsible for their ideas about them.

I now use the critical notebook and allied workshops in all of my undergraduate courses. I typically assign a topic suitable for development in a short paper and then require students to bring detailed notes on the topic to a subsequent class during which the workshop is to be held. The notes serve as the basis of their participation in the workshop, which in turn generates more ideas which they can incorporate into the final product before they hand it in. They are permitted to submit the entries only if they have prepared the notes in preparation for the workshops and have participated in them. I award term marks for this participation as well as for the notebook entries themselves.

It occurs to me now that the theoretical underpinning of the learning journal was different from that of the critical notebook. The implicit assumption behind the learning journal was that students would encounter and express their autonomous, if still developing, inner selves through their engagement with equally autonomous, timeless masterpieces. The tacit hope was that, if the students could commune honestly with themselves and speak with an authentic voice in the act of writing, they could then say something meaningful about the literature. The critical notebook was the product of a competing view, which I believe to be more credible: that students do not so much use their pre-existing identities as a key to unlock the riches of literature as they do enlarge and even alter their identities as they learn the habits of mind and regimens that will open up the literature for them. Students' identities are, to a significant extent, shaped and changed by the process of socialization within the institution of the university and the disciplines that comprise it. The literature on the syllabus of English 1100 is no more free-standing than are those identities, because the wherewithal to make sense of it is dependent on mutable, historically situated, institutionalized ways of knowing. People don't possess these inherently; they acquire them gradually as they are educated, both formally and informally. To one degree or another, students begin this process of acculturation in high school (though many, as we know all too well, actively resist it), but for most it accelerates dramatically in university, perhaps because upon entering most students are on the threshold of adulthood. My primary goal in using the critical notebook is to support this process by systematically helping my students to take on new identities as fledgling members of some of the "interpretive communities" that constitute the discipline of English (Fish 1980, p.14). I try to make English 1100 an environment in which my students can begin to experience the intellectual excitement and fellow feeling that make such membership worthwhile.

IV. JEANETTE LYNES: "PORTFOLIOS AND THE 'IRON MAIDEN' MOMENT"

From 1991 to 1994, the period during which I taught the English 1100: British Authors survey course, the learning journal, in my classes, was conceived of as a "portfolio." I had imported the term from composition programs in the U.S., where I taught from 1989 to 1991. The "portfolio," in those contexts, represented a body of work — typically, writing assignments from a variety of courses and disciplines — which was compiled and submitted to a WAC (Writing Across the Curriculum) evaluation committee. The heterogeneity of the "portfolio" appealed to me, since, underlying the WAC philosophies to which I had been exposed, was the conviction that a competent writer should be able to adapt his or her skills to a *variety* of rhetorical situations and audiences. I was also attracted to the artistic connotations of the word "portfolio," the notion of writing as an art or craft malleable enough, like making a work of sculpture, to be honed and perfected.

Thus, I endeavoured to offer, through the portfolio medium, a variety of compositional opportunities or "prompts" within the context of the British survey course. To put this in fairly bald terms, I envisioned the portfolio, in part, as simply one way of injecting some variety into what could otherwise become (or be perceived as) a plodding course with an unvaried lecture format. I hoped, too, that varied composition prompts might, if even implicitly, discourage the formulaic kinds of writing that students seemed all too familiar with, and uninspired by, from past experience: for example, the "five paragraph essay," the theme paper, the book report. It was time, I told my 1100 students, to move beyond those valuable, though monolithic, forms of composition. What I had not anticipated was that many students were in fact quite fond of those forms. They represented tangible, manageable tasks, familiar and safe. A small minority of students had experience writing some kind of journal entries, but most had not. The "portfolios" were given a holistic score out of 15 or 20 at the end of the year; points were deducted, however, for incomplete portfolios. Some entries were written in class, some out of class (this was one aspect of the diversity I was attempting to build into the writing activities on the course). Nearly all the prompts were instructor-driven.

Along with the first goal of increasing the flexibility and adaptability of student writers, I also believed that instructors of first-year students can make a real difference in terms of whether students get "turned on" to the English discipline, motivated to read, write, and delve deeper into the study of literature. There is a good deal of anecdotal evidence around universities to suggest that first-year courses are critical testing grounds that either "make or break" a student's interest in a subject. Since English 1100 is, as mentioned, a required course for English majors at Lakehead, some students were already "converts"; but still, the first-year university experience is a decision-making site — even "converts" might opt for alternate disciplines.

Of course, as instructors, we have limited control over what our students choose; and of course, we are teachers, not recruitment officers. But surely all of us, to recall the film "Mr Holland's Opus," have a little "Mr. Holland" in us; to some degree, we hope to pass some spark of our own passion for our discipline on to our students, our own pedagogical "opus."

At the level of first-year teaching, then, student motivation was a key concern for me. The motivation issue was attached, too, to broader questions: how can we make English studies relevant to the everyday lives of nineteen-year-olds, and to what extent should we even try?

Re-enter the portfolio assignment, and its second purpose. I envisioned portfolio writing as forming a potential bridge between the discourse of the academy — the critics, experts, and the "major authors" (the subtitle of the *Norton Anthology* used in English 1100) themselves — and student writers who, as Kim Fedderson has pointed out, come to us "already situated in a variety of communities."

One community in which our students are "already situated" is surely the world, or worlds, of popular culture which, as well as being manifested through music, film, the internet, and various other aspects of consumer society, is simply their everyday lives, and the artifacts therein. As Ray B. Browne and Pat Browne put it: "popular culture is the everyday, vernacular culture that comprises virtually all our lives… the everyday culture of existence" (p. 1). I would include here, too, the particularities of students' experiences in terms of place, race, gender, and sexual orientations. Thus, while some of the prompts in the course's portfolio component were, in my view, more restrictive literary-analysis prompts, others invited students to draw direct correlations between the literature studied on the course and the more personal and experiential aspects of their lives.

To summarize my discussion thus far, I used essentially two types of writing prompts: first, prompts which directed students towards more detached, critical analyses (the explication of a passage, for instance); and, secondly, prompts which encouraged more first-person "input" (for example, a viewer-response reaction to a film adaptation of a novel) in conjunction with the literature on the course.

When I reevaluated my use of learning journals, I realized that although I had tried to vary writing situations, the portfolio writing done in my courses was not as wide-ranging or multi-faceted as I had hoped it might be. It seems self-evident to me now that the kinds of writing done within the context of a single literature course are destined to be less diverse than those done "across the curriculum." I had tried to make my 1100 class a kind of "writing across the curriculum writ small," the curriculum being the span of centuries encompassing the literature studied. I had to re-think the question of how much diversity, how many different rhetorical situations and writing occasions could be crammed between the book-ends of one literature survey course.

My answer to that question now is "some." Portfolio prompts might invite students to write using different points of view: from the point of view of one of Chaucer's pilgrims, for instance. Though I think now that my concept of the "portfolio" was over-reaching, it is clear that, for me, the second, more personal type of prompt produced the most exciting pieces of student writing. I will refer to these as "bridging prompts" since they rested on the hope that students might discover continuities between the literature in the formidable *Norton* and their own experience: might discover that, as Herbert J. Gans (1974) puts it, "no culture is ever entirely new... What is new, however, is the expansion of... high culture forms into the lower taste cultures" (p. 94). My portfolio prompts then, which frequently encouraged "bridging," invited students, for example, to tease out analogues between, say, Chaucer's use of folk forms and comparable forms in contemporary culture, Matthew Arnold's concerns about literary standards and the degree to which those concerns have currency in the late twentieth century.

Of course, a careful and ongoing balancing act between the worlds depicted in *Norton* and the worlds in contemporary culture or "real life" is crucial, but having their own cultures legitimated through writing assignments did seem to motivate students, and I believe that portfolio writing played some valuable part in this.

Let me provide several brief examples. After a class during which the lecture subject had been Coleridge's "Rime of the Ancient Mariner," a student approached me and asked if I was familiar with the version of "Rime of the Ancient Mariner" done by the heavy metal band Iron Maiden. I was not, but I encouraged the student to bring the lyrics to class. He obliged, and a portfolio prompt shortly thereafter invited students to "write about the differences and similarities between Iron Maiden's version of "The Ancient Mariner" and Coleridge's version. This popular culture prompt seemed to help rekindle the energy levels of some students. Also, I believe that this student would not have approached me if he had not detected some connection between what he was studying and his own vernacular experience.

Another portfolio assignment which attempted to bridge cultures invited students to assess Matthew Arnold's fears in *Culture and Anarchy* (excerpted in *Norton*) concerning middle-class reading material with respect to people's perceived reading habits in the late twentieth century. Students often take the safe route of agreement, but portfolio writing seemed to offer more potential room for dissent. As one student wrote: "...to be frank, I did not like reading Arnold. He has either an attitude or an ego problem. I also felt he was unduly harsh on Chaucer. It is unfair to say that his works are not worthy of the title of 'classics' just because they have a sense of humour. Arnold is judging works written in the 14th century on the basis of the standards of the 19th century. Personally, I think that Arnold was just being insecure about a potential lack of market for his works... " (Terri-Ann Barlow). Although this writing still operates on a rudimentary level of "likes" and "dislikes," and although the critical vocabulary needs work, sophisticated concepts pertaining to issues of literary value and the ways in which texts are ideologically motivated are beginning to form, and the writer is learning to take a position.

The same student-writer continued, throughout the portfolio assignments, to engage with the literature in a way which legitimated her own positioning with respect to the text. Her willingness to take writing risks increased, and in her final portfolio entry, which invited comparison between some aspect of D.H. Lawrence's "The Horse Dealer's Daughter" and some aspect of students' own lives, she wrote:

> For my last journal entry, I have decided to do something a little different. "The Horse Dealer's Daughter" takes place in a small mining town in England. Coincidentally, I happen to have grown up in two small mining towns in Northern Ontario. I thought it would be interesting to compare my real life experience with that portrayed by Lawrence. (Terri-Ann Barlow)

This entry suggests to me that the student is beginning to take charge of her own discourse, to learn how to draw discursive parameters and carve out a focussed line of discussion. The remainder of the entry contains some fairly detailed analyses of the Lawrence story. Clearly, the student was able to use the particularities of her own experience to bring the literature to life in a meaningful way.

The above examples reflect what I believed to be strong portfolio writing; however, many pieces of "stock" writing were submitted as well. In my experience with learning journals, the most uninspired pieces of portfolio writing were usually generated by the more conventional "essay"-type prompts. Having said that, the prompts which invited a more personal response did not always lead to exciting writing; some students were simply unwilling or unable to engage with the literature in any meaningful way, or to conceptualize some kind of link between themselves and the literature they were reading. Of course, a precondition for establishing that link is reading the literature, and in a class of 80-100 students, it can be difficult to monitor reading habits.

I have not taught English 1100 since 1994 because of other course responsibilities, but if I teach a section of it again, I believe I will use portfolio writing. However, I will need to consider some issues: the extent to which gender might impact on "life-writing" (i.e., the use of personal prompts), since I did notice that females seemed to orient more comfortably to personal modes of discourse than did males; the degree to which the "bridging" of literature and "real life" or lived experience might detract from the importance of understanding writing as convention, invention, artifice (even though I am not convinced that that was the case). I believe, too, that I would dispense with the "essay-like" portfolio prompts altogether, and restrict the teaching of English-studies-discourse to the essay assignments instead of trying to create a portfolio with possibly too many mixed modes.

At its best, the portfolio experiment carried out during my three years of teaching English 1100 was a form of life-writing which revealed that composition is multi-faceted; that writing is a kind of positioning; that the "positions" we assume as writers are grounded in the particularities of our own lives; that discovering continuities between cultures which initially seem remote — Iron Maiden and Coleridge, Coles Books and Matthew Arnold — is pleasurable, valid, and capable of opening doorways for further discovery.

AFTERWORDS

What do these four pedagogical accounts tell us about the possibilities for student writing within the context of first-year literature courses? Although these accounts approach this question from different angles, they all reveal that "alternative" forms of writing such as learning journals, critical notebooks or portfolios — "alternative," that is, to the traditional research essay and exam — can have a place, even in large survey classes. Having said that, more than one instructor found small-group workshopping to be a valuable component, in terms of increasing students' sense of accountability and responsibility for their own writing, and raising their awareness that, as Kim Fedderson puts it, "writers are embedded within communities."

Each discussion tracked a shift, or shifts, in pedagogy with respect to using writing in undergraduate English courses. These shifts, in turn, meant that we, as instructors, were continually re-negotiating our own positions with respect to student writing and their classroom practices. Changes in nomenclature ("reading log," "critical notebook," "portfolio," for example) underscore these negotiations.

In Bill Heath's experience, what was initially envisioned as a "reading log" evolved into a form of journal writing which would emphasize "the *process* of thinking" rather than a "repository" of "arrived-at thoughts." Thus, Heath's *pedagogy* around journals moved towards a meshing of teaching writing and critical thinking skills. For Heath, too, journal-writing can create a more interactive space in the classroom. Frederick Holmes set aside journal-writing as a means of documenting the "autonomous" "inner selves" of students, and adopted instead the "critical notebook" as a means of helping students "take on new identities" as "fledgling members" of the discursive communities of English study. Kim Fedderson shares Holmes' reservations around the value of journals as essentially a private, expressive mode; as Fedderson discovered, "the goal of having students find their individual voices was ill-conceived." His pedagogy shifted towards a conception of journal-writing as collaborative. Thus the journal, for Fedderson, did not negate the notion of "finding a voice," but rather re-envisioned it as "finding a voice that worked within the community of the classroom." Jeanette Lynes experimented with the way journal — or "portfolio" — writing might enhance the perceived relevance of English studies for first-year students, and how it might help expose overlaps between historicized, literary "high" culture and everyday, vernacular culture. She also found that writing prompts grounded in personal experience could help students write with greater authority and, by legitimating the particularities of students' own cultures, could increase their self-confidence as writers.

Despite the range of emphases and approaches reflected through the experience of these four instructors, their work with learning journals attests to the conviction that, even in the era of increased class sizes, facilitating student writing remains a crucial component in developing the skills required to exist meaningfully within the discursive communities within and outside of the university. Finding effective ways of teaching these skills, Lakehead's learning journals project suggests, is itself a process, and one that has been enriched through dialogue and collaboration.

Notes

i   Lakehead University, located in Thunder Bay, Ontario, is, for the most part, an undergraduate institution with a full-time enrollment of approximately 6,000. All English majors at the undergraduate level are required to complete English 1100, a full-year survey called Major British Authors. Most students in English 1100 are in their first year of study; the course does include some non-majors. English 1100 is a multi-sectioned course, with about 80-100 students in each section. The department may run as many as nine sections per year. Texts in the course are usually taught with emphasis on historical development, and generally, poetry, fiction and drama are included in the course. Typically, a main text such as *The Norton Anthology* is adopted which may be supplemented with several novels and/or plays. One or two graduate teaching assistants (the English Department has a Masters program) are assigned to each section wherever possible.

References

Barlow, T. English 1100 portfolio entries: Feb. 19, 1992: Arnold: Did his fears concerning middle-class reading material come true?; March 24, 1992: Lawrence: A comparison of factual/fictional small towns." Quoted with permission.

Browne, R.B., & Browne, P. (1991). Digging into popular culture: Theories and methodologies in archeology, anthropology and other fields. Bowling Green, OH: Bowling Green University Popular Press.

Burke, K. (1957). The philosophy of literary form: Studies in symbolic action. New York: Vintage.

Cooper, M. & Selfe, C. (1990). Computer conferences and learning: Authority, resistance, and internally persuasive discourse. College English, 52, 847-869.

Csikszentmihalyi, M. (1991). Flow: The psychology of optimal experience. New York: Harper Perennial.

Fish, S. (1980). Is there a text in this class? The authority of interpretive communities. Cambridge: Harvard University Press.

Frost, R. (1995). Collected poems, prose, and plays. R. Poirier & M. Richardson (Eds.). New York: The Library of America.

Gans, H.J. (1974). Popular culture and high culture: An analysis and evaluation of taste. U.S.A.: Basic Books.

Gold, J. (1992). Reader response and experiential learning. English Studies in Canada, XVIII, 1-19.

Harris, J. (1989). The idea of community in the study of writing. College Composition and Communication, 40, 11-22.

Knutsen, E. (1996, January). Emily and Elizabeth: Sisters of paradox. In Learning journal: American literature. Quoted with permission.

Monk, R. (1991). Wittgenstein: The duty of genius. London: Vintage.

Postman, N. (1979). Teaching as a conserving activity. New York: Delacorte Press.

Postman, N. & Weingartner, C. (1979). Teaching as a subversive activity. New York: Delacorte Press.

Disrupting Fairy Tales and Unsettling Students

William H. Thelin, University of Akron
Wendy Carse, Indiana University of Pennsylvania

We actually thought it was going to be easy. With Wendy teaching the class and Bill taking an active participant-observer role in it, we thought students would respond to the relatively low-risk venture of comparing different versions of the "Cinderella" fairy tale and analyzing the story's possible role in acculturating children. Wendy had used a similar assignment previously and felt the students were able to relax and have some fun exploring the ways in which the changes from version to version influenced not only the intended moral but the meanings that could be read into it. We both believed the readings were less difficult than the ones accompanying the assignments that had preceded the "Cinderella" segment of the class: Stanley Milgram's "The Perils of Obedience" and a series of articles that focused on the decline of America and the role of women in the country. Surely this assignment would have to be perceived as a break.

But we had not counted on something important: the relatively comfortable relationships students had with fairy tales as contrasted to the increasingly uncomfortable relationship they were experiencing with the university and its discourse. Not only would we be turning the fairy tale on its head to reveal how it mediates gender and class tensions, but we would be disrupting yet another icon of the students' lives, so many of which had already been challenged through their courses in history and science. On top of that, we would be doing it in a first-year writing course, a class in which their peers in other sections seemed to be held less accountable for the type of critical thinking being demanded here. Yes, we thought the assignment could be both fun and challenging. We believed that with the use of something familiar to the students, a certain comfort zone could be reached. They then could experience the sensation of criticizing an object they were deeply invested in, thus exposing to scrutiny the contradictions abounding in our postmodern world (see Sells' 1995 critique of *The Little Mermaid* for an example of the tensions that can surface when examining a fairy tale). We ended up engaged in more resistance than we had encountered in any of the other assignments for the course.

In constructing this research project, Bill was looking to uncover student reaction to English courses in which the professor carried through with a political agenda. Although much has been written about political pedagogies, little classroom research is available. The few studies that have been published are generally instances of professors reporting on their own classrooms or programs (see, for example, Bauer, 1990; Berlin, 1991; George & Shoos, 1992). Through the participant-observation method, Bill hoped to glean information that would not be subject to criticisms of bias. He approached Wendy and explained that he was looking to study a teacher who used political readings to create uncertainty in student convictions. He wanted to see how this uncertainty manifested itself in student texts and classroom decorum. Wendy's pedagogy contained many political elements, as one of her goals was to disrupt complacency in her students through her writing assignments. She agreed to allow Bill to conduct a semester-long participant-observation in one section of her writing course.

Our conclusions on the issue of resistance to the "Cinderella" assignment are derived mostly from Bill's data, including notes from all the class sessions, interviews with the students, analyses of their essays, and end-of-semester student evaluations. In coming to our conclusions, we focused on the atmosphere of the classroom during this essay assignment, the students' opinions as expressed during the interviews, the implicit and explicit attitudes towards the topic as forwarded in their essays, and references to the topic in their evaluation of the course.

The "Cinderella" paper was assigned in the middle of the semester, immediately before and after the Spring break of that year. The university is located in a small Pennsylvania town, northeast of Pittsburgh, with a population of predominately white, working class, first-generation students. Wendy's class, however, was more diversified than the average first-year writing course at the university. Five of the 21 students who completed the course were African-American, and many of the students, based on information given during the interviews, were probably from upper-middle-class homes and had at least one parent who had attended a college or university.

The course is called "College Writing" and is required of all students, unless they test out of it through an entrance exam taken during the summer. Although the English Department has graduate programs in literature and composition, most professors teach the entry-level writing courses. Thus, the course assignments and textbook selections are the instructor's choice, as long as the syllabus and goals fall within the departmental description of the course. Within this situation, Wendy chose to use the 4th Edition of Behrens' and Rosen's (1991) *Writing and Reading Across the Curriculum* and composed a syllabus that required five essays, along with summaries, quizzes, a group project, and other activities designed to ensure the students were engaged in critical reading. Assignment #4 was the one that involved comparing five versions of the "Cinderella" story, as presented in Behrens and Rosen.

Assignment #4 had been preceded by an assignment that asked the students to argue about the accuracy of Masters, Johnson, and Kolodny's description of the pressures teenagers and young adults face in becoming masculine or feminine. A second option had them focus on a handout from the *UTNE Reader* and argue about its contentions regarding male-female friendships. A third option, which none of the students chose, had them argue about the appropriateness of American morality tales and whether they amounted to self-congratulations or warnings about how far the country has fallen in following through on its ideals. The classes devoted to this assignment were quite lively and led some students to explore gender roles further in their group projects. While Bill noted the usual amount of student inattention during group work, he also saw discussions much more involved than is normally the case. Several students debated the impact of Barbie dolls on gender roles, for instance, while others tried to figure out what was acceptable for society in terms of socializing children into traditional gender values. The papers were stronger than the previous group for Assignment #2, and the students seemed to pay more attention to surface details as well as to content and form.

In constructing Assignment #4, Wendy tried to use the momentum from this gender paper to help the students analyze the sequence of "Cinderella" tales. Her assignment read as follows :

The one thing that people who study folktales agree on is that fairy tales like "Cinderella" appeal to some basic social needs. One of those needs can be seen as a means of acculturating children — that is, to familiarize children with the roles expected of them in their culture. Write an essay in which you argue that the fairy tale "Cinderella" in the forms we are most familiar with contains elements that demonstrate *either* [emphasis hers] (1) acculturation of children in terms of gender roles, or (2) acculturation of children in terms of American values.

Her instructions also explained to the students that the assignment was meant to be a synthesis, so the students should refer to specific elements in more than one variant of the fairy tale. She also required them to refer to Jane Yolen's "America's Cinderella" or other essays in the text, including those used for the previous assignment.

The students had enjoyed the reading and had participated in the first group assignment in which they compared and contrasted five versions of "Cinderella" given in the text — Charles Perrault's, the Grimm Brothers', Disney's, Giambattista Basile's, and Tuan Ch'eng-shih's. They noted the absence of violence in the versions with which they were more familiar and listed obvious differences, such as the lack of a fairy godmother in the Grimm's version, the forgiveness Cinderella displays in Perrault's, the different names for Cinderella, and the cat characters in Basile's Italian version. However, our first clue that we would be meeting resistance also occurred in the second half of this session when Wendy asked the groups to discuss how these versions related to cultures and times. Bill stimulated some discussion in the groups he visited by asking about gender roles, but other than the feedback he received, the students waited for the synthesis of the group sessions to relate it to cultural lessons and values.

Wendy ended up leading the class discussion more than she normally did. One student, an outgoing woman named Mary, indeed saw the way the tales represented their cultures in the tales' perceptions of the aristocracy, the influence of World War II, and the role of magic. Aside from her, though, only two students spoke. Wendy asked many pointed questions regarding the role of religion and the varying beliefs regarding vengeance, the stepsisters' reward of marrying noblemen, and the role of the father. The students resisted all attempts at her incorporating the Chinese and Italian versions of the fairy tale into the discussion and did not respond to Wendy's specific citations from the text that they might have found relevant. Slightly frustrated, Wendy ended the session by instructing the students to read Yolen's article, then to reread the differing versions of the "Cinderella" tale for the next class session.

The dramatic drop in participation caught us off guard. In discussing it after class, we assumed that the level of difficulty had increased when Wendy asked them to construct a relationship to the cultures and times of the different versions. We wondered if they had understood the assignment or knew enough about the cultures surrounding the times to see a relationship. It was a cognitively much more sophisticated task than the previous ones. Later, when looking back on the session, we found ourselves analyzing the students' sense of their place in the knowledge-making of the university. It seemed to us that the students were familiar with the comparison and contrast ritual that marked the first part of the class session. However, they were uncertain as to what the second task implied about the type of knowledge they were expected to generate. In their personal registers, comparison and contrast could be located and categorized as a tool for analysis. But what was taking a fairy tale and showing how it reflected the culture and times it was written in? It did not fit into any of their preconceived notions of how knowledge was produced. Without knowing it at the time, we had ventured into the crucial area where academic knowledge threatens the certainty of the models students had previously constructed.

Wendy gave a reading quiz the next class session and followed it up with an individual exercise for the students to summarize the main points of Yolen and then to react to her argument. During the second half of the class, Wendy started the synthesis of the exercise by discussing the different views of children in the stories. A male student, Jake, quickly brought up the passivity of women Yolen had referred to in her argument. Yet, despite some connections made to the American morality tales found in Behrens and Rosen, the students still seemed uncomfortable. When Wendy stated that the rags-to-riches story was false, everyone nodded their heads and seemingly agreed, albeit in a very passive way. Despite the fact that Wendy had made the claim to generate disagreement, nobody attempted to dispute it. Wendy continued to prod them until a student named Janet, slightly off-topic, said that she would not want her children to read the Grimms' version of "Cinderella," called "Ashputtle." This prompted another fairly active student named Rachel to talk about the forgiveness aspect of one version and how she thought that it contained a positive message for children. Some head-nodding and murmurs indicated that several members of the class agreed with this assessment of the texts.

However, one student, a woman named Toni, ridiculed the whole notion of children learning from fairy tales. "Kids don't get into messages," she said. "They don't analyze stories. There's a moral at the end and that's it." Wendy's eyes widened, as the opportunity for a meaningful discussion had emerged; however, there was also the chance that Toni's comments could shut down further analysis. Wendy had to choose her words carefully.

"Do people learn whether they analyze a story or not?" she finally asked.

Some of the students seemed to consider this perspective, as Bill noted the pensive looks on many faces. Jake, however, turned the conversation back to the issue of raising children with the fairy tales. He liked the "Ashputtle" version, as he felt the morals of vengeance and justice were important. The stepsisters, having their eyes pecked out by doves on the day of Ashputtle's wedding, got what they deserved, according to him. Only two students, an often-disgruntled woman named Desiree and a frequently absent student named Mark, agreed with Jake.

Wendy was happy to have any feedback and said with some degree of hope, "All right. A fight." But instead, the students focused on the issue of violence, contributing comments on how children would react to it, rather than what Wendy had hoped for, to examine what children were learning about the codes of their society. She mentioned how Yolen did not promote violence, but the class ended before she could turn the conversation toward American attitudes about violence in society. Prewriting for the synthesis essay was due for the next class period.

In constructing this narrative of the class, we were very aware of Maguerrite Helmers' critique of how students are typically portrayed in composition research. Helmers (1994) argues that in most written testimonials of pedagogical insights, students are reduced to stock characters who are most notable for what they lack, whether it be grammatical correctness, the ability to use detail, or thinking in ways relevant to the instructor's agenda. Helmers claims that this construction of students enables the hero narratives of composition to unfold. Students are seen as deficient in an area, the instructor devises and implements a plan, and the result is the enlightenment or rescue of the students. Our narrative, we were afraid, was heading in this direction, as the students so far in our representation had appeared listless, bored, and unappreciative of the dynamic being set up in the classroom. However, no rescue was imminent. Our goal, then, was not to turn the students into stereotypes and show how Wendy's pedagogy saved them, but rather to display the degree of discomfort they were experiencing and to try to explain it. Thus, we realized, our narrative necessarily at this juncture had to continue to show the students as they were, or at least how they appeared to be, and follow through as honestly as possible with the details of how the class proceeded. We feel the result does not elevate either Wendy as a teacher or Bill as a researcher/facilitator, but rather explores the complexities of the interaction between the students, the material, the historical moment, and us. And from our perspective, the students' resistance seemed to be getting worse.

The next class was complicated somewhat by the presence of a tenured professor conducting Wendy's bi-semester observation. As often happens, the students were wondering what he was doing there, whether Professor

Carse was in trouble, and whether they should behave as they normally did. After the students shuffled the desks into a circle, the class started with Wendy asking about the types of arguments emerging from the students' prewriting. Dead silence was the response. To ease the burgeoning tension, Wendy explained that there was no need for the students to have complete arguments right then, but that they should have questions about key issues, based on their prewriting. After yet another palpable pause, a usually re-served student named Christopher said he had looked at the father to see if the many versions deviated from patriarchal expectations. A shy student, Christopher did not venture too much further into this area of analysis, not really saying what he had found. Wendy affirmed that looking at the father was a good starting place. She repeated Christopher's observation and wait-ed for the students to elaborate on it, as she saw many potential questions springing from this area of inquiry. The feedback was minimal, however.

Throughout the class, Wendy showed great patience during the points that Bill observed as dead space. In fact, when she reviewed Bill's notes at the conclusion of the data collection, she was surprised at how often Bill had commented on the silences in the class, often in negative terms. She was not as uncomfortable with silence as Bill was, and she felt that allowing the students to come out of the silence on their own was important for their de-velopment. Perhaps because of the professor observing the class, however, she felt an added impetus to keep this class lively. She thus interrupted the si-lence with several questions about Cinderella's father. "What is the expected gender role?" she wanted to know.

There was no response. One student asked which version of the tale she wanted them to look at, but Wendy's question remained unanswered. "There's a lot that could be argued," Wendy said. "C'mon. What about the father's lack of active participation in raising Cinderella?" Many students took notes as Wendy referred the class to sections in the text, but there was no vocalizing of agreement or disagreement.

"Let's talk about American values," she said, exasperated by their lack of interest in the gender roles' option. "How does 'Cinderella' participate in acculturating students into traditional American values?" No one responded. Wendy looked around the room, but students stared at their books or looked away. "Okay, let's take five minutes and write down what you're thinking and how you're interpreting 'Cinderella'."

The class was evenly divided between those who diligently wrote dur-ing this period and those who did not. Wendy asked the students to put their names on the papers. She collected them and distributed them randomly among the class, asking students to comment on the ideas now in front of them. She wanted to pick up the strand started by Christopher and tried to find who had gotten his paper. No one volunteered the information, so she called on Laura to initiate a conversation.

The paper in front of Laura talked about "Cinderella" not reflecting the American value of hard work. Wishing hard was not the same as working hard. Wendy again thought she saw something to build on, but when she asked a question based on a comparison between wishing and playing the lottery, the students persisted in their silence. Jake finally broke the ice with a comment about the differences in the separate versions of the story. Instead of talking about working hard, though, he concentrated on the lessons about "rot at the top" and "guts and gumption," both terms coming from the text's discussion of American morality tales. Jake believed that Perrault's and the Grimms' version reflected these while Disney's did not.

Wendy used these ideas to return to the issue of forgiveness versus vengeance, since that topic had sparked interest previously. She tried to correlate it to the "guts and gumption" tale and showed the difference or compared to the "triumphant individual" moral. Yet again, nobody responded. Bill could see the frustration etched on Wendy's face.

"What do you think about some of Cinderella's actions that do show guts and gumption?" she asked. "If you want something, do you go for it, no matter what? Triumph is not necessarily ethical, you know. Do you think we need to explore what it takes to get to the top?" She was greeted with more silence. "Think about some of the morality tales surrounding the Wild West. Could triumph be explored?" She waited for response and received none. "Well, I think we have some ideas that could form arguments. Does anybody have anything else they want to talk about?" No one apparently did.

She collected the papers and passed them back to the students who had written them. She then asked for a paragraph on a separate piece of paper, explaining which option they intended to choose so she could review them over the weekend. She told them they could share ideas, and some students worked with each other to help in constructing their paragraphs. The class ended with Wendy reading out loud Rachel's paragraph about materialism and American values to help the others if they were stuck.

The resistance to analyzing "Cinderella" first appeared in this week of class time, but emerged as well in the writing of the papers. In trying to figure out the problem of lack of participation, Wendy speculated that perhaps the students had not done their reading, so she asked for re-readings and gave a pop quiz. She then thought the students were blocked and thus attempted various classroom workshops and freewriting sessions to stimulate them. What Bill was noting through his interviews and his role as observer, however, was not that the students were blocked, but that they simply did not want to explore the connections between "Cinderella" and ideology.

As a student named Bob worded it, "'Cinderella' was the least interesting [of the paper topics]. I thought fairy tales were just there for entertainment... It [the assignment] was the hardest. It ["Cinderella"] is not there to teach children values." He claimed to have "no difficulty" in writing on any of the topics, though, so when he talked about Paper #4 as being the hardest, he seemed to be talking about his objections to analyzing "Cinderella" for its role in acculturating students to gender roles and American values. He was not saying that he didn't see the connection, but rather that he did not find it interesting to look too deeply into what was for him and other students only a form of entertainment.

Similarly, Mark said it was hard to progress as a writer "when you disagree with the topics ... I never looked at fairy tales like that and I didn't take it too seriously. How could you? I mean, I saw her points, but come on." He did not necessarily dislike writing about "Cinderella," but connecting it to gender roles and American values disturbed him. "You kill the story by dissecting it," he said.

A student who rarely spoke up in class, Jean, complained, ironically in our perspective, that there was not enough discussion about the connection to American values. She disliked the assignment and spoke to Wendy about it. She believed that Wendy "looked too deeply into things," and Jean felt "funny" writing about "Cinderella." "It's innocent," she claimed. "Kids know the difference between reality and fantasy." Toni simply said that "fairy tales are fairy tales." She felt it was "hard" connecting fairy tales to gender stereotypes, "hard" here again signifying, we believe, a resistance to disrupting the innocence the students in general had attached to fairy tales. She, too, said that analyzing "Cinderella" took the enjoyment out it. "I never had to analyze it ['Cinderella'] the way we had to," she said, admitting that she was not "true" to herself when writing her paper.

Wendy's class proceeded with draft workshops and peer group revision discussions the next week. Student attendance was spotty, and the atmosphere of the classroom did not return to its pre-Cinderella level. When the students turned in their papers, it was apparent that the resistance during class discussion had seeped into their writing. The quality of the prose and form of the papers was quite high, however, eight students earning "A's" or high "B's" with nine others receiving "B's" or high "C's." The "D" and "F" papers, with one exception, were turned in by students who had struggled throughout the quarter on the other topics. The resistance we noted, though, surfaced in the blandness and what we feared was a lack of sincerity in the students' arguments.

Typical of the "A" papers was Toni's. During her interview with Bill, she said she hoped to write something that stood out from the rest of the papers, whether or not it reflected her beliefs. In her paper, she attacks the message that "Cinderella" sends to children, framing it through Margret Edwards' discussion of the "Little Woman" in her essay, "Is the New Man a Wimp?" Toni's argument is that girls today are being taught to take initiative rather than letting men run their lives. She contends that Cinderella's passivity and reliance on men might have been appropriate characteristics for women to possess "years ago," but that "to try to feed them this message now would be a step in the wrong direction." The dominant structure of the paper reflected this idea. Throughout, she makes broad generalizations about "today's woman" and compares it to places in the various versions of the "Cinderella" tale that denounce women's assertiveness and glorify the virtue of waiting.

The lack of critical insight in Toni's paper is masked by this focus. When she needs to get deeper to support her argument by more fully explaining the meaning of her comparison, she cannot sustain her focus. When talking about the stepsisters, for instance, Toni compares their assertiveness in trying to win the Prince to Cinderella's helplessness in improving her lot in life. Toni astutely points out the punishment the stepsisters receive in the Grimms' version (which she mistakenly calls the original), but then switches her focus to obvious rhetorical questions, such as, "Are these the type of lessons that we want our children to learn from fairy tales?" and "Do we want our children to grow up … helpless and passive?" Wendy's comment in the margin reflected her concern with this avoidance of analysis, as she wrote, "Why not come back to the point about assertive women?" Elsewhere, though, Wendy praised Toni for her clarity and use of supporting textual detail. Based on the features Wendy used on her grading sheet (Thesis, Organization, Sentence-Level Issues, and Readability), Toni had indeed written a relatively strong paper. Throughout the four pages of text, though, Toni succumbs to repetition or generalization when the opportunity for critical analysis presents itself.

Despite telling Bill in the interview that fairy tales were harmless, Toni states in the paper that "young children … will read fairy tales, such as 'Cinderella', over and over again. This is what makes fairy tales an important part in shaping our children's attitudes about male/female roles and responsibilities." Thus, her essay does not reflect her genuine thoughts on the subject. In fact, she said that she wanted her own daughter "to be soft and nice, to be a more traditional woman." She went on to claim that she had no problem with traditional gender roles and had not paid attention to them prior to this course.

It is incumbent upon us here to explain what we feel are the differences between Toni's apparent insincerity in her paper and Maxine Hairston's (1991; 1992) claims that politicized classrooms silence dissenting opinions, reduce creativity, produce writing blocks, and force students to mimic the teacher's belief when that belief conflicts with their own. Throughout Bill's interviews, the students consistently said that Wendy's opinions were not forced on them and that they felt free to write what they wanted. Toni emphatically stated that "Professor Carse never grades on her opinion." Wendy's fairness in grading is clearly seen through the grades she gave students who felt "Cinderella" embodied a positive message.

Mavis, for example, believed that Cinderella was a good role model because of her virtues of patience and determination. Mavis shows that Cinderella acted intelligently and even "took things into her own hands" by going to the ball. She compares the tale to the "Triumphant Individual" morality story and says that Perrault's version, at least, shows a generosity of spirit lacking in today's society. Mavis' ultimate belief is that "Cinderella" teaches children to work hard to allow good things to happen. Wendy believed this was a very clichéd argument, but she admired Mavis' support for her position, including relating it to her own life. Mavis received an "A-" for the assignment. Students obviously, then, were willing to risk opposing the professor's opinion and were not punished for doing so.

A further piece of evidence from our data that counters Hairston's assertion is Toni's statement that she "had fun doing" the paper on "Cinderella" and that she did not change her opinion from fear of a bad grade. She made a rhetorical decision to try to stand out from the crowd. In other words, she was experimenting with a different voice, a voice best facilitated by an oppositional stance to her own beliefs. Toni, thus, certainly did not have a block that hindered her development as a writer and was demonstrating creativity.

This is not to say that we are unconcerned with her resistance to looking deeper into the issue. Rather, we feel that the resistance was not as debilitating as Hairston would lead us to believe and that the political nature of questioning gender roles and critiquing American values is not at the root of the resistance. Our concerns were instead located in why analyzing fairy tales specifically seemed to produce this sort of resistance. The next assignment focusing on advertisements, highly political in itself and more so with the twist Wendy gave it, did not produce nearly as much resistance, nor had the previous assignments, as the students seemed to be more willing to scrutinize the subject matter. It was only with the "Cinderella" papers that we noted on the whole a lack of depth.

Mavis' paper was perhaps the most superficial of the ones receiving high marks, but others showed similar tendencies. Janet and Jake, taking opposite positions on the issue of vengeance, avoided the crucial question of the assignment: how does the fairy tale acculturate children in terms of gender roles and American values? By doing so, they did not have to tackle the more difficult ideological issues inherent in analyzing "Cinderella." By claiming what amounted to "'Cinderella' is good for children" and "'Cinderella' is bad for children," both students kept their distance from a more substantial analysis by simplifying their themes. Janet bases her analysis on the Christian value of forgiveness, quoting scripture throughout her paper and saying that the Disney and Perrault versions of "Cinderella" give a "new magic" to the fairy tale. She assumes, apparently, that Christian values equal American values, although no such interpretation was discussed in class nor can be found in the reading. Jake tries to work his appreciation of the punishment and justice features of the Grimms' versions into a discussion of gender roles, but as Wendy reminded him in her comments, he loses his focus, claiming that the Perrault and Disney versions substitute "wonderment and magic" for the more valuable lessons of "realism and responsibility."

In and of themselves, these analyses have some substance, but it is telling that both students seem to ignore Wendy's prodding in class to think about the value Americans attach to vengeance and justice and how that value connects to American morality tales or concepts of femininity. The deeper dissection of "Cinderella" never takes place in either of these papers. Both merely compare versions of the tale to their personal belief systems and remain relatively safe.

Other students strayed even farther from the assignment. Jean very forthrightly argues against the assumptions of the topic, as she claims that fairy tales provide a needed escape from the hatred found in the world. She believes that fairy tales are "innocent, imaginary worlds that we may enter and leave without effecting [sic] our everyday lives." The purpose behind them is to "entertain, not to project a blueprint of life." Therefore, she does not discuss how fairy tales acculturate, but rather narrates a fond childhood memory of "Cinderella" and defends dreams against the analysis of Yolen. Another student named Carl also wrote off-topic, but without directly confronting the assignment as Jean did. Championing the role of men as rescuers, Carl compares his mother's life to Cinderella's. His mother was saved from a dismal life by the intervention of Carl's father and now lives a successful life, full of love and happiness. Nowhere does Carl analyze gender roles or American values, nor does he make any reference to the assigned readings. Carl seemed to feel the impact of fairy tales could best be felt by showing how their patterns could come true if men behaved gallantly and women were appropriately submissive. But he was unwilling to explore the "Cinderella" tales and never makes an explicit argument.

Another type of resistance could be seen in some of the students in the lower half of the class. They unearthed some lessons from "Cinderella" but rejected the conclusions they had found. A student named Natalie, in a paper she titled "Cinderella, Good or Bad?", isolates many separate lessons that can be learned from the tale but fails to compare it to any other readings from the book. After a point-by-point discussion of what the fairy tale could teach children, such as passivity in women and the vulnerability of the family unit, she concludes by saying, "We must remember that it is just a story and it is meant to be read for fun and enjoyment." In her interview, Natalie said she was not interested in feminism or in discussing "America in decline," which might account for her unwillingness to extrapolate a conclusion from her analysis.

Christopher, who had definite insights regarding the absence of a father figure in "Cinderella," also explored the story, showing how the many versions give misleading and outdated accounts of "realistic family roles." Yet, he too denounces his own analysis by saying that fairy tales are "not meant to be picked apart and scrutinized." Instead, they are "meant to be bedtime stories for children," something that will "foster their imagination." Taking an antagonistic turn in his concluding paragraph, he again reverses course:

> ...fairy tales should be left as is, and not [be] seen as examples of "sibling rivalry" or "misleading family roles." For the purpose of this essay, however, a sacred fairy tale had to be examined under a microscope. This examination has proven certain facts; that "Cinderella" is outdated in many ways, especially in its view of women, and it shows a confusing male/female role reversal. Young children may be confused by these elements, but most children will not think about it that much because it is, after all, just a fairy tale.

Christopher's devotion to "Cinderella" stunned us, especially since he was so subdued during class discussion. Clearly, the assignment had made him do something he considered profane, and he could not do it without comment, which muddled his focus and made us wonder what he actually believed.

But within Christopher's conclusion lies a tension that nearly all the students felt. They were not amazed by the paradox of how a person could critique an artifact of culture to see its ideological implications yet still feel deeply invested in that artifact's preservation. And they certainly were not having fun finding meaning in explorations of culture in this assignment. They were, instead, sensing a danger of losing innocence. The university, as is part of its function, was already distancing the students from some of their childhood beliefs and expectations. One line the students appeared hesitant to cross was the sense of idyllic simplicity they felt with fairy tales. For them, morality in fairy tales was not a guessing game and the way to pursue happiness was not complicated. Implicating "Cinderella" in the oppression of women and the reproduction of jingoistic American ideology was akin to defiling a religious icon — notice Christopher's use of the word "sacred" when describing the "Cinderella" tale. Simply put, fairy tales' simplicity mattered to these students. Professors could complicate students' lives when it came to issues such as gun control or foreign affairs. Students on some level knew they would have to question their beliefs and adjust some of their expectations in life. But professors could not enter the domain of childhood wistfulness. Such analyses were going "too far."

Despite the students' resistance, we see great value in assignments that, in essence, cut to the core, as a critical pedagogy cannot function if it must restrict itself from the very ideological terrain professors and students must explore in order to pursue a democratic, just society. The question one might ask, then, is what should be done in order to cut through the resistance. How, in other words, can a professor get such an assignment to work? The answer is not so apparent.

We can start by talking about the mistakes that occurred throughout this assignment, many of which should be evident by the narrative of the three classroom sessions. We clearly did not anticipate the students' rejection of fairy tales as agents of acculturation, despite the fact that Wendy had taught a version of this assignment before. Believing an examination of "Cinderella" would be fun for the students, we would have been much wiser to understand the rigors of the assignment. In Paulo Freire's (1970) terms, we were asking the students to "develop their power to perceive critically *the way they exist* in the world [emphasis his]" and "to see the world not as a static reality, but as a reality in process, in transformation" (pp. 70-71). In having the students examine "Cinderella," we were investigating not just an acculturating feature of society, but an oppressive acculturating feature of society. In exposing oppression, we were obviously hinting at the possibility for change. In retrospect, we realize that we should not have expected the class to be full of laughter and merriment, and instead should have prepared for students to be thrown off guard by their discoveries.

We were also perhaps guilty of "frontloading" our desires as to the direction students took in critically approaching this subject matter. Ira Shor (1996) discusses the differences between the problem-posing method of critical pedagogy and the authoritarian model of preset subject matter. Shor believes that critical student discourse must evolve through a process of the professor speaking first in questions then "backloading" his or her comments based on student responses, rather than the more prevalent model of professors frontloading their beliefs through lectures and then expecting students to respond. Wendy's assignment did not really allow the students to explore whether or not fairy tales acculturate children into gender roles and American values. She instead asserted that the one thing the experts on folktales agreed on is how they fulfilled basic social needs, such as acculturating children, and took this as a given. Thus, her agenda was frontloaded. Similarly, throughout the three class sessions, Wendy tried to guide the students towards what we considered to be the more critical matters of fairy tales. She did not want the students to dodge difficult questions by steering classroom discussion towards easier analytic tasks.

However, Wendy's teaching methods during this period can hardly be described as authoritarian. Within the scope of the assignment, she tried to frontload their interests without ignoring her responsibilities as a legitimate teacher, one who has knowledge, experience, and authority. As Shor (1996) reminds us, a critical pedagogy differs from the "anything-goes class," where the teacher loses the respect and confidence of the students. In a critical pedagogy, the teacher intervenes to challenge the status quo and shares power in order to transform power (p. 20). To have succumbed to the students' wishes, to have let them off the hook, in other words, would have been to deny them the opportunity to engage in transformative critical discourse. Pressing students to think through complicated issues, then, is not the same as exerting an authoritarian discourse. Judging by the interviews, the students certainly did not perceive Wendy as an authoritarian, and her choice to grade them on what they produced rather than on what she wanted them to produce further argues against her implication in an authoritarian model. Still, more time devoted to the assumptions behind the assignment might have helped include a wider range of student voices in the classroom dialogue and have enabled the students to write more critically on the topic.

As has already been noted, though, the type of resistance we saw during this assignment did not crop up in the other four essay assignments. Bill's classroom observations confirm that Wendy did not teach the "Cinderella" topic any differently from the other four. The students, then, were probably not reacting against the teaching method or a perceived lack of choice. This brings us back to the question of how this assignment could be made to work. Our response, though, is that we need to problematize what it means for an assignment to work.

Resistance can take many forms. Beth Daniell and Art Young (1993) argue that resistance can be both healthy and unhealthy, delineating between resistance to abusive situations and resistance that springs from habit. The resistance we saw seems to lie somewhere in between, in that zone occupied by uncertainty and anxiety. It was not a student game, but it was not the type of civil disobedience that leads to change, either. In an important sense, however, the resistance we saw may well be part of a process of incorporating new knowledge. Daniell and Young feel that blatant resistance in the classroom is an "opportunity to analyze the circumstances in which teachers and students now find themselves" under the new paradigm of writing instruction (p. 233). Such resistance can be taken a step further, though, beyond merely an opportunity to a necessary step in resolving the conflict between the students' expectations upon entering the university and what the university deems as knowledge.

The students in Wendy's composition class will not be able to deny what they found during this assignment, even those whose writing seemed to show little exploration. Their uncertainty about the role of fairy tales in acculturating children to gender roles and American values is something that they will build on, one way or the other. We do not know whether it will lead to the type of critical consciousness Freire (1970) advocates, or a reaffirmation of more traditional values, or just a continual feeling of uneasiness when they come in contact with "Cinderella" or other fairy tales. We do know, though, that our role, and the larger role of the university, should be to urge students to question assumptions in the pursuit of a better society. This often means making them uncomfortable and dealing with the concomitant resistance we should see in their writing.

References

Bauer, D. (1990). The other 'F' word: The feminist in the classroom. College English, 52 (pp. 385-396).

Behrens, L. & Rosen, L.J. (Eds.). (1991). Writing and reading across the Curriculum (4th ed.). New York: HarperCollins.

Berlin, J. (1991). Composition and cultural studies. In C.M. Hurlbert & M. Blitz (Eds.), Composition and resistance (pp. 47-55). Portsmouth, NH: Boynton/Cook.

Daniell, B. & Young, A. (1993). Resisting writing/resisting writing teachers. In W. Bishop (Ed.), The subject is writing: Essays by teachers and students (pp. 223-234). Portsmouth, NH: Boynton/Cook.

Freire, P. (1970). Pedagogy of the oppressed. New York: Continuum.

George, D. & Shoos, D. (1992). Issues of subjectivity and resistance: Cultural studies in the composition classroom. In J. Berlin & M. Vivion (Eds.), Cultural studies in the English classroom (pp. 200-210). Portsmouth, NH: Boynton-Cook Heinemann.

Hairston, M. (1992). Diversity, ideology, and teaching writing. College Composition and Communication, 43, 179-193.

——————— (1991, January). Required writing courses should not focus on politically charged social issues. Chronicle of Higher Education, B, 1-2.

Helmers, M. (1994). Writing students: Composition testimonials and representations of students. Albany: SUNY Press.

Sells, L. (1995). 'Where do the mermaids stand?': Voice and body in The Little Mermaid. In E. Bell, L. Haas, & L. Sells (Eds.), From mouse to mermaid: The politics of film, gender, and culture (pp. 175-192). Bloomington: Indiana University Press.

Shor, I. (1996). When students have power: Negotiating authority in a critical pedagogy. Chicago: University of Chicago Press.

The Personal and the Academic: Construction of School and Self in First-Year University Writing

Judy Hunter
Ryerson Polytechnic University

LITERACY EVENTS IN FIRST-YEAR READING AND COMPOSITION

"Response to Rubin and Thompson"

Nowadays, learning a foreign language is becoming a must to all well educated men and women. But some people fail in their try to learn a foreign language; mostly society is to be blamed for that. Moreover, it is society that discriminates against those whose English is their second language.

Rubin and Thompson forget an important factor in the language learning process, which is society. In fact there are so many people whom I know, faced discrimination in their way of learning English.

In my high school years I found it hard to deal with some teachers. Those teachers discriminated against any student with an accent; for instance, they refused me the right to take some courses; and they advised others who were good students to drop school and work instead.

Of course, when a student faces that kind of discrimination he or she tends not to be sociable, and that means he or she wouldn't have that much opportunities to use the new language and then master it.

Therefore, discrimination is caused by the society is an important factor in the language learning process[i] .

This essay, a strong critique of Canadian school experience and of the underlying assumptions of a respected book on second language learning, was written early in the term by a first-year engineering student. A Somalian refugee, Aman[1] was in my first year writing-intensive English as a Second Language (ESL) course, Reading and Composition. Although credited as a liberal studies elective, in 1992 the course was required for students who received an adequate, but not high entry score on our pre-admissions English proficiency test. Thus, they were not beginners; many had attended high school in Canada; most had extensive previous English language education. They needed not another grammar course, but refinement — instruction, guidance, and practice in the use of English in the university. Class membership covered a variety of language groups and professional programs.

My approach to the course and to this assignment included building from the students' background and knowledge to introduce them to analytical inquiry. In fact, the liberal studies policy at Ryerson is "to develop the capacity to understand and appraise the social and cultural context in which graduates will work as professionals and live as educated citizens" (Ryerson, 1997, p. 348). Accordingly, one of the first assignments involved students' critical appraisal of a reading (Rubin & Thompson, 1982) on strategies and techniques for learning a second language. With the assignment, I hoped to provoke students' reflection on their individual experiences as language learners in light of the recommendations of the text. I pointed out, as did the authors, that there was a range of successful strategies for language learning, and that they should examine their own or try out new ones suggested in the text. They were to respond to the reading in terms of their own experience of learning English or additional languages, to recall their own successful or unsuccessful strategies, and to analyse how well these corresponded to Rubin and Thompson's. I added that we might share the results in the class. In sum, my construction of the assignment rested on the assumption that even first-year students were capable of critical thinking and writing about topics relevant to their lives.

Three sections of the course received this assignment (over 60 students), and all but two wrote essays praising the strategies in the text, promising to try them and berating themselves for not having been more successful language learners. One of the two papers to depart from this pattern was barely comprehensible. Aman's essay, above, was a short, not well-developed five-paragraph theme typical of students directly out of high school. In fact, all the students in the course initially wrote to this five-paragraph formula, relating that it had been taught explicitly. Nevertheless, I was pleased; I considered his paper the only "success" of the assignment. I tried to encourage him, for I saw, despite his imperfect English, a message that was in vogue in much of the academic discourse on the topic: the debate between individual cognitive processes and social context as explanators of language and literacy development. I was impressed not just because Aman dared to be critical of the textbook reading but also because he had identified the issues of a broader debate.

At first, I was tempted to see Aman, as compared to the others, a more critical observer of life, who had the confidence and sophistication to respond critically to the topic. I saw him as capable of coping with his experience in Canadian schools and taking advantage of the assignment to express it in a critical analysis. On the other hand, he was a student who only sporadically came to class; and shortly after this assignment, he never returned. His essay may have arisen more from a deep anger and disaffection with school than from a commitment to the task or willingness to take learning risks.

Why, then, did the overwhelming majority not fulfill the assignment? I might have suspected they were not able to think critically about a topic relevant to their lives. But I would like to explore two alternative possibilities. One source of the assignment failure may have been the students' own cultural and experiential knowledge about school settings. In other words, their prior school experiences contributed to their perceptions of what would be valued in my university course. For example, they may have previously acquired the notion of the instructor as authority and the text as the source of factual truth and thus been unable to consider critiquing the text. The second alternative involves "face," the desire to protect their dignity and establish identity as diligent students. In reading their essays, I would be assessing not just their English writing and their understanding of the text, but also their worth as students. What's more, the possibility of sharing essays in class with unfamiliar classmates made their face vulnerable to peers, which could consequently display their social position in the classroom as well. Such a situation might well have constrained the students' willingness to deviate from the text or to make claims about their successes that others might not have seen as evident, because they had been placed in an ESL class.

"THE DIFFERENCES BETWEEN CANADIAN AND IRANIAN POLITENESS"

At the time my concern as a teacher was how to turn around the results; I continued to believe that first-year students could write critical appraisals, not necessarily with great depth or sophistication, but that they would learn to do so by beginning with discussion and practice. I looked to modify the course content so that engagement with the topic would not cause them to risk losing face. At the same time, they would need to draw on adequate experiential knowledge of the topic and personal investment to be able to engage with it in a critical way.

Consequently, when the course became an official liberal studies elective, and was retitled Language and Identity, I incorporated a section on language and social distance. I had listened for years to students' anecdotal complaints about the Anglo Canadian practice of warm conversation among recent acquaintances, the "invitations" to "do lunch" or to "drop over," suggesting an incipient relationship that never develops. My focus in one section of the course outline became language of relationship, of distance and intimacy, of status and solidarity in English. We read Scollon and Scollon (1995) and Lakoff (1990) on camaraderie politeness, i.e., politeness strategies that signal friendliness and social involvement, as opposed to distance and deference politeness, which respect privacy, independence, and hierarchy. We discussed address forms, and the possible meanings of the discomfort caused to many students by the practice of university professors and students and employers and employees addressing each other by first name. The students were also anxious to talk about the cultural differences they saw in the ways language and behaviour marked friendship relationships.

The following passage was written in the 1995 Fall term by a Computer Studies student. Her paper compared interpersonal politeness strategies in Iran to those she had observed in Canada. She dealt with address forms in institutional settings, politeness between genders, and the following discussion on communication practices that signal friendship as opposed to friendliness.

What confuses me the most in Canadians' attitudes is their camaraderie politeness in distant relationships. In Iran after the first few steps of friendship the idea of distance politeness is broken and people develop genuine friendships. After reaching this stage of friendship, the preservation of space and maintaining distance has no meaning. They use a genuine friendly attitude towards each other without any hidden meaning of distance in it.

When I first came to Canada as a tourist, people seemed so friendly and helpful. Whenever I asked for direction[s], people answered me with open faces. If my destination was close, they even accompanied me to it, but since I have started my life as a part of Canadian society everything seemed to change. In each relationship at first everything seems nice and friendly, but when it reaches a certain stage I cannot take any step further. It's like they have barricaded themselves behind walls of glass. I can see them smiling at me and each time I think that this time I can reach them, but finally I only feel the coldness of the glass on my skin. At first I thought that something was wrong with me that I can't make any close relation with people, but now I know that they just wanted to be polite and everything was a part of the Canadian camaraderie strategy of politeness. Now this attitude of Canadian people really scares me. When they are friendly it confuses me. I don't understand the meaning of their attitude and I always wonder if I am pushing too hard or if I am near their forbidden territory of privacy. That kind of thought always makes me hold back and not trust people's attitudes.

This essay was among the best in the class. Nevertheless, this time, essays that incorporated discussion of the principles with experiences illustrating the concepts were much more the norm. There was a mixture of positive and negative outlooks. I believed I had found a topic that engaged both academic and personal interest, a mode of presentation that combined these two spheres, and a set of related academic readings that engaged the students. This time the topic didn't require a risky display of self along with language proficiency; rather, it allowed for a detached but reflective observation of social interaction and social relationships. Moreover, it seemed to be a topic that concerned them all, that they had an emotional stake in or at least puzzled over, which was legitimated through academic discourse as well. It did not require students to critique the information presented in the text, but to use it as a framework for structuring and understanding their own experiences. The task gave scope for distancing, both from the personal involvement of the earlier assignment, and also from the subject-matter itself, thereby creating the opportunity for some kind of academic interpretation.

CONTRIBUTING TO A FRAMEWORK FOR UNDERSTANDING WRITING DEVELOPMENT

What can we draw from these two classroom literacy events that might deepen our understanding of the writing development of non-native English speakers entering university? So far, I have noted that prior learning may shape text structures, such as the five-paragraph formula. In other words, at least some students acquired knowledge and skills that may be directly represented in their writing. But I have further suggested that task interpretations may be influenced by cultural and other experiential constructs of what is valued in school situations. I have also suggested that students' desire to maintain face with teachers and peers and identify themselves as worthy students may affect the way they take up assignments. If we consider the university as text, then, it is not just composed of writing skills and knowledge, but also of translations of prior notions of "school" to the university context and of the way students see themselves as situated in the university context.

PRIOR EDUCATIONAL EXPERIENCE AND THE UNIVERSITY CONTEXT

Ample evidence exists in the research on literacy development to suggest that when the literacy practices and values of students' cultures differ from those of the school, students are often evaluated by school standards as deficient. One of the best known studies in this area is Heath's 1983 ethnography of children's language and literacy development in the Appalachian area of the U.S. Heath researched three communities: rural whites, rural blacks, and middle-class townspeople. She found that the two rural communities followed distinctly different language and literacy practices from the townspeople. In Heath's (1983) view, for one rural community, "the written word limits alternatives of expression; ...[for the other], it opens alternatives. Neither community's ways with the written word prepares it for the school's ways" (p. 235). She contrasts them to the middle-class children, who at home "learned the rules for talking about and responding to books and writing tasks.... In school, they found continuity of these patterns of using oral and written language" (1983, p. 262). The result of the mismatch between home and school literacy practices of the rural children was, according to Heath, negative evaluations of their literacy skills. Although Heath's research focuses on children, it shows how previously acquired literacy practices can conflict with the school's. Furthermore, it shows that reading and writing are not just skills; rather, they embody ways of dealing with print.

Other studies of cross-cultural language education complement Heath's perspective. Young (1987) reports on the findings of his own and other research on Chinese classrooms. He maintains that the "interaction of Chinese teachers and learners in the [Chinese ESL]... classroom is... a balanced eco-system of reciprocally defined behaviours, attitudes, and interpretations of reality" (p. 27). He particularly notes that Chinese teaching style favours control and direction of students more than North American teaching does. Moreover, he believes that other, Western style instructional approaches may not necessarily be successful with Chinese students unless these deeper differences are taken into account. Ballard and Clanchy (1991) support Young's view in their discussion of culturally different attitudes to knowledge, learning approaches, and learning strategies. Also describing Asian cultures and contrasting them with Western Anglo cultures (in this case Australia), they maintain that fundamental differences along these lines tend to be deeply ingrained, often unconsciously held, and can play an important role in the misassessment of language and writing competence.

Communication and cultural theorists attempt to define analytical frameworks for what Heath, Young, and others may loosely refer to as culture. They often refer to "frames" (Agar, 1994; Goffman, 1986) or "discourses" (Gee, 1990, 1992a, 1992b), and propose models of their nature and relationships to each other. Gee (1992b), for example, defines "Discourse" as:

> a socio-culturally distinctive and integrated way of thinking, acting, interacting, talking, and valuing connected with a particular social identity or role, with its own unique history, and often with its own distinctive "props" (buildings, objects, spaces, schedules, books, etc.). Socio-cultural approaches to literacy argue that literacy is inherently plural (literacies) and that writing, reading, and language are always embedded in and inextricable from Discourses (social practices, cultures, and subcultures, or whatever analogous term is used). Writing, reading, and language are not private psychic possessions of decontextualized heads, nor are they generalized skills from specific contents and contexts. (p. 33)

Gee has a great deal more to say about the nature of Discourses, but two aspects of his theory seem particularly relevant to the literacy events described above. The first is that individuals have multiple social identities, for instance as family members, employees, and as rock music fans or chess players. This implies that they are members of and operate in multiple Discourses — in the family, in the workplace, and in leisure activities. Second, Discourses are hierarchically placed in society, with mastery of dominant, status-giving Discourses leading to social goods and empowerment. Gee (1990) elaborates that dominant "Discourses empower those groups who have the least conflicts with their other Discourses when they use them" (pp. 144-145).

How might Gee's model apply to the student writers in Reading and Composition? We can begin by considering that they have come to a Canadian university as reasonably successful members of school Discourses that are foreign to ours. They may harbour, as Young's article illustrates, different perceptions about what school is, the roles and responsibilities of students and professors, and the expectations and demands placed on them. When these perceptions conflict with the Canadian university, they may place themselves at cross-purposes when participating in the new Discourse. Students, for example, from Discourses where the teacher is an unquestioned authority may find themselves in great conflict being asked to critique a text the teacher has selected. Gee's model can also apply to the student writers in Language in Social Identity. The students in this revised course were asked to analyse politeness practices they had observed and experienced in Canadian society. This assignment required them to observe Anglo-Canadian Discourses as outsiders and to interpret them according to a framework presented in the course. It didn't demand, as the language learning assignment did, that they take on a role as members of Discourses that may have conflicted with their own. Instead, it allowed them to speak from their own Discourses.

SOCIAL IDENTITY AND MAINTAINING FACE

I have suggested in discussion of the language learning assignment that the ways students see themselves positioned in relation to others in the university Discourse may bear on their writing development. The overall importance of friends and supportive peers in first-year university is affirmed in the results of a recent Canadian survey by Gilbert, Chapman, Dietsche, Grayson and Gardner (1997). The importance of university as a community is cited by Boyer (1990). Further insight into this area may come from a research project I carried out among my own first-year ESL students. In 1995 and 1996, I conducted 39 ethnographic interviews with first-year, non-native English-speaking students in my courses in order to understand more deeply how they saw themselves as university students, what they considered their needs to be, and what part they considered their language competence to play in their university lives. I asked fairly open-ended questions, with no preset categories to fill; I looked for recurrent patterns rather than statistical results.

   Like Gilbert et al.'s (1997) research, my findings suggest that the sense of belonging to a university community and having a friendship group as a supportive resource are important to many students. Similar to the general first-year university population they studied, the ESL students were undergoing a transition that often left them feeling isolated. Although both the university and I labelled them ESL students, the students didn't consider the L_2 as part of their identity — for them, language for accomplishing school work was rather a practical hurdle for them to overcome. Social needs, particularly a feeling of belonging, seemed to be at least as salient in their lives as academic language needs. What the interview data also indicated was trends in the students' responses to these needs. One response was to retreat to social groups of the home culture; they were familiar and often supportive. In fact, several students mentioned peer pressure from the home culture group not to use English, for the use of English represented snobbishness, an attempt to be "above" one's background. The results were that English for these students remained a foreign language, a language of study but minimal everyday use.

Yet living in a dominant English context, along with English assessment of their school performance, put them in a state of paralyzing tension, a condition exacerbated by their retreat from English. One student commented in a wry understatement, "When you can't socialize with other students — I don't know, it feels strange, it feels weird, to live somewhere and not communicate with those people." The tension also invaded the classroom setting. Many avoided talking to their professors. For example, another reported: "I feel shy to ask my professor, because if my talk is not related or if there's a mistake or if he couldn't understand, then I feel sorry, so that's why I do not go." Others commented on classroom joking that they couldn't follow, fear of speaking in class, Anglo-Canadians who avoided them in group and lab work, embarrassment at being slower than their Anglo peers to process language, imitation of their accents, and unsuccessful attempts to join Anglo peers' conversation groups. In other words, many echoed the sentiments of the dispirited Iranian writer on camaraderie politeness. Some recognized the underlying cultural differences that had to be bridged in order to join informal social groups, pointing out that they didn't know anything about hockey or baseball, nor were they interested. In labs and group work, they clustered together or joined other non-native English speakers. Overall, these students tended to withdraw in situations where they had to rely on English — not just to display knowledge, but to participate in everyday classroom interaction. Not all students reacted this way. Others seemed able to adapt to university more easily. Some had stronger English proficiency when they arrived, not necessarily from English study, but from extensive social or workplace interaction. Some seemed more independent. They were more effectively resourceful at solving problems; or they had strong, supportive family ties or other existing social networks that may have buttressed them in stressful English situations.

The interview data do not show that the students in Reading and Composition were interpreting the assignment in a face-saving way. But they do

suggest that social dignity in relation to teachers and peers is quite important. What's more, these students' withdrawal from situations, their coping
response to the immediate possibility of losing face, may at the same time
potentially jeopardize their academic success. Even for students who were
less intimidated, though, an assignment carries more weight in the long run
than everyday classroom encounters. For this reason, the language learning
assignment may have been interpreted by both types of students as personally threatening. Of course, face may be equally important to all of us, yet we
are not saddled nearly as obviously with the additional, highly visible factor
of language for success or failure, acceptance or rejection.

IMPLICATIONS FOR A MODEL AND A PEDAGOGY OF WRITING DEVELOPMENT

In summary, I have looked at the writing of two first-year university students
in courses designated for those who speak English as a second language.
I have attempted to show that although their writing reflects their learned
knowledge and skills to some extent, other important variables are at play in
their interpretation and fulfilment of written assignments. First, membership
and experience in other Discourses, upon which students may base their
understanding of school and education, figure in their perception of writing
purposes. Second, the degree to which they perceive a potential effect on
their identity in relation to others may influence their participation in school
activities. Whether or not they are constant, highly powerful elements in
students' writing, these underlying forces do suggest that students' ongoing
positioning of themselves and their mental constructions of what university
is contribute to their writing. Although I have focussed on ESL students, it
is likely such factors influence native speakers as well, but are simply more
visible among the students I observed. This may be a direction for future
investigation.

My interpretation of these two writing events implies that we as writing teachers need to be sensitive to and respectful of students' dignity in all
aspects of our work. For often we tend to consider respect and community in
terms of polite classroom interaction, when it may be much more. We need to
reflect on the ways personal writing may expose and burden students unnecessarily. We can also work toward making our classrooms and our programs
an inclusive community. As well, we might incorporate explicit discussion
and instruction about how we view students' and teachers' roles, responsibilities, and purposes. Considerations like these are part of the constant

reflection called for in our work. In reviewing the cross-cultural politeness assignment, one can see that whereas the students were more successful at critical analysis and fulfilling the assignment, students like the Iranian writer seemed further discouraged by her own analysis. For those of us who invoke personal writing as a bridge to the academic, there's a clear need to avoid exploiting the personal in emotionally damaging ways. These points may seem obvious to many of us, for good teachers seem to take them for granted in their approach to teaching. But they are easy to disregard if we focus our teaching too rigorously on the task at hand without trying to see the learners as they see themselves, or in other words, trying to take into account their identities and backgrounds. Especially when faced with distracting pressures of an era in which we are required to be more accountable, to meet "standards" with measurable outcomes, and to defend our professionalism, the significance of less tangible qualities can be unnecessarily swept aside.

Notes
1   All student names are pseudonyms.

I would like to thank David Cooke for his support and critical comments during the preparation of this paper.

References

Agar, M. (1994). Language shock. NY: William Morrow.

Ballard, B. & Clanchy, J. (1991). Assessment by misconception: Cultural influences and intellectual traditions. In L. Hamp-Lyons (Ed.) Assessing second language writing in academic contexts (pp. 19-35). Norwood, NJ: Ablex.

Boyer, E. L. (1990). Campus life: In search of community. Princeton, NJ: The Carnegie foundation for the Advancement of Teaching.

Gee, J.P. (1990). Social linguistics and literacies: Ideologies in discourses. London: The Falmer Press.

————— (1992a). The social mind: Language, ideology, and social practice. NY: Bergin and Garvey.

————— (1992b). Socio-cultural approaches to literacy (literacies). In W. Grabe (Ed.), Annual Review of Applied Linguistics, 12, 31-48.

Gilbert, S., Chapman, J., Dietsche, P., Grayson, P., & Gardner, J.N. (1997). From best intentions to best practices: The first-year experience in Canadian post-secondary education. Columbia, SC: University of South Carolina.

Goffman, E. (1986). Frame analysis. NY: Harper and Row.

Heath, S.B. (1983). Ways with words. Cambridge: Cambridge University Press.

Lakoff, R. T. (1990). Talking power. The politics of language. NY: Basic Books.

Rubin, J. & Thompson, I. (1982). How to be a more successful language learner. Boston: Heinle and Heinle.

Ryerson Polytechnic University. (1997). Toronto: Ryerson Polytechnic University.

Scollon, R. & Scollon, S. (1995). Intercultural communication. Oxford: Basil Blackwell.

Young, R. (1987). The cultural context of TESOL — A review of research into Chinese classrooms. RELC Journal, 18(2), 15-30.

Provisional Knowing and Exploratory Narrative: Positioning Uncertainty in Academic Inquiry

Jaqueline McLeod Rogers
University of Winnipeg

For many students, the first year of university can be characterized as a time of uncertainty. When a student is enrolled in a mandatory composition course that constitutes a degree requirement, this attitude of uncertainty can manifest in an inability to recognize the high stakes attached to writing well not only within the academic system but also in the working world. On a more personal level, many first-year students are unclear about how to identify their own writing weaknesses and developmental needs and consequently struggle to make use of the instructional support. Finally, students who are uncertain about their goals do not always know what course of study they will pursue, and thus it is not especially helpful for them to think about the discipline-specific nature of interpretive strategies and writing conventions.

Despite posing some obstacles to growth, uncertainty can be viewed as a positive student characteristic — as an attitude constructive of learning. Remembering Burke's description of the novice's struggle to find a way into the ongoing conversation of disciplinary experts can help us to understand why many students assume that they do not know it all and why their prose may be halting or sketchy as a result. Remembering Mina Shaughnessy's argument that structural errors signal sites of possible growth can lead us to consider whether students show signs of disorientation or misdirection because they are responding to discourse conventions that they have noticed but not understood fully during the relatively limited time that they have been exposed to university-level readings.

UNCERTAINTY, KNOWING, AND NARRATIVE INQUIRY

Rather than encouraging our students to cultivate taking a position and seeking firm ground, it might be more useful to help them to understand uncertainty as a postmodern condition of knowing, in the sense that "researchers and theorists with a postmodern orientation have questioned the neutrality and objectivity of the researcher, writer, or teacher" (Flynn, 1997, p. 540). It is also the case that many feminists prefer to avoid what Jane Tompkins (1993) calls "the authority effect, which ignores, among other things, the human frailty of the speaker" (p. 31). Instead, feminist theorizing ascribes "as much value to interpretive, provisional theories as to grand all-encompassing ones" (Ray, 1993, p. 35), and maintains writers "start their inquiries on the ground of their subjectivities" because "the mystery of identity and its relationship to culture can never be banished from scholarship" (Young-Bruehl, 1986, pp. 15, 18).

As we introduce students to academic writing and research practices, we can point out how recent scholarship has been influenced by postmodern-ism and feminism, particularly in the turn away from rigid conclusions and toward raising questions or offering provisional perspectives. We can point out how an attitude of self-reflexivity can help a writer to recognize and re-vise his or her assumptions and hence to develop ideas that are responsive to new information and particular contexts. Students with an interest in doing research that involves interpreting some element of human experience might benefit from learning that writers are often encouraged to reflect on how their experience may be shaping their response to a text or site. A stance of self-consciousness rather than confidence is often intellectually appropriate to the process of sorting out old assumptions from fresh understandings.

Indeed, an attitude of uncertainty is something of a necessary stage for a field researcher, according to the recent text *Narrative Inquiry: Experience and Story in Qualitative Research* (2000), whose section "Writing Research Texts in the Midst of Uncertainty" describes how writers frequently let go of their original suppositions and plunge into a welter of observations that appear to be without pattern or meaning: "the writers are less confident of what they are doing and what they want to say than they were when they entered the field, and most certainly, they are less secure and at ease with themselves than they were as the field experience, if successful, unfolded" (Clandinin & Connelly, 2000, p. 145) When observational research is focused on human activity, another source of uncertainty is the relationship between writer and participants, so that the "researcher learns that people are never only (or even a close approximation to) any particular set of isolated theoretical notions, categories, or terms" (Clandinin & Connelly, 2000, p. 145). This description recalls Robert Coles' (1989) story about why he gave up writing crisp theory-driven psychological accounts of the state of mind of polio-stricken children. His wife, working as an engaged educator with the same cohort, chided him for turning the children they knew into clinical cases, and for thus reducing the complexity of human response: "she suggested that I wasn't really speaking about them at all; I was, rather, 'making reference to them' as I showed 'those doctors' how dutifully I could mobilize a theoretical apparatus to the task of 'explaining' what was going on" (pp. 28-29). As Coles' story begins to illustrate, a reluctance to examine human questions through a lens of theory and a recognition that one's knowing will be partial has accompanied the shift away from relying on empirical models of knowing.

Narrative is a form of thinking and writing that enables the making of personal and provisional observations about human situations. In *Actual Minds, Possible Worlds*, Jerome Bruner (1989) observes that narrative appears to be more of a way of thinking than a style of writing, and links the concept to telling stories rather than constructing paradigms (pp. 12-13). It can also add to our understanding of narrative to think of how European formalists "defined story as the sequence of events, plot the way a story is narrated, and narrative as the manner of the telling" (Lewieki-Wilson, 1999 p. 107), thus raising issues of interpretation and perspective. More recently, and applied to educational research practice, Clandinin and Connelly (2000) define narrative as an inquiry form and point out that its great strength is in being responsive to change. This responsiveness is also a source of struggle for researchers who try to find a way to place their story in time: "Their task is not so much to say that people, places, and things are this way or that way but that they have a narrative history and are moving forward. The narrative research text is fundamentally a temporal text" (pp. 145-46).

FROM EXPRESSIVISM TO PERSONAL VOICE INQUIRY IN COMPOSITION

In the 1970s and early 1980s, personal-voice narrative essays had a place in most first-year composition classrooms, too often on the basis of being a "feel-good" foray into writing for an academic audience. Because this form of writing bore little resemblance to the writing students practiced in their course work outside, many instructors were willing to abandon it. In a watershed debate, Donald Bartholomae represented a social constructivist approach recommending that students attempt to learn academic conventions and enter into academic discourse, a position that received more widespread support than Peter Elbow's expressivist views. Within the social constructivist composition classroom, students were often introduced to the interpretive strategies and writing conventions of a discipline-specific community and encouraged to develop an awareness of the forces of politics and culture.

The pendulum appears to be swinging away from a wholly constructivist approach and back in the direction of seeing purpose in cultivating personal voice. Yet, this development is not really a return to expressivism, so far as this term is understood as referring to a student's exploration of a unique self and voice. There is a recognition now that rather than encouraging students to record and crystallize ready-made opinions, self-reflection is a critical act helping them to understand their assumptions and change their views. As Sherrie Gradin (1995) points out in presenting an approach that she calls "social expressivist," "the expressivist classroom can resist disempowering social influences, use interdisciplinary classroom methods, and posit a social understanding of the self "(p. 112).

Perhaps the most significant development in personal-voice writing is that it is more firmly linked to public discourse in its current forms. By contrast, non-academic personal writing was often the centrepiece of earlier expressivist curriculums that featured exploratory, writer-based journals and freewrites. The personal voice was connected to self-examination and self-development, rather than to inquiry and argument, a division that is captured in the title of Peter Elbow's (1995) side of the debate, "Being a Writer vs. Being an Academic: A Conflict of Goals."

ASSIGNMENT: TO (SELF-CONSCIOUSLY) LINK PRIVATE AND PUBLIC WORLDS

Some time in the late 1990s, I went back to teaching a unit of personal-voice narrative as the first writing assignment in my writing classes. When I didn't have it, I missed it. I ask students to find a connection between some element of their reading or writing experience and the public issue of literacy. Reading their personal-voice essays, I appreciate learning something about students as individuals with stories, rather than looking at a sea of faces. I also appreciate being reminded of the challenges of writing from a student's perspective, and have found that this vantage point can sometimes correct my thinking, as in the following example where the writer puts student enthusiasm for academic writing into a practical perspective: "My writing skills are not as sharp as some people I know, but as far as enthusiasm goes, we are a lot alike. I have never met anyone or heard of anyone getting excited about writing assignment essays."

In the older version of this assignment that I gave several years ago, I asked students to write about a learning experience narratively and to point out how their experience could be meaningful to others. Responding to this assignment, students often wrote stories that were rather pat, since they were choosing moments of experience that were easily generalizable. Many stories ended by tacking on a sentence or two intended to establish universal significance. In general, the manner of telling conveyed the sense that writers were not exploring experience to consider its meanings, but writing a story intended to demonstrate a "truth."

The wording of the current narrative assignment places emphasis on the need for writers to explore experiences that have influenced their attitudes toward reading and/or writing. They are asked to write an exploratory rather than a thesis-driven narrative in the process of linking private to public world. The assignment also stipulates that the telling of events needs to be accompanied by some analysis of the significance and implications of these events.

In presenting the current narrative assignment, I begin by establishing literacy education as a social issue that directly involves students. We talk about such things as the gatekeeping function of the recently implemented grade twelve English exit test and of mandatory university-level writing courses, about the way in which culture influences the texts we value and call "classics," and about more composition-specific questions like whether there is a link between reading and writing ability or between confidence and writing ability. We also look at several examples of literacy narratives, where individual experience shines a light on an epistemological question. Students' inquiries into their individual experiences is framed within this larger context.

At the same time as they are asked to be continually mindful of the public dimension of their experience, writers are also instructed that such enlargement is not always developed explicitly. They are also asked to think about the problems associated with a writer's setting him/herself up as a universal figure rather than as one whose experience represents that of some others. The point here is that the students are not exploring the self and idiosyncratic experience, but are interrogating the way their experience says something about how we learn and the way we are educated.

The assignment is also exploratory in nature, which means that students are encouraged to begin drafting with a willingness to discover patterns and meaning rather than from a vantage point of knowing. This is different from simply following an inductive pattern of development, because an exploratory approach affects conceptualization rather than surface arrangement.

EXAMPLES OF SELF REFLECTION AND NARRATIVE ARGUMENT

Examples from these literacy narratives help to demonstrate how students can use personal voice to explore public issues and how doing so requires a critical stance and active self-reflection. In the following passage (written by an Education student), the writer looks at the effect of grading on performance. This anecdote about the writer as a grade five student receiving a bad mark for a story that he has enjoyed writing completes the narrative:

> Usually when I got something back from the teacher, there were plenty of red marks and things crossed out. Those I expected. What I didn't expect was what Mrs. S. delivered: a single, bloody "f" at the top of the page with the words "too long" written underneath it. My heart skipped a beat, and for a second I was sure that I passed out. I went numb and lost all awareness of where I was. When the bell rang, it was like swimming in very cold water, as I retrieved my jacket and walked home.
>
> As I entered the house, my mom asked me the familiar question: "How was your day?"
>
> I didn't respond, only handed her my sheets of crumpled paper. She gasped when she saw the mark that awful Mrs. S. had given me. I collapsed in the living room chair, too confused to care what was going on.
>
> I was still there an hour later when my mom handed back my paper. I took it and started to shove it under the chair when she motioned me to look at it. At the top, where the horrid blemish had been, was a new mark. Mom had erased the ugly red mark and replaced it with a "B+." Underneath the mark was a short phrase, "Too many spelling mistakes! Be more careful!" I looked up at her and smiled.

This student is exploring how grading has a strong influence on writers and writing and implicitly how praise should be part of the feedback if it is to be helpful; also implicitly, the story conveys the idea that a child with supportive parents has a chance of withstanding harsh treatment at the hands of overly critical educators. Because it moves beyond simply blaming the teacher, the narrative does more than reproduce the feelings of anger and frustration the writer had as a boy.

In another story, the writer tells a series of school-based vignettes, most of which explore the effect of brutal teaching on a shy student. Here is the first of several vignettes:

> I attended kindergarten in a First Nation Community. I remember enjoying the first part of kindergarten. There were two teachers; one was nice and friendly and the other was mean and strict. I made sure to keep my distance from her.
>
> During the first days of kindergarten the nice one taught us how to count and spell our names. She was preparing us to go into the structured program with the strict teacher. Once a student learned how to print their name they were moved to that classroom. I didn't know this until it happened.
>
> I thought that the nice teacher was always going to be my teacher. I felt proud to accomplish the task of printing my name. She encouraged me and was happy for me. The experience was a positive one, although short lived.
>
> The strict teacher informed me it was time to go into her classroom. I was horrified. I thought there must be some mistake. The nice teacher was mine and I didn't want to change. I shook my head that I did not want to go. She raised her voice and demanded that I obey her. I began to cry. The strict teacher seemed to be impatient with me. She grabbed my arm and pulled me towards the classroom. I remember trying to resist. The next thing I knew, she had me under her arm and I was now crying even harder and trying to wiggle free. She marched straight into the classroom full of other students; they were sitting straight and silent. She literally plunked me in an empty desk so hard, I felt my stomach jerk to the thump in the chair.
>
> She won; I couldn't stop her from taking me. I felt embarrassed, angry and scared. All I could do was to ignore her and stay out of her way. From then I thought it was a punishment to learn and master ideas at school. The other children seemed to be just as wary of her as I was.

These paragraphs about teacher brutality are primarily self-story, although there is an element of generalizability, particularly when the author notes that other children seemed "just as wary." Later in the essay, toward the end, the writer connects her experience to that of others more directly and raises the question of whether mistreatment was the result of racism. Here the link between self and others joins private experience to public issue (racism):

As an adult, I have talked with other people that had bad school experiences with teachers or bullies, and how it influenced their behavior. This made me feel that I was not alone and maybe my perceptions about my personal reading and writing were wrong. I was a small, shy, quiet student and did not cause any trouble. My school years were between 1965 and 1978. I think back and wonder how much of the attitude of teachers was related to racism.

In "Reflecting on the (Re-?)Turn to Story: Personal Narratives and Pedagogy," Cynthia Lewiecki-Wilson (1999) expresses the concern that storytelling often crystallizes a student's opinions rather than encouraging fresh thought: "often students will not reflect on or budge in their beliefs" (p. 108). By raising the issue of racism as a possibility toward the end of the narrative, the writer avoids telling stories with predetermined meanings; she does not insist that a story means one thing or demonstrates a ready-made point. She is following an exploratory form of development wherein she examines what her experience may mean and how parts of it may be connected.

Apart from addressing public issues from a complex personal perspective, these stories reveal writers in the process of reinterpreting their experiences — of using "writing as a means of creating a self, not for expressing a self that already exists" (Zawacki,1992, p. 37). In both cases, writers tell about younger selves, yet they have to struggle with the time-bound nature of narrative, sorting out how to tell about what they felt back then from what they now feel about that moment in the past. These two perspectives meeting creates something new.

Often, writers learning about themselves and changing their minds is evident in the narrative itself. For example, one student begins her narrative by saying that the assignment has prompted her to think for the first time about writing: "I have never really had a passion for writing. Before today, I can honestly say I have never given much thought to writing." By the end of the paper, she reaffirms that she is unlikely to become passionate about writing, but points out that she now recognizes its value. Her comment is earned rather than tacked-on because stories about the disadvantages of not writing well as a student and as a working person are at the centre of the narrative.

During workshops for early-, middle-, and late-stage drafting, I ask students to explore the process of writing the narrative by responding to these three freewriting prompts:
1) early stage — When I think about writing, I feel...
2) middle stage — As a reader/writer, I was most influenced by...
3) late stage — What was easy/difficult about this assignment...

Responses to the first freewrite often begin with lame observations to the effect that nothing much has happened or that the writer finds writing dull. By the end of the first freewrite or into the second, however, writers usually have a sense of purpose or are finding stories. This excerpt, from a response to the final freewrite prompt, is evidence of the reflective process of forming ideas rather than simply crystallizing old thoughts that students can go through: "It made me reevaluate my ideas towards reading and writing."

SOME IMPLICATIONS OF PERSONAL VOICE WORK

Donald Murray (1991) makes the case that "All Writing is Autobiographical" largely on the strength of his contention that our experiences shape our interpretations and values; from this standpoint, he argued there should be more not less personal writing. Coming from another direction, a recent composition text by Lunsford and Ruszkiewicz (1999), entitled *Everything's an Argument*, develops the perspective that all discourse is ideological. If we bring these two perspectives together, we have the connection between personal voice and critical inquiry, between narrative and argument.

Completing his appointment as editor of *CCC*, Joseph Harris (1999) says in his final editor's notes that contentions surrounding personal voice writing were consistently debated in the articles he has published: "In reviewing the issues of CCC that I have edited, I am struck by a kind of simultaneous exclusion of and focus on the role of the personal voice in writing and teaching" (p. 8). Because narrative writing is not only much discussed but also frequently practiced, students who are learning about real academic writing need guided opportunities to work with this form. Given that personal-voice narrative is moving in from the margins of scholarship, so that it is now more of an interdisciplinary than an alternative form, I agree with Donald Murray (1991) that we should not "move away from personal or reflective narrative in composition courses, but closer to it" (p. 73).

References

Bishop, W. (1999). Places to stand: The reflective writer-teacher-writer in composition. College Composition and Communication, 51, 9-31.

Bruner, J. (1989). Actual minds, possible worlds. Cambridge, MA.: Harvard University Press.

Clandinin, D. J. & Connelly, F.M. (2000). Narrative inquiry: Experience and story on qualitative research. San Francisco: Jossey-Bass.

Coles, R. (1989). The call of stories: Teaching and the moral imagination. Boston: Houghton-Mifflin.

Elbow, P. (1995). Being a writer vs. being an academic: A conflict of goals. College Composition and Communication, 46, 172-183.

Flynn, E. (1997). Rescuing postmodernism. College Composition and Communication, 48, 540-555.

Gradin, S. (1995). Romancing rhetorics: Social expressivist perspectives on the teaching of writing. Portsmouth, MA: Boynton.

Harris, J. (1999). Teaching writing creatively [From the Editor]. College Composition and Communication, 51, 7-8.

Lewiecki-Wilson, C. (1999). Reflecting on the (re-?)turn to story: Personal narratives and pedagogy." College Composition and Communication, 51, 96-109.

Lunsford, A. & Ruszkiewicz, J. (1999). Everything's an argument. Boston: Bedford/St. Martin's.

Murray, D.M. (1991). All writing is autobiography. College Composition and Communication, 42, 66-74.

Ray, R. (1993). The practice of theory: Teacher research in composition. Urbana, IL: NCTE.

Rose, M. (1989). Lives on the boundary. New York: The Free Press.

Tompkins, J. (1993). Me and my shadow. In D.P. Freedman, O. Frey, & F.M. Zauhar (Eds.), The intimate critique: Autobiographical literary criticism. Durham and London: Duke University Press, 23-40.

Young-Bruehl, E. (1986). The education of women as philosophers. In M.R. Malson, J. F. O'Barr, S.Westphal-Wihl, & M. Wyer (Eds.), Feminist theory in practice and process (pp. 35-49). Chicago: University of Chicago Press.

Zawacki, T.M. (1992). Recomposing as a woman—An essay in different voices. College Composition and Communication, 43, 32-38.

The Art of Rhetorical Deception and Modification

Robert S. Vuckovich
Brock University

> Let us suppose that I ask you: "What did the man say?" And that you
> answer: "He said 'yes.'" You still do not know what the man said. You would
> not know unless you knew more about the situation, and about the remarks
> that preceded his answer.
>
>   - Kenneth Burke, *The Philosophy of Literary Form*, p. 1.

*A*s Kenneth Burke attests, uncertainty can arise with respect to an individual's response to an apparently simple question. One possible response, as in the above instance, is to provide simple, unimaginative "answers to questions posed by the situation in which they arose" (Burke, 1973, p. 1). But, by these very terms, answers indeed arise from questions, and questions arise out of settings. So, Burke would have us thoroughly analyze a question situationally before responding to it.

Burke's case reflects my first experience as a teacher's assistant in two introductory philosophy seminars at Brock University in St. Catharines, Ontario: my job was to determine students' understanding of the lectures they were attending and texts they were reading and to assist them if they had difficulty with the material assigned. By raising strategic questions, I attempted to assess the students' knowledge of those materials (on the basis of whether they understood what I was asking them). Yet, I was uncertain myself about how to carry out this task "accurately." I wanted to bring my students to an understanding and appreciation of the history of moral philosophy. Note that successful learning to me entailed knowledge and value: knowledge *as* value. For 50 minutes, twice a week, for 23 weeks, I prepared for discussion on a broad range of material, from Plato, Buddhism, Islamic philosophy, Descartes, to modern and postmodern thought. There was a problem: my students rarely spoke. My first reaction was to wonder whether the material was too complex for them — or were my students simply uninterested? My next move was to probe their silence. Their silence, then, for me became a text.

The seminar format is an integral part of first-year education at Brock. A seminar, in theory, is where students openly express their thoughts on philosophy and on the course. I usually started a class by asking whether there were any difficulties either with the lectures or the readings. Not to my recollection did one student raise any concerns. Some students, as the year progressed, adopted a non-verbal strategy for registering their failure to engage: they shrugged or nodded. At issue here was, how could I get them to express concerns in order to generate not just philosophical discussion but what I would call "a philosophical mood." From my perspective, it was necessary to manipulate, i.e., to coax out what I assumed lay buried: namely their issues and interests. As an open forum, the seminars at Brock were definitely not set up to test *my* understanding of the material. I did not assume, in other words, that my authority or expertise was in question. Underlying this thought, however, was my liberal assumption that neither was the students' (or if not their expertise then their responsibility to, or interest in the subject). So, instead of lecturing, I invited students to show me what they knew about the material they had covered. It was their turn to speak. I concealed my relationship with the subject, tried to be mediator, keeping in mind Robert Con Davis's (1987) claim that what is "[i]mportant to pedagogy is the sense in which the teacher does not convey information to students but only helps students situate themselves in relation to knowledge" (p. 749).

What I was trying to be was less an informant than a doorman, one who opened the subject for the student. But from the students' perspective, my position made no sense. The course, they would argue, was their first exposure to the subject: without providing them with pertinent, which is to say stable, knowledge, I left my students in a state of confusion. What I kept in abeyance, however, was my stronger knowledge that confusion marks the site where intellectual development begins. Following Davis, one would say that learners must reformulate their belief in the total authority of the instructor by replacing it with their own articulations. The successful teacher is the one who disappears at the crucial moment. Davis (1987) wants the "teacher… [to present] knowledge as a kind of bait that lures the student… [such that] the student will find a place from which to produce (rather than merely repeat) language" (p. 752). In a seminar setting, this production founded on absence is trickery. The important thing to note, though, is that the instructor's method of encouraging student discussion involves deception.

I resorted to deception as a means of promoting uncertainty. But here, an aspect of my own desire surfaces: I encouraged identification with the subject, not critical detachment but immersion in the drama of philosophical crisis. The question arises, is this strategy legitimate or misleading, not only in terms of how students relate to their instructors, but by compelling them to accept partial rather than full knowledge?

MOTIVATIONAL DECEPTION

As I say, I, as instructor, presented myself duplicitously as one who knows and does not know. To define myself in terms of opposing predicates is, to say the least, a rhetorical ploy. Burke (1969) affirms the practicality of enlisting opposites, because toying with opposites is an invitation to generate new output (p. 58). Non-participation was not an option. My show of ignorance acted as an opportunity for the students to participate. Ignorance in such an instance is not associated with being incompetent, unless one is not a good rhetorician. While some students engaged each other in debate, I kept track of what was said and plotted the next area for discussion. The game was partly successful — there were still several students who rarely contributed. Here is another dimension of my desire as teacher. Students could enter into a fragmentary relation with knowledge, but the classroom must be all inclusive.

As some of my students gained confidence responding to my questions, I continued to play devil's advocate to spark arguments, to situate learning in the interstices of classroom discussion, in concrete exchanges between students. For instance, discussing Glaucon's account of the myth of Gyges from Plato's *Republic*, students initially agreed that it is "wrong" for one person to take advantage of another — for whatever reason. In response, I expounded on how wonderful it would be to live advantageously by satisfying one's desires. By advocating the opposing view, I established myself as the corrupt character in the text. Unlike the Socratic interlocutors, who typically gave either affirmative responses or objections, I pressured students to explain their positions fully. Likely some students learned to dislike my portrayal because I was confrontational. When we were discussing Plato's stance on censorship, I stirred up further heated debates. For the benefit of students favouring censorship, I argued how unfair it would be for any person or political establishment to determine the rights of an individual. On the other hand,

I pointed out that there are problems with people acting freely and doing what they wanted. One student vehemently disagreed with my advocacy of censorship, not perceiving the ambiguous or, let's say, dramatic ingredient behind my presentation. Occasionally, I acted more "aggressively," because my points were not being addressed in discussion — so, I did attempt to control the content of discussions. Also, though, by creating friction I hoped to recruit less vocal students. So I was motivated by extreme cases: to what extent I was returning students' attention to the subject at hand and to what extent I was departing from, and thus betraying, the text and the felicities of serious discussion — not an issue I was willing to pursue at the time. Was I seeking to replace the text with my own personality?

At one level, the challenge was to place students in a contemplative situation where only one view could ultimately prevail. In essence, I was demanding that my students come to decide on a philosophical issue. At the same time, some students got the hidden lesson: they began to recognize how this challenge was saturated with uncertainty. The instructor, as the deceptive instigator of discussion, enlivens discussion by indicating that there is more than one perspective to consider. We should realize how an audience is contained within extremes, in the Burkean sense. Students have to decide which perspective, over and above mere subject matter, suits their own personal beliefs. Without wanting to appear demonic, I confess that I took enormous pleasure in disturbing students' perceptions.

Eventually, as one student said, "what comes around goes around." This motto expressed her brand of moral justice, as it then stood. She thought that justice meant that every person would be punished for wrongdoing. As I remember, the discussion dealt with the establishing of objective moral codes. Ironically, after lengthy discussion, her exact words came back to haunt her. She argued that there were circumstances when people cannot be held accountable for their actions.

This growth of insight becomes a way of measuring progress. What is at stake though, too, is the strictly detached or impersonal perspective on knowledge. This detachment is replaced by agon: one becomes partly, or also, the enemy of what one thinks one knows. In effect, what this student thought was certain was undermined so as to reveal that she was never really certain in the first place. Uncertainty situates itself at the doorstep of knowledge — in such close proximity to knowledge that it almost goes unnoticed. Belatedly, uncertainty is revealed as having been there all along.

For me, the main point to consider when using this approach is to make sure that the students re-evaluate their way of thinking. Students are now *confronted* with a challenge of interpreting reality from multiple perspectives. What is desired is an introspective dialogue. Students must privately ask themselves whether I, as the instructor, am right and envision how I could be wrong. Here the rhetorical audience is personal, singular. In "Confrontational Teaching and Rhetorical Practice," Virginia Anderson (1997) suggests that effective teaching manifests itself when the instructor encourages a student "to create an inner authority by answering [and questioning those perspectives] for herself" (p. 210). Likewise, I thought that it was necessary for students to re-examine their comments in the same manner as the student mentioned above did. In the *Republic*, Socrates never tells Thrasymachus that he is wrong; rather, Socrates dialectically guides Thrasymachus to reconsider his own position on justice. I often expressed the need for my students to be objective when assessing their own or another's position.

Such an exercise reveals an interesting fact, namely, that the students' involvement mimics the text they are studying. My students acted as if they had adopted the views expressed by Socrates, Glaucon, Adeimantus, or Thrasymachus. One assignment that I had my students do for participation marks was to write down a question pertaining to any passage from the *Republic* that either they did not understand or for some reason found interesting. Attention now focussed on what the text omitted, not on what it said, on potentially subversive moments in the source. Again, I distinctly requested that they question their own question in order to earn full marks. I also introduced a methodological dimension: I wanted students to explain the rationale behind their questions. By having students each present one question to the group, we invented our own Socratic dialogue — beyond the source text, yet inscribed within it. This dialectical drama unfolds when students, from a Burkean standpoint, understand "the maieutic... of philosophical assertion, the ways in which an idea is developed by the 'cooperative competition' of the 'parliamentary'" (Burke, 1973, p. 107). For Burke, this democratic drama demands that opposing assertions help the initial assertion to mature. Reflecting on the entire experience, I think that not only were my students made more aware of the views of Plato and company, but they each had to take notice of the views of their colleagues — insiders who nonetheless dwelled outside the text, beyond its hermeneutic circle, as it were.

Rhetoric, as Burke (1984) sees it, is mobile: it is that which establishes shifts in thought, especially "since motives are distinctly linguistic products ... [that] lead to different conclusions as to what reality is" (p. 35). Admittedly, some students failed to recognize that Plato's thoughts have contemporary applications; yet, Burke himself recommends that we ought to "apply to our old vocabulary in new ways, attempting to socialize our position by so manipulating the linguistic equipment of our group that our particular additions or alterations can be shown to fit into the old texture" (p. 36). Through discussion, then, it is possible for students to develop an appreciation of past ideas after the fact — in much the same way that I reconstructed the lesson of the course from a hypothetical future viewpoint — as I do now. Nostalgically, I look back on what was stated, accomplished, as I look forward to this "present" encoding of the course's aims and objectives. But my reflective position is also a creation of what transpired in the class. I am an outcome of this mechanism — and a chancy one at that. Following Burke's recommendation, we see that it is the instructor who has the responsibility of motivating students to participate because it is the instructor who reads the performance. The instructor is no longer in command of the text but of communication "about" the text, which places instruction in a suspended position. Now, the task for us is to see whether it is possible to motivate reluctant students, to get them to exchange silence for articulate uncertainty, by employing Burke's methodology.

THE STRATEGIC INTERACTION OF RHETORICAL GUIDANCE

Confucius (1938) remarks on his own role as instructor:

> I won't teach a man who is not anxious to learn, and will not explain to one who is not trying to make things clear to himself. And if I explain one-fourth and the man doesn't go back and reflect and think out the implications in the remaining three-fourths for himself, I won't bother to teach him again.[i] (p. 112)

Although the instructor influences the student's incentive to learn, for Confucius, the onus is on the student to be responsible for learning, for independent learning. Confucius's insights are not that different from Davis's notion of transference and Anderson's views on inner authority. The instructor's guidance is only instrumental up to a point. Still, there is reason to believe that, for Confucius, while the instructor gives away authority, the search for authority remains as an active, supportive principle. It is not the *ultimate* intention of the instructor to undermine or mislead a student.

In guiding the seminar, I knew I had to choose my words carefully; otherwise, I might discourage students from following along. Again, my conscious motives played a role in influencing the direction and outcome of learning. Yameng Liu (1997), in an inquiry into how authority can produce inventive discourse, recognizes that the rhetorician invents discussion by selecting appropriate words. Instead of leading discursive discussions, the rhetorician, according to Liu, "is defining and redefining her own rhetorical responsibilities in such a manner that she is justified, or, we may say, *authorized*, in saying what she has to say, stopping where she feels like stopping, and bypassing what she does not want to touch on" (p. 421). This need for authority reveals how well selected words open up further discussion. (Note that Confucius penalizes students for not learning by withholding further instruction: they are even denied an opportunity to repeat the lesson.) The distinction here is between knowledge in itself and the motive to re-engage the learning process. One may know without being able to create knowing in others. In Plato's cave allegory, the individual enlightened by Truth is unable to directly convince the others inside the cave to follow.

By posing strategic questions, I encouraged my students to know less, not more. To be specific, their lack of certainty related to how students were, in Confucian terms, expected to make sense of the one quarter I gave them and to configure, independently of my instruction, the remaining three-quarters. One student made it known that it took a while for the process to sink in. Moreover, this student admitted that he had to think about the discussion after the class was over: taking education seriously means taking the subject of inquiry outside the seminar. Most of our discussions started near the end of each seminar. Factoring in Joseph Sen's (2000) insight, I should have realized that "genuine philosophising cannot be rushed. It takes time and there are no fixed boundaries to the amount it may require" (p. 607). One thing I initially overlooked was the possibility that fifty minutes was insufficient to cover as much of the material as I intended. Also, it is worth mentioning that I never had an opportunity to return to the previous week's discussion without falling behind the lectures.

Ludwig Wittgenstein (1997) offers an interesting account of how teaching and learning proceed under such conditions. "Let us consider," he writes, "the experience of being guided, and ask ourselves: what does this experience consist in when for instance our course is guided?" He asks us to image the following:

> You are playing in a field with your eyes bandaged, and someone leads you by the hand, sometimes left, sometimes right; you have constantly to be ready for the tug of [the guide's] hand, and must also take care not to stumble when [the guide] gives an unexpected tug. (p. 70e)

Notice how the relationship between the guide and the blindfolded person complement each other. This scenario depicts the relationship between student and instructor insofar as students expect their instructors to provide them with finished knowledge. Their relationship, in fact, is initially constituted by this expectation. Since Wittgenstein calls for caution, we might conclude that trust is the crux of the relationship. It is a curious feature — this trust — if we consider that deception can also be used as a guide.

To layer Wittgenstein's vision on Burke's: let us first identify how the student/instructor relation develops autonomously. According to Burke (1969), "two students, sitting side by side in a classroom where the principles of a specialized subject are being taught, can be expected to 'identify' the subject differently, so far as its place in a total context is concerned" (p. 27). For Burke, then, rhetoric not only accommodates each student's individual concern, but also enables each student to develop a unique way of thinking about the subject. In an actual argument about whether human beings have souls, I admit I found it amusing to witness two students pitted against one another, each failing to recognize the context. Their argument began when I questioned why one male student thought that the brain was in control of behaviour and emotions. He stuck to his views when I asked him whether the brain was responsible for a person's falling in love. A female student, who normally remained silent, lashed out at him, saying "That's sick." Impressed by her reaction (contribution), I took my leave of the ensuing debate. She took over, opposing his strictly empirical conception of human beings with the view that one cannot reduce "human feelings" to neural firings in the brain. Another student soon interjected with his own views in support of the female student. None of the students seemed to be aware at the time that I had orchestrated the digression. At the end of the seminar, one student charged me with having played the role of devil's advocate. Did this student expect me to provide the class with a summation? Or was he trying to pull me back from the marginal, dislocated position I had placed myself in, rescuing me from oblivion?

Let us return to the subject of rhetorical deception. Dialectical opposition furnishes a ground for further deliberation. Just because the instructor stands firm on a particular claim, there is no reason for anyone to accept the claim as truth. One can be consistent *and* mistaken. For a student to oppose an instructor's claim potentially signifies that the student has taken a matter into consideration. Similarly, if it is fair to have the instructor demand answers, then how is it not fair for a student to challenge the questions? In Wittgenstein's case, the person responsible for guiding the other must be prepared to deal with the misgivings, hesitations of the one being guided. Again, the motivational residue, the tacit performative dimension of speech, is brought to the fore. Mind you, the instructor's plan ought, ideally, to have been formulated in advance, especially since the instructor assumes — or is expected to assume — control over the discussion. Moreover, as the one in charge of the game, the instructor must allow for challenge, of changes in directions, reversals, and so forth. It is in the nature of a plan to be subject to alteration. There is no point in presenting a question, a problem, or a situation without being prepared to offer reasons why the question needs to be addressed at all, why there is a problem in the first place. Behind each query is another query, so we come to face the danger of an infinite regression. Under such conditions we may ask: does someone really have to be in charge? Or, does inquiry itself become a battle for control of the forum of discussion? Whose desire is responsible for the flow of the inquiry? Whose desire has the final say?

In practice, I found that deception is instrumental in presenting ideas that might otherwise be ignored. Or, it directs attention to the seams, the tears, the gaps within discourse and within a classroom practice. Not only does the material being covered leave an impression on students, but so does the technique of delivery. Rhetoric is integrated into the lesson as new content. From the students' standpoint, there is a drama to watch unfold between a philosopher and the philosopher's rival. Imagine the possibility that Socrates was pitted against someone with equal skill and knowledge. It makes sense to suggest that the dramatic performance, the presentation of conflict in action, would be interesting. But such dramatic thinking is not always thought of as being applicable to the game being played between an instructor and a group of reluctant first-year students.

Despite this seemingly difficult project of encouraging student participation, the rhetorician can appeal to other works that are not typically regarded as philosophical. Such an appeal aims to discover what students find practical, believable, especially if the subject matter is presented as theoretical. I am thinking of how a contemporary moral issue can be introduced through the mechanism of a short story. How does the rhetorician fare when dealing directly with a fictional source? During a discussion of the Buddhist conceptions of causality and moral responsibility,[ii] I related the moral predicament of Varka, the nursemaid in Anton Chekhov's "Sleepyhead," as a case for either justifying or condemning infanticide. In this extraordinary story, Varka, a servant to an abusive couple, cannot find a moment's rest. Her desire to sleep is always thwarted by the couple's baby, who never stops crying.

The pressure finally is too much to bear, so Varka takes matters — and the baby — into her own hands. To me, "Sleepyhead" illustrates Chekhov's conception of moral ambiguity. The story ends tragically, and the issue of moral responsibility is left unresolved. Chekhov's story works as well as any moral philosopher's argument does in that its realism surely appeals to the nonspecialist. An audience, according to Aristotle (1994), is affected by and can easily identify with stories, which "are suitable for [the general public] ... " (p. 277).

The rhetorician can strategically select those stories that seem to convey the same thought found in a philosophical text. Students, as we will see, then have to decide for themselves whether a link between a story and a philosophical "truth" can be made. What they are unsure of is how one text can become the key to unlocking the mystery of the other. There is absolutely no guarantee of either success or failure in carrying out this exercise. Even though I did not think of it at the time, I could have asked students themselves to find situations in selected literature that resemble problems found in the philosophical text. Students might have realized that literature thus acts as a supplement to the philosophical text.

Literature supplied my students with an alternative perspective on the same moral dilemmas they were engaged with. Instead of bombarding first-year students with highly specialized concepts and jargons, I sought out literary works that could treat these dilemmas in concrete terms. Rhetorically, this approach is plausible, though not unproblematic, because it develops students' level of understanding of more formal philosophies through an alternate. Identifying a moral theory through literary examples helps students assess the theory. For Davis (1987), reading literature "tends to emphasize a large margin of undecidability in the [students] as a kind of textual decentering, or the degree to which a text escapes the conception of form altogether ... " (p. 753). Here, an instructor presents the material in a dynamic fashion whereby students are not subjected to a fixed interpretation of a text. Decentering the text encourages students to expand their own interpretations, but, importantly, it does so by positioning them within the literary text, by compelling them to adopt one or more of the perspectives made available by the text.

Exploring literary sources in order to establish a bridge between literature and philosophy can sometimes be tedious. It was, I admit, shocking to discover that some students had little knowledge of literary works such as William Golding's *Lord of the Flies* and Harper Lee's *To Kill a Mocking Bird*. These are fictional works that cross the border into polemics. They escape from their narrative design, aspiring to the status of didactic or ethical argument. Part of their meaning, or conscious intention, is outward — towards the reader and the reader's world. Students can ask themselves: Can fiction support and/or criticize a moral position beyond its own parameters? In the seminar, I — providing my one-quarter — promoted myself as one who continually reads literature and finds links between literature and philosophy. In essence, I was asking them: Could you create a conversation between two distinct texts? By showing students how the two overlap, by blurring the boundaries between them, I raised another uncertainty. I personified the momentary intersection of two academic disciplines. In terms of my performance at the graduate level, I see myself as having a broader range of academic resources to rely on because of this connection. I become, or am in danger of becoming, the virtuoso, the one whose expertise lies not in knowledge possessed but in an instrument mastered. As with Confucius, the instructor provides a starting point, while the students construct/narrate their own process of understanding. And it is the narration, as distinct from the outcome, that is crucial. In this sense, rhetoric emphasizes that students have to become creative in thought, speech, and writing. To my surprise, one student, in his last essay on postmodern ethics, did make reference to the *Lord of the Flies*, comparing the characters of Piggy and Jack with Nietzsche's camel and lion — images, in *Thus Spake Zarathustra*, of the cultural transformation of morality. I would have evaluated the essay more highly than I did if the student had developed the comparison with specific references to both Golding's and Nietzsche's text. Still, I was delighted by this comparison, by the fact that he had made it at all. He had discovered a devious, yet nonetheless profound connection. He had transgressively linked two texts, or found a way of placing one text inside the other. Actually, I would like to have been notified of his ideas beforehand, so that I could have encouraged him to expand on his project. (Notice how I was projecting my desires onto the student's performance — wanting to be involved in his process of learning.) Instead, he was secretive about his thoughts — more silence. Presumably, ideas can function as either blockages or incentives to further exploration. Effective criticism, on my part, might have been a form of encouragement, might have extended, refined the student's insights, subjecting them to more self-criticism.

Wittgenstein's comments on guidance show us that the uncertainty that students are confronted with can be therapeutic, in that uncertainty leads students to diagnose their own capabilities and, presumably, deficiencies. They can retain, or carry over into future performances, the strengths they have developed, even as they overcome what they perceive as shortcomings. (There is indeed the chance that some students may come to reconsider whether they are meant to survive in the university environment.) But even Wittgenstein would agree that the instructor should resort to the occasional "unexpected tug," which would serve to show students that academic work is to be taken seriously. This lesson effectively transforms students into researchers. The climb out of Plato's cave itself is no easy task; but though the lone individual is capable of accomplishing such a feat, it is comforting to have another person along for the journey — a Vergil to the learner's Dante. Recalling that Aristotle (1994) regards "Rhetoric [as] a counterpart of Dialectic" (p. 3), we might say that rhetoric prefers that students not fend for themselves. Motivation is collective.

In practice, I found myself motivating students to overcome their uncertainties, not only about the material of the course but also about the university as a whole. Such motivation included my adopting both persuasive and dissuasive methods. When it came to writing their postmodern existentialism essays, I provided them with two options: they could argue in favour of or in opposition to the philosopher's position. I never intimated that one or another perspective was more or less correct; rather, I instructed them to assess both perspectives and to choose which perspective they thought was more worthwhile. It was even possible to argue against both positions, such that students could devise their own rhetorical criticism and use it not only against the philosopher but against the structure of the question itself. Some students wanted to explore their own ideas, though, which definitely digressed from the task. Isolation thus becomes superfluous: community is all. As I noted earlier, one student did incorporate Golding's text into his essay. I felt myself disapproving of how he, and some other students, had been overly ambitious, attempting to write the essay without my guidance. I foresaw that the essays would reflect my students' own brand of philosophy as opposed to Nietzsche's or Kierkegaard's. By limiting their options, I was requiring students to show me that they could converse with the subject material. By doing so, I was imposing an arbitrary, artificial limit on their thinking. But this limit was an outcome of the fact that I myself was limited in my role as seminar leader. I was demanding that they internalize my deficiency, my descent into uncertainty.

PROVISIONAL CONCLUSION

It is by no means assured that students' academic standing will improve on account of having rhetoric as a feature of their educational experience. Rather, rhetoric presents itself as a means, instead of a certified end in itself. Nonetheless, one fundamental question has still not been fully answered, namely, what difference does rhetoric make to learning? Can students learn from a rhetorical approach?

As Confucius stated, any improvement is, in part, really up to them (i.e., students). As for the instructors, Burke (1969) warns of the possibility that the "same rhetorical act could vary in its effectiveness, according to shifts in the situation or in the attitudes of audiences" (p. 62). Therefore, rhetoric is inappropriate at times. But Burke's warning also signifies that rhetoric should be aware of its own situation. By way of inversion, the audience's feedback is, of course, an indication of what direction to take. Burke shows us how rhetoric's flexibility follows no analytical rules or absolute doctrines. Rhetoric requires an open-minded attitude from both instructor and students in order that they all may become more productive, individually. Rhetoric is, on occasion, best suited to handle uncertainty. We come back to the idea that proper guidance is an attempt to ensure that productivity is never counterproductive. Our wish is still to eliminate uncertainty, to rid ourselves of the anomaly.

Ineffective guidance would seem to result from an instructor's resistance to the interpretations of students. There is a difference between this type of resistance — really a type of ignorance — and the constructive or informed ignorance deployed by the instructor, which leads to learning. Pedagogically, seminars are inverted versions of the lectures. Seminar and lecture are in a kind of Lacanian mirror stage. Authority remains, but its specific location is uncertain, provisional. It is not knowable in a finite sense; rather, it is an aspect of the culture, the lore, contained within the teacher-student contract. I, as seminar leader, instigated dialogue in order to avoid direct participation. I became deceptively involved (present and absent) when I asked tactical, timely questions to perpetuate student discussion.

Depending on the context of one's course, rhetoric can be quite accommodating for a general audience. Rhetoric is a crafty method, useful in assisting an instructor to get recalcitrant students to participate. Notice that one begins by assuming a recalcitrant audience. Still, is it possible to fuse rhetoric with the material being taught, such that the method inundates course content? Can students distinguish the means from the end? It is not typically the case that if an instructor employs rhetoric, then the course automatically becomes a course in rhetoric. According to Burke, in *The Philosophy of Literary Form*, rhetoric consists of stylized strategies, which express real life situations to a public who might have some type of a relation to those situations. On this account, rhetoric establishes a sense of familiarity. In a classroom setting, rhetoric allows students to identify that which they do not understand with that which they do. It should again be noted that this manner of understanding involves a comparing of opposites, uncertainty and certainty. There is, from an epistemological standpoint, a transformation of the unknown into the known. Rhetoric plays only a supportive role in such a process.

By studying the *Republic*, my students were exposed to the dialectic approach. By attending the seminar, they became an integral part of the rhetorical method of learning. To correlate these two approaches: we discover that students are individually capable of identifying themselves with the university. From a Burkean perspective, students do this to see themselves (note the reflexive) within this "wider context." Also, Anderson's notion of students' possessing an inner authority invites them to investigate how wide the context can be. The way I see it is that rhetoric first deals with the practical, yet specific, parts of a subject matter, then leads to more theoretical speculation. This development, in my assessment, rightly characterizes how rhetoric can be employed as an educational vehicle for first-year students. Consider also that this progression functions inductively, in that an instructor starts with the part then moves to a construction of a larger picture, namely a student's relation to the university experience. But now the picture contains the student's experience: the picture is also reflective: again, like a mirror. One should notice that this situation resembles the epistemological transformation that occurs with the individual's trek out of Plato's cave, whereby opinion ripens into knowledge. (Remember Plato's individual, once outside the cave, sees himself in the pool of water as image — a figure who is part of a much bigger picture.) The thing is, Plato, perhaps due to his bias, never thought the "wider context" could be expressed rhetorically. This inability to expose the truth through deceptive means may be why Plato's lone individual failed to educate those who remained in a state of delusion, who remained, simply, satisfied with their opinions.

I would like to add a personal remark. What may be the defining moment of such a transformation is anticipation. Plato's lone individual, ascending to the unknown world outside the cave, must have anticipated something more than what he already knows. This lone individual metaphorically represents Plato's vision of the ideal student of philosophy. Instead of focusing on this idealistic view, we might ascribe these qualities to regular students, that is, to any students at all, who are students simply because they are in the classroom. If students develop a desire for learning, this desire, stimulated by the rhetorician's words, would also involve the eventual quenching of that desire. If the Burkean notion of rhetoric is a call for action, then anticipation reflects students' deferred understanding of the academic situation. They anticipate looking back on where they are now. The academic situation can be seen, then, as a counterbalance to their grander expectations. The instructor on one side has expectations regarding the aims of a particular course, while students come to seminars with the expectation of understanding the material from the lectures on the other.

Finally, we must examine the question of whether Brock's seminar format is an appropriate setting for rhetorical discourse. The seminars provide students with an opportunity to come to terms with what they may not fully understand. Although in my case students were hesitant at first to speak up, some students in the second term did take up the challenge of asking for help. Even on a one-to-one basis, I made use of my role as trickster, so those students could learn from what they recalled having been said in class. Thus, the class context became mobile: it was transferred from the classroom setting to the one-to-one forum. In this way, classroom dialogue became another text, something to be recalled and applied. Here, too, I had recourse to the uncertainty principle, guiding students only to a limited extent, then abandoning them, as it were, to their own devices. Remember that one of my students commented that he took the topics brought up in the seminar home to think about, analyze further. Generally I found that whenever students were preoccupied with uncertainty, this preoccupation contained the motive and means to rise above it. Rhetoric, we might say, as an uncertainty-generating instrument, operates as a motivational force that impels or enables students to act, reflect, and think. Uncertainty, through reflection, leads to its opposite, or double: the purging of uncertainty in the name of higher knowledge. Although it can be argued that not every student functions at the same level, we might also take into account this paradox: the unique aspect of rhetoric is that it appeals to a general audience. And what audience could be more general than first-year students?

Notes

i   I mention Confucius because as the graduate representative for the Philosophy Department, I presented this exact quote on the poster for a social event sponsored by Brock University's Graduate Student Association. I recall that a graduate from the science program wrote Confucius's saying down because she thought that it reflected her role as a teacher's assistant.

ii   This discussion arises from one of the assigned texts for the course, Thich Nhat Hanh's *Being Peace* (1989). Hanh relates an incident of a young girl's being raped and claims that not only are the perpetrators of the act responsible, every human, whether directly or indirectly, throughout the world has played a part in this offense (pp. 61, 62). Though a majority of the students disagreed with Hanh's reasoning, I in order to support Hanh's position resorted to Chekhov's story to illustrate that if one were to pass moral judgment, it is not always easy to arbitrarily resolve such a dilemma. Connecting the two writers involved my reading Chekhov prior to the start of the course — in other words, the connection made was, on my part, coincidental.

References

Anderson, V. (1997). Confrontational teaching and rhetorical practice. College Composition and communication, 48, 197-214.

Aristotle. (1994). The "art" of rhetoric. J. H. Freese (Trans.). Cambridge: Harvard University Press.

Burke, K. (1969). A rhetoric of motives. Berkeley: University of California Press.

——————— (1973). The philosophy of literary form: Studies in symbolic action. Berkeley: University of California Press.

——————— (1984). Permanence and change: An anatomy of purpose. Berkeley: University of California Press.

Confucius. (1938). The Wisdom of Confucius. L. Yutang (Trans.). New York: The Modern Library.

Davis, R.C. (1987). Pedagogy, Lacan, and the Freudian subject. College English, 49, 748-753.

Hanh, T.N. (1989). Being peace. A. Kotler (Ed.). Berkeley: Parallax.

Liu, Y. (1997). Authority, presumption, and invention. Philosophy and Rhetoric, 30(4), 413-427.

Sen, J. (2000). On slowness in philosophy. The Monist, 83(4), 607-615.

Wittgenstein, l. (1997). Philosophical investigations. G.e.m. anscombe (trans.). Oxford: Blackwell.

"All the World's a Stage": Performance, Audience, and A Room of One's Own

Carrie E. Nartker
University of Toledo

> Every time a student sits down to write for us, he has to invent the university for the occasion.... The student has to learn to speak our language, to speak as we do, to try on the peculiar ways of knowing, selecting, evaluating, reporting, concluding, and arguing that define the discourse of our community. Or perhaps I should say the *various* discourses of our community, since it is in the nature of a liberal arts education that a student, after the first year or two, must learn to try on a variety of voices and interpretive schemes....
>
> - David Bartholomae, "Inventing the University," p. 134.

One of the first classes most students take in college is a composition class. Advisors, counselors, and even the title, College Composition 101, assure students that these classes are "where they will learn how to write." Armed with this information, students enter the composition classroom only to realize that writing expectations vary from instructor to instructor. Students begin, as David Bartholomae (1985) suggests, to "invent the university," building it to meet the expectations they have constructed. The university they build, however, is only a construction that lasts for a moment; as they move through the curriculum, they will have to construct many sets. Like performers, students will learn the moves, the lines, and the roles for each class until they equate school with a kind of performance and themselves with performers. An examination of a composition class demonstrates how these performances secure popular myths of learning and thus undermine the university.

Theorists, such as Linda Flower and John Hayes, and Sondra Perl, have termed students new to colleges and universities and composition classes "basic," or "unskilled," writers. If by these terms theorists are including students who cannot use or define a thesis statement or focus on organization or ideas, I can agree with them. However, because the nature of our work creates categories like these, many instructors lose sight of students as individuals who bring with them a multitude of possibilities, and instead see the students as characters in their classroom worlds.

When students recognize these roles, they begin to focus on two important aspects of performance the instructor has (often unknowingly) set up for them: script and audience. Because they have been given the roles already, the students immerse themselves in the character to which they were assigned. They lose sight of their original, "naïve" notion of learning to be a good writer, and instead focus on how to most please their director and their audience. Students become performers because, certainly in composition, we give them the vocabulary: "audience."

Perhaps it would be best to "cut" here and examine some of the reasons why students see composition classes in this way. One of the significant problems I have found with both students and instructors stems from a misunderstanding of who their audience is, and this idea of audience is troubling to many students. What experiences have our students had so far with audiences? It has probably been with audiences who watch a play or audiences who attend a concert. If we continually remind our students to focus on audience, we are inevitably setting them up as performers — although we may not call them performers outright. Inadvertently, we put them in that position because, if there is an audience, then someone is performing. In this case, it is the student.

In his article, "The Writer's Audience is Always a Fiction," Walter J. Ong (1975) discusses the idea of "audience" in relation to writers:

> Although I have thus far followed the common practice in using the term "audience," it is really quite misleading to think of a writer as dealing with an "audience," even though certain considerations may at times oblige us to think this way. More properly, a writer addresses readers — only, he does not quite "address" them either: he writes to or for them. The orator has before him an audience, which is a true audience, a collectivity. "Audience" is a collective noun. There is no such collective noun for readers, nor, so far as I am able to puzzle out, can there be. (pp. 10-11)

Ong mentions that it is "misleading to think of a writer as dealing with an 'audience'." If this is true, why do instructors continue to use this term?

Perhaps the idea stems from a time when "rhetoric" was an oral practice with real audiences. However, writers new to colleges and universities cannot take the time to reason through the term audience as thoroughly as Ong has. Ong says earlier in his article that, "It would be fatuous to think that the writer addressing a so-called general audience tries to imagine his readers individually" (p. 10). When I asked one of my students what came to mind when she thought of the audience for her paper she told me, "A large crowd of people of all different races. They're looking at me. It's scary." Who that "large crowd of people" is for our students presents another problem.

Students in composition classes are really writing for an audience of one, the instructor. However, that instructor "constructs" herself as a multiple audience — as a critic who has multiple views. When an instructor reads a paper, she is looking at it from perspectives of all of the people she creates in her head to make sure the paper is written clearly enough for many different people to understand. Perhaps, then, the student's anxieties are not unfounded.

This idea of being a performer whom people are watching would, of course, be very unnerving for students in their first composition classes. Students have already been part of an audience, so they are very aware of the scrutiny the performer undergoes, and the role filled by the critic or teacher. The students realize the importance of pleasing the audience; therefore, they study very hard to perfect the "character" the instructor has created for them, and their sole focus becomes the intended performance. Their individual ideas and needs must be pushed to the wings, as these would cause a deviance from the script; they focus on what is expected of them, not what they have to contribute. Since the instructors have determined who students are — or what roles they will be playing — it is not worth the student's efforts to do otherwise. The critic will retaliate. While these students have had to invent the university, their instructors have already constructed the script and given them roles into which they fall: the Othello, the Iago, or the Desdemona.

OTHELLO

One of Othello's chief downfalls is that he listens faithfully to everything Iago tells him and never listens to his own instincts or inclinations. Othello trusts Iago (never suspecting Iago has his own agenda) as a friend and a guide and, because he does this, Othello loses confidence in his own abilities.

One of the ways students may react to the pressure of being "performers" is to submit to the ideas and whims of their instructor, or, in the students' minds, the director.

> In addition to the descriptive and prescriptive standards, we also find what we might term the perceived standard, that is, what speakers and writers believe Standard English to be. Here we find such myths as "Never start a sentence with and," and "Never end a sentence with a preposition," as well as patterns of conscious analysis that leads writers to mispunctuate the dependent clauses beginning with "whereas" or "which is to say" as if they were sentences. (Moss & Walters, 1993, p. 146).

This scenario most often happens when extremely shy or insecure students interact with overzealous instructors who make suggestions as directors. Instructors — unaware of their power — pursue their own agenda by way of the student, oblivious to the surface performance their directions elicit.

One example of this is seen in Joseph Harris's book, *A Teaching Subject* (1997). In one of his "Interchapters," Harris responds to a student's letter of complaint about a composition class he took at a university, though Harris quickly points out that it was not a composition class that *he* taught. The student begins his letter by explaining his most important grievance with the class:

> I am extremely disappointed in the composition course here at the University. It fosters an exceedingly stifling environment with respect to creativity and personal opinion.... The only way to get an 'a' in this course is to write what you know the teacher wants to hear. What the teacher wants is always obviously pointed out in the instructions....

He goes on to be more specific:

> I was criticized for "hiding behind my vocabulary" because I used "big" words. (What ever that means. The language employed was similar to that used in this letter.)... To conclude, I charge that the University's composition course is wholly inadequate. It's curriculum and goals should be seriously reevaluated. The primary interest of writing about texts in a fashion compatible with a university setting in a way that allows creativ-

ity and independent thinking to take place unhampered by non-professional teachers...." (pp. 91-92)

While Harris uses his response to this letter to model evaluation responses, he actually demonstrates his own use of the student in pursuing an agenda. Harris writes,

> His letter [the student's] is instead something far more *cranky* and remarkable: an *unsolicited political critique* of the account of the class he took.... This doesn't mean that I *fully* trust his account of the class he took.... (my italics p. 93).

By saying that the student's complaint is "cranky" and that he does not fully "trust" the student's account of the class, Harris seems to be a frustrated Iago who is not happy with what Othello is doing. Harris, like Iago, wants to be in control of the situation and of the student.

Harris has another instance in one of his "Interchapters" where he attempts to reconstruct the student's ideas and make them his own. After reading an introduction to Dave Marsh's collected writings on rock and roll, *Fortunate Son*, Harris says, "I ask them to write an essay in which they talk about some of the ways music has entered into and affected their lives" (p. 19). Although Harris claims he finds the piece "intriguing," he goes on to make suggestions that would make the work his own, instead of the work of his student.

> ... what I think David needs to do with this piece is to say more about what he thinks his experiences mean or add up to, to move from narrative to idea, to show how what he has to offer here is something besides one more zero-to-hero story. In my comments I urged David to try to do so by relating his story to the one told by Marsh. (p. 22)

Although he seems to appreciate the idea behind the student's essay, Harris again, like Iago, wants to take charge of the student's work to make sure it turns out exactly how Harris thinks it should. Although the "Interchapter" does not go on to relate how the student reacted to Harris's comments, there is a good chance the student, like Othello, trusted Harris because he was the instructor and the student changed his work to conform to Harris's ideal. The irony here is that Harris's book, and others with similar examples, is used to train composition instructors.

Students are insecure about their own abilities in college, and instructors do not realize that "Collaboration is in danger of dissolving anytime a tutor [teacher] imposes his or her will upon a client, or when a client surrenders his or her will...." (Jacoby, 1994, p. 140). Although Jacoby's article refers to students interacting with writing center tutors, this situation is also detrimental, perhaps even more so, when this happens between a student and her instructor. The students focus on these submissions as a means to an end: ultimately the grade they will receive in the class. Therefore, the student does not have to worry about offending the audience with what they perceive as their own crude thoughts and gestures. Instead, they trust their instructor to guide their every movement in the hopes of pleasing their audience, which, their instructor has told them, is their ultimate goal. In this situation, the student need not trust or attempt to explore her own ideas.

On the other hand, it is easier for the instructor to take over and develop the work, rather than guide the student through what can at times be a tedious process. An instructor has the vision — she can see the end product needed. She has only to guide the character development, whereas the student does not have to interact with the script at all, except to memorize it and respond as directed. She is not learning how to write and develop her thoughts and ideas. The presented text ends up looking staged and artificial in its presentation. Although from the audience's perspective the performance may look flawless, the student has become the character she was directed to be. The question to be asked here is, can she write?

IAGO

Another way students react to the pressure of being labeled a "performer" is to become the "constructor." What I mean by constructor is that the student becomes focused on the idea of a multiple audience and her role as a performer, constructing that outside audience, rather than the teacher, as the purpose for performance. Ong (1975) makes this point in his article, but twists the idea of role-playing.

> What do we mean by saying the audience is a fiction? Two things at least. First, that the writer must construct in his imagination, clearly or vaguely, an audience cast in some sort of role — entertainment seekers, reflective sharers of experience... and so on. Second, we mean that the audience must correspondingly fictionalize itself. A reader has to play the role in which the author has cast him, which seldom coincides with his role in the rest of actual life. (p.12)

Here Ong places the audience and writer in the position of role players and identifies a common dilemma: figuring out the role in this fiction for
which they (the audience or writers) were intended. The audience forces the
writer into the role of performer, because they are out there, in the darkness,
waiting for the performance. However, to further complicate this matter,
Ong also suggests that the writer casts the audience into a role as well, a role
that is tailored to the performer's script. The student invents the university
even as the university has invented her. If the performer is indeed having to
interact with the audience in this manner, she will certainly be working to
make sure the audience, like herself, is following along with the script. Some
instructors even encourage this type of behavior, but this construction can be
more problematic than helpful.

Constructing an audience takes time and energy that could be better
spent working on developing ideas for the writing assignment. When students construct audiences, they can lose sight of what they are trying to say
and become overly focused on their audience. The student may replace her
intended text with a text she thinks this imaginary audience will enjoy more.
If a student is on this stage, there will most likely be a large number of asides
and soliloquies. Like Iago, students want to reassure themselves that this
vast audience is following along with the plot, or they may not trust in their
own abilities as communicators, so they rely on explaining the plot to the audience directly. These asides can cause the text to become tedious and over-
simplified because the student is trying too hard to communicate the script
— rather than her ideas — clearly.

I once conferenced with a student who was writing an analogy paper
comparing a thunderstorm to a band concert. He was explaining, in great
detail, the percussion section of a band. I suggested that his audience would
probably know of what a percussion section consisted when he looked at me,
completely serious, and said, "No, one of the members of my audience has
never been to a band concert before, and he has no idea what a percussion
section is." It was here that I began to rethink the concept of having students
"create" the audience for which they were writing. Although not all students
take the concept of audience so literally, it did make me more aware of the
possible impact words and ideas can have on students new to this genre.
Creating an audience for which she writes can inhibit a student's natural
inclinations and cause her to construct an irrelevant paper for an imaginary
group in a fictitious setting.

DESDEMONA

A third problem students have is working with an already constructed audience. Often, an instructor may assign an "audience" for whom the student is to write, or, in the student's mind, perform. Their instructor may tell them that they are supposed to write for a middle-aged, college-educated audience. With this information, the performer begins to see the audience in specific shapes and sizes. Instead of worrying about whom to put in her audience, as do students suffering from the Iago Syndrome, the student takes on the responsibility of tailoring her work to fill the needs of her already constructed audience.

> Even when writers have access to an abundance of verifiable information about their audience, even when they are addressing classmates or friends, their sense of audience is not simply the sum total of all the factual information they have access to. It is, rather, a mental construct, a product not merely of "facts" but also of the writer's processes of selection, synthesis, and inference. (Odell, 1993, p. 294)

Like Desdemona, the student is again too focused on everyone but herself.

Because the student is not aware of what is going on around her, she does not teach and delight the audience as she had intended, but instead stumbles awkwardly around the stage not noticing trap doors or curtains. In her quest to please the audience, the student completely loses sight of what her goals and objectives are, and instead works to fulfill the needs of the preconstruted audience. This stumbling and bumbling takes away from what the student is trying to communicate. Instead of focusing on the content, the audience only sees awkward transitions and disjointed ideas. There is no smooth flow of ideas because the student is thinking too much about what the outcome of her performance will be: that is, whether or not she will please this particular group. Ironically, the audience notices only the flaws in the presentation — the very thing the writer is trying to avoid.

If students are getting the sense that they are performers, and if these performances are true for composition classes, they are also true for the university as a whole: students are constructed, they take on roles, and do, as Bartholomae suggests, invent the university. As they do so, learning becomes a performance.

How do we then, as instructors, move students off of the stage and into the classroom? One way to do this in the discourse of composition may be to shelve the idea of audience and focus on the different voices of experience students bring to their writing. Perhaps as instructors, we need to focus more on what is inside our students, and help them explore that, rather than direct their attention on outside audiences that do not really have much to do with the ideas the students bring to the classroom.

> Though the folk wisdom of our profession holds that students are permitted to break the rules once they have mastered them, we are never able, or never willing, to specify the point of mastery. We postpone discourse in the name of discourse when we silence those exterior voices our students bring to class without knowing it, nearly forgotten voices from the home and from the past which our own words might reanimate. (Spellmeyer, 1993, p. 78)

Rather than acting as directors who guide the students through a series of rehearsals to ultimately please an imaginary group of people, we need to find alternative ways to take the spotlight off students.

So then, what is the solution to students' problematic ideas that they are performers for an audience that scrutinizes their every move? We, as instructors, must avoid the implication of performance while maintaining the genre. It is of course not feasible to not give beginning composition students any kind of guidelines for writing their papers. Different styles of papers require different styles of voices. One alternative that I devised during my senior year of college happened during my honors seminar. There were seven students in the seminar, all seniors, and each week we would bring our progressing theses to the meeting and critique them. In the initial meetings of our group, there seemed to be (or so it seemed to me) an undue amount of attention placed on audience. One student in particular would repeatedly confront other members of the group: "What's your audience like? Who's in your audience? What do you know about them?" She even went as far as to suggest to one student that he cut out faces of famous intellectuals and paste them on a piece of paper so he could look at them when he was writing.

After several weeks of listening to this student make suggestions about audience to the group, I proposed the idea that perhaps we should not be focusing on an audience while we were writing our papers. Surprised, my instructor asked me for whom then I would be writing. I did not have a conceived audience for my thesis, which incidentally was entitled "Hawthorne and Poe: The Beautiful, Frightening, Brilliant, and Evil Women Who Inhabit Their Stories... A Materialization of Misogyny." I told my instructor and group that I did not have someone I was writing for, but a place I was writing in. Each time I began working on my thesis I would imagine myself in a room that suited the mood of my subject matter. For me, it was a dimly lit Gothic library with bookcases that stretched to the cathedral ceilings that seemed to erupt from the crimson-colored walls and carpeting. I transported myself to this place each time I began to write, and my language and tone became naturally attuned to this "room." Perhaps one alternative is to have students think of a place, a room, that is appropriate to the tone or mood of the paper they are trying to write. I did not consciously try and create the atmosphere I wrote my senior thesis in, nor did anyone suggest doing so. However, this "room" I was writing in was virtually pressure-free. I did not feel like I was performing for anyone, or being scrutinized by a group of people I could neither see nor hear. Thus, I was very aware of the language I was using and the tone I was setting for my paper. Here, in essence, I was my own audience. I was very engaged in the content of my paper and had a vested interest in its outcome. I was real.

Because this worked for me, I suggested this strategy to one of my students who was having a difficult time finding the right "tone" in which to write her paper on capital punishment. She thought the first draft of her paper sounded too "happy." I suggested that she could imagine herself in a setting where her mood would be more somber and dark. Her second draft, which conveyed her ideas much better than her first, had a darker tone. I asked her if my suggestion had helped her, and she said she had imagined herself writing at a cold metal table in a dingy, damp, grey room. She said that the "room" helped her convey her mood about her subject much better than the actual environment of her dorm room, a place which was pleasing to her. She told me that after a few times of actually picturing herself in this "room," she automatically began to feel herself there whenever she would work on her paper. She said there was no pressure to think of her audience and if they were understanding the words she was putting down on the page.

This "room" of one's own can be a sanctuary for writers struggling with the idea of audience and the pressure of performing for that audience. In the "room" they create for themselves, there is an opportunity for a student to explore voice and tone without a teacher or director trying to "improve" their work before it is on the page. This "room" is not illuminated by spotlights that overlook an abyss of darkness but, rather, is a place to listen for rhythms. If the student is her own audience, she can listen to the words she is putting down on the page. There is no script to follow and no audience to please. Here she writes for herself and not others. This "room" gives a student the opportunity to vary sentences and test out new ideas without being chastised or scrutinized. There are no footprints on a stage to help her be in all the "right" places, nor is there an anxious director whispering directions from the wings.

To some, this idea of creating a "room" where a student can pursue her own agenda, rather than one for a teacher or an imaginary group of people, may seem unstructured or chaotic. "While writing can become the 'practice of freedom' no writer is unconstrained by other voices, by discursive conventions, by institutional regulations" (Spellmeyer, 1993, p. 81). Ideas such as thesis and organization are still important concepts — worthy of class discussion. However, after all of the guidelines have been established, the student can feel free to move to somewhere that creates a mood for the paper she is going to write, and choose to construct her own set, if perform she must.

By walking onto artificial stages, students accept scripts instead of ideas; they mimic, not learn. This is not very different from partaking in a laboratory experiment where the answers are already in the workbook, or plotting data when the outcome has already been graphed. Composition is an opportunity for students to explore their ideas and learn to communicate those ideas, as other classes should be as well. Classrooms should be learning environments, not stages. Rather than a performance opportunity, the university must become an opportunity for students to see ideas of their own come alive.

References

Bartholomae, D. (1985). Inventing the university. In Mike Rose (Ed.), When a writer can't write: Studies in writer's block and other composing process problems (pp. 134-165). New York: Guilford.

Harris, J. (1997). A teaching subject: Composition since 1966. Upper Saddle River, NJ: Simon and Schuster.

Jacoby, J. (1994). The uses of force: Medical ethics and center practice. In J. A. Mullin & R. Wallace (Eds.), Intersections (pp. 132-147). Urbana, IL: NCTE.

Moss, B. & Walters, K. (1993). Rethinking diversity: Axes of difference in the writing classroom. In L. Odell (Ed.), Theory and practice in the teaching of writing (pp. 132-185). Carbondale, IL: Southern Illinois University Press.

Odell, L. (1993). Writing assessment and learning to write: A classroom perspective. In Lee Odell (Ed.), Theory and practice in the teaching of writing (pp. 289-313). Carbondale, IL: Southern Illinois University Press.

Ong, W. (1975). The writer's audience is always a fiction. PMLA 90(1), 9-21.

Spellmeyer, K. (1993). Common ground: Dialogue, understanding, and the teaching of composition. Englewood Cliffs, NJ: Simon and Schuster.

Falling Through the Hoops: Student Construction of the Demands of Academic Writing

Robert Runté, University of Lethbridge
Barry Jonas and Tom Dunn, Alberta Learning

A first-year student prepares to write yet another assignment. She has retrieved half a dozen relevant texts from the library, and spread these out before her on the kitchen table. Using the index or table of contents to zero in on the most relevant passages, she quickly scans each of the texts for an opening sentence. Finding one she likes, she paraphrases it slightly for the opening of her own paper, then begins scanning the other five books for a second sentence that might reasonably follow. Sentence by adapted sentence, she painstakingly builds up a paper that appears to meet the demands set forth by her instructor. In spite of this tedious effort, however, her grades remain disappointing and she wilts under the marker's withering comment that her papers "are growing increasingly stodgy."[i]

This common scenario reveals a student who lacks all confidence in her own voice. Intimidated by the diction and convoluted style of the academic reading that confronts her, she has become convinced that academic writing is something distinct from normal communication and completely beyond her own writing abilities. And yet, this is a student perfectly capable of holding her own in classroom discussion or of writing clearly in other contexts. It is her perception of the academic writing task as alien, arbitrary, and daunting that undermines her achievement.

In this paper, we wish to accomplish three things: to identify the characteristics that distinguish successful from less successful student writers; to relate these categories to the lived experiences of university students; and to suggest some instructional remedies that may assist students in becoming more comfortable with university-level discourse.

THE "BEFORE" PICTURE

As it happens, our research did not start out to be about student approaches to writing. Instead, we were part of the team investigating changes in achievement over time on the Alberta provincial Diploma Examinations. In June of 1990 and again in June 1991, a comparison study of student writing was done in Social Studies 30, English 30, and English 33. In the first case, papers from June 1984 were compared with those from June 1990. In the second case, papers from June 1987 were compared with those from June 1991. Teams of teacher-readers led by personnel from the Student Evaluation Branch of Alberta Education (now Alberta Learning) described features of writing in three general categories: Thoughtfulness, Effectiveness, and Correctness. The two questions that guided the original study were: "Did students who wrote diploma examinations in June 1990 and 1991 produce better compositions than did their 1984 and 1987 counterparts?" and "Have the standards of expectation for written responses at the Satisfactory (3) and Excellent (5) levels of performance changed since 1984 and 1987?" Both questions were answered in the affirmative.[ii]

Alberta teachers subsequently began to refer to the qualities of "3ness" and "5ness" that distinguished "satisfactory" and "excellent" papers respectively. Analysis of these characteristics yielded four major themes or dimensions: ownership, ambiguity, risk-taking, and specificity. These findings are summarized in Table 1 (facing page).

Although issues of confidentiality prevent us from directly quoting student papers, it may be useful to reconstruct two examples to illustrate some of the characteristics of "3ness" and "5ness." Typically, a paper exhibiting qualities of "3ness" will begin its discussion of, say *MacBeth*, with an opening sentence such as:

> In the great play *MacBeth* by that great playwright Shakespeare we see just how really great Shakespeare (the greatest playwright in the English language—maybe in any language ever!) was, because it is a really fantastically great play.

One is immediately struck in these essays not only by the meaninglessness of such verbiage, but also by the desire to please the marker. One gets the strong impression that such students have simply *memorized* the fact that teachers think Shakespeare was a great playwright (why else would they have included him in the curriculum, after all) and are determined to assure

Table 1: Qualities of "3ness" and "5ness"

LEVEL OF ACHIEVEMENT	
(3) Satisfactory	(5) Excellent
OWNERSHIP	
Lack of ownership • Little depth of thought or internalization of idea • Inflated language, attempt to impress, trying to enter a relatively foreign world of thought and language without really having the keys. May rely on what seems to belong in that world (inflated language, for example) but that is not connected to the writer • Confident, but not engaged • Lack of ownership of idea and language	Desire to accept ownership • Originality within a defensible context • Ownership of idea; writers are engaged with their ideas and the material • Ideas are the writer's own and have merit • Personal voice, but not inappropriate; these writers speak as themselves and believe that their ideas merit discussion • Appreciative of the material under discussion
AMBIGUITY	
Comfort with absolutes • Need to "nail things down" in concrete black and white terms — a need for absolutes • Little acknowledgment of ambivalences, dilemma, ambiguity, uncertainty, possibility, inconclusiveness, subtlety • Judgmental and/or moralizing (perhaps moral judgment to these thinkers is a substitute for exploration of idea; it may justify the exercise) • Information is skewed or manipulated to fit a formula, form, or limited idea — not internalized or interpreted	Comfort with ambiguity • Aware of subtlety • Value and seek out irony, ambiguity, intricacy, contradiction, ambivalence • Argue balanced positions (not only/but also this/but that) • Do not attempt to resolve or judge paradox or areas of gray, yet acknowledge and understand these complexities • Do not seek absolute closure; comfortable with open-endedness, unfinished business
RISK-TAKING	
Need for certainty • Reluctance to explore • Sincere • Determination to do what has been asked • Methodical, mechanical approach	Need for exploration • Willing to take risks • Comfortable with exploring ideas in their complexity, not seeking narrow, literal, defined right answers • Able to set a context, redefine topic
SPECIFICITY	
Need to assert/generalize • Generalized language, ideas, information • Apparently no need to elaborate, explain, or develop	Ability to support/specify • Apply knowledge, evaluate, analyze, and *relate* • "show" rather than "tell"

the teacher that they think so too. In truth, these students would rather impale themselves on their protractors than voluntarily read *any* Shakespearean text. The lavish praise these students heap on the texts such as *MacBeth* have little relation to their own opinions, as becomes painfully evident when they reveal their lack of understanding of what the play is about. These are the students who believe it is possible to summarize *MacBeth* in a single paragraph, who adopt the safest interpretation they can grasp, and who leave the examination hall convinced they have aced the test.

In contrast, the "excellent" papers generally take an original, and occasionally contrary, position on what has been taught. A typical "excellent" paper might start by complaining that *MacBeth* is over-rated compared to Shakespeare's other tragedies, and that the standard interpretation entirely misses the significance of the symbolism of the witches. The "excellent" student takes risks, and is confident that the marker will reward such risk-taking. Reading these essays, one knows that these students have internalized both the play and its meaning: they have made *MacBeth* their own.

For example, one year the examination asked students to discuss the theme of "alienation" in literature. One student chose the poem "Examiner" to illustrate his argument. This already indicates a willingness to take risks, because poetry is almost always more difficult for students to interpret than a prose piece. Furthermore, it was a unique and daring selection. The poem, the student argued, is about the alienation felt by a teacher who is forced to proctor an examination, but who sees himself doing to his students what the gardener outside his window is doing to the grass: scything it to an even height. At one level, the paper was a straightforward discussion of a poem that met all the requirements of the question posed; but at another level, the student had built in a complete subtext, that of blowing a giant raspberry to the examiners marking the paper. Pretty sophisticated stuff for a Grade 12 student writing a first draft in an hour-and-a-half examination. The teacher-markers loved it. They gave the paper the highest mark in the province. And yet, we would not be surprised to learn the student had left the exam with a certain amount of trepidation, perhaps even thinking, "They're going to crucify me."

Although the characteristics outlined in Table 1 were derived from an analysis of school-leaving examinations, they are likely to have considerable resonance with anyone teaching at a post-secondary institution. Our findings are especially relevant to those dealing with first-year students because Table 1 essentially describes the range of student writers that constitutes the universities' intake. In other words, the Diploma Examinations provide the "before picture," the starting point from which students enter the university system. It is therefore worth examining how students' first-year experiences contribute to, or undermine, growth along the four major dimensions identified in this study.

GIVING THE INSTRUCTOR WHAT S/HE WANTS TO HEAR (CONTENT)

I'm feeling good about my teaching. Class discussion has gone better than ever. As the class files out, still debating the issue of the day, a couple of students hang back. "That was a great debate," says the first student, "but I must have missed something at the end there. I never got down in my notes what the right answer is."

The other student is more direct. "I think you forgot to say. You got all the students to talk, and that was great, but you never said at the end which of us had it right."

I reply, "Well … I don't think there is one right answer. The answer depends on one's beliefs, on one's underlying values. As we saw in the class, everyone has a slightly different take on this issue."

"Yes, yes," says the first student, "I get all that, but which of all of those viewpoints is the right one?"

I try again. "Well it's not the kind of issue anyone can tell you what the answer is, you just have to work it out for yourself."

Frowning in obvious frustration, the student blurts out, "But why won't you just tell us? I've already told you I can't work out what the answer is supposed to be. A lot of what was said today sounded convincing. How am I supposed to be able to work out which is the right answer?"

"Look," I said, a bit frustrated myself by this point, "There is no right answer. Or they're all right. I can't tell you which one because there isn't one. Or not just one. Pick the one that's right for you!"

The other student, seeing that the two of us are talking past each other, holds up her hand in the universal gesture of "I've got it" and asks a question that cuts to the core of the issue. "What he means, professor, is 'what is your stance on this issue. What do you want us to put down on the exam?'"

I try valiantly to convince them that it doesn't matter what stance they take so long as they are able to make an articulate, well supported argument. They may not say it out loud, but their body language is clear enough: "We've heard that speech before, and we know it's a crock." I feel oddly deflated.[iii]

How does one convince students that they do not need to agree with the instructor to do well in a discussion course? Whenever students are challenged to take ownership for their assignments and write what they truly believe, the vast majority complain that their past experiences have shown that to do so is to take unacceptable risks. One must, they argue, agree with the instructor's opinions or pay a heavy penalty.

This nearly universal perception on the part of students does not accord with the experiences of most instructors, who generally feel they bend over backwards to accommodate other viewpoints. Similarly, there are always a few top students who will attest that no one has ever failed *them* for disagreeing with their professors — and that they routinely play devil's advocate and attack all their instructors' pet theories because they find arguing *against* a known position helps to focus their own thinking. Have these students been outrageously lucky in their selection of courses and instructors, or are all these other students wrong when they claim they have to "suck up" to do well? What we have seen at the high school level, what we know happens there because we have been part of the team that designs the exams, that trains and supervises the markers, and then does follow-up research, is that the students who do the best almost never spout the party line.

On the other hand, there may be just enough truth in the students' fears to perpetuate this paranoia. We all have our suspicions about one or two of our more opinionated colleagues, and it is quite possible that a few bad apples could be tarring the reputation of the entire professoriate. More likely, however, is that we are all a bit biased, whatever our intentions. We may think we are basing our marking entirely on the sophistication of the students' analyses, but it is obviously easier for them to be sophisticated if they base their approaches on sophisticated theorists: that is, those with whom the marker agrees. Students can adopt a contrary position and do well, but only if they address the weaknesses inherent in the out-of-favour theory, or anticipate and refute the instructors' potential counter arguments; only, in other words, if the student does more work than one who simply reiterates the positions with which the marker agrees.

We suspect, then, that what is happening is that stronger students do best when they demonstrate their independence of thought by taking the instructor on, while weaker students' papers collapse under the rigorous examination that follows their adoption of an unpopular position. Weaker writers who toe the party line get mediocre marks for lack of originality but are accepted as basically correct. Stronger students who adopt the party line do better than weak writers, but not as well as they could have done had they written from their heart. The instructors and top students are then confirmed in their belief that the system is completely fair, while the lower students learn that schooling is about compliance and conformity.

(Which, as it happens, is what one would expect from the work of correspondence theorists such as Bowles and Gintis (1976) or Jean Anyon (1981), who see schools streaming students into separate tracks for workers and managers. The potential future managers are taught self-reliance, independence, and critical thinking while the workers are ground into obedience. Nice to know we are doing our bit.)

GIVING THE INSTRUCTOR WHAT S/HE WANTS TO HEAR (PROCESS)

I have been going over a student's paper with her. I am concerned with her lack of voice, with her over-reliance on secondary sources. She nods as I explain that she needs to bring her own ideas forward more, that the secondary sources she is citing can provide support for her ideas, but should be left as background information. She asks the reasonable question of how she might accomplish this goal. I take her over-reliance on quotations as an example. "Why did you quote this author?" I ask. "What does he say here that you couldn't have said just as clearly in your own words? Then it would be your voice, rather than his voice."

Her eyes widen as if I had just suggested she plagiarize her entire essay. Mistaking her look of horror, I launch into an extended lecture on the difference between citation and quotation, and how the former can be accomplished without the latter. I explain that a good rule of thumb is never to quote anyone unless they've said something so original, or so cleverly, that one could never hope to duplicate it in one's own words.

Her expression growing continually darker as I speak, she finally interrupts with the angry, frustrated exclamation: "But the last professor told me I wasn't using enough quotations! He told me he had to dock me because I just summarized without quoting my sources directly! He wanted to hear the people in their original voices, without my introducing my own biased interpretation!" Left unsaid, but nevertheless hanging in the air between us, was the obvious question, "Which one of you idiots am I supposed to believe?"

It was the first time anyone had challenged the maxim I had always lived by, that I had had pounded into my brain all through my undergraduate training and grad school and even in my initial forays into academic publishing, that one should resort to quotation only when absolutely vital. Taken aback, I blurt out, "What idiot told you that?"

"My history prof," she said.

"Oh well, history … That's different. Lots of quotations are normal in a history paper. Quotations are your data."

In the discussion that followed, it slowly dawned on both of us for the first time that each discipline might have its own taken-for-granted rules.[iv]

It should come as no surprise that many students believe that they have to conform to the arbitrary and idiosyncratic demands of their instructors when no one has ever explained to them that different disciplines, traditions, and paradigms may call for different approaches to the writing task. The student who has successfully internalized the post-modernist concern that writing preserve the voice of those quoted with as little interference by the author as possible is likely to be frustrated by the business instructor who declares that s/he "stopped reading after the second page because no executive summary should be longer than 1000 words." The business student is similarly confounded when told by the comparative literature professor that a concise two-page summary of complex material is unacceptable because it lacks sufficient embellishment and fails to allow for a multiplicity of discourses. Overgeneralizing the feedback received in one course to assignments in other disciplines where the advice may not apply, students naturally conclude that these contradictory directives reflect the personal prejudices of individual instructors rather than systematic differences between disciplines.

Indeed, many university teachers, isolated within a departmental organization that restricts their interactions to colleagues within their own or related disciplines, may themselves be only vaguely aware that other departments require significantly different approaches to written assignments. Secure in the knowledge that all their close colleagues stress the same attributes, many instructors do not even articulate these criteria for students ahead of time, but simply dock marks after the fact for any deviation from their discipline's implicit standards. Because grading criteria are not made explicit, and explicitly linked to the particular assumptions of the discipline that provide their rationale (or at least their history), students have no basis on which to predict these hidden criteria.

When students experience variations in the writing task as something imposed by the instructor, rather than as defined by the logical requirements of particular applications, they have no basis on which to make informed decisions for themselves. Instead of being provided with a set of tools from which they could reasonably choose the most appropriate tool for the task at hand, they are left with the mistaken impression that all writing tasks are the same, and it is only the instructor that changes. It should be obvious that it is impossible for students to take ownership of their writing if they feel its characteristics are arcane and dictated by the instructor.

GIVING THE INSTRUCTOR WHAT S/HE ASKED FOR

I have arranged to loan a weaker student copies of the three top student papers written for the assignment. She turns them back in even angrier than before. "I admit those were really good, but... *two* of them went completely off topic! All that stuff from Chapter 2! And I don't even know what Mary has been reading! I thought this assignment was supposed to be on material from the last half of the course, but they wrote on stuff I haven't even heard of. I stayed on topic, and did everything that you asked for, and yet you gave them the "A"s![v]

Paradoxically, when instructors are clear about the discipline-based requirements for their assignments, many students at the "3" level take the directions too literally. Instead of producing an integrated and coherent argument, they mechanically reproduce the assignment structure or scoring rubric, often even adopting the descriptors from the rubric as their topic headings. Such methodical approaches do allow limited success, because it is clear to both the student and instructor that the student has met the assignment's *minimum* requirements. This approach is further reinforced by reasonable success in those course components (such as labs) where essay-style integration is not required. Their unwillingness to take risks, to bring their own out-of-course knowledge to bear, or to push the envelope, however, restricts their grades to the "C" and "B" ranges. For students who religiously follow the structures set out in the assignment, it is frustrating to be told that they received only a minimal pass because they "failed to go beyond" the requirements as set out in the assignment. "Tell me what you want," they complain, "and I'll do it!"

WRITING "LIKE AN ACADEMIC"

Having reviewed the student's first draft and declared it a perfectly satisfactory paper, I watch as he pulls out his thesaurus and begins the painstaking process of replacing as much of his own language as he can with what he con-

siders to be the more properly impressive vocabulary of academia. When I pro-
tested that he is ruining the paper, he appears startled. "But I want it to sound
good, like it wasn't just written by me, but by somebody who knows stuff."[vi]

A somewhat related problem is that in trying to enter the relatively foreign world of academic discourse, many students fixate on the tropes without understanding their substance. The most obvious and most frequently
encountered example is the inflated diction of students who lack confidence
in their own voice. Faced with readings that appear nearly incomprehensible,
students often strive to make their own writing sound equally important.
In attempting to emulate this supposed academic style, they often sacrifice
what clarity of thought and language was available to them.

Similarly, some students adopt the stylistic devices of particular paradigms — such as the jargon and rhetoric of post-modernism, Marxism,
feminist critique — without mastering the content that underlies these specialized discourses. Fending off constructive feedback with accusations of
marker bias, they often fail to improve.

WRITING TO THE INSTRUCTOR

"But why would I need to talk about the stuff from the textbook? Don't
you know that already?"

Because students know that the instructor is the only person to read
their paper, they often mistakenly treat their assignment as a personal communication, rather than as an essay intended for "publication." This unfortunate confusion of formats often undermines student success. Weaker students are unlikely to grasp the importance of specificity, for example, when
their only audience is the professor, whose assumed expertise in the subject
seems to the student to make it unnecessary, and perhaps even presumptu-
ous, to provide supporting detail. Similarly, students occasionally document
their process — listing every book read and web site viewed in the order in
which they were encountered, describing how each draft has been revised
in light of new insights, and asserting how much they have learned — without actually making a coherent argument or directly answering the question
posed.

INSTRUCTIONAL IMPLICATIONS: MOVING STUDENTS BEYOND "SATISFACTORY" WRITING

We have argued that the most crucial feature of writing at "3" level is the absence of "ownership." If our diagnosis is correct, then the question becomes, how can our instruction encourage and develop independence of thought and internalization of ideas so that the ideas are meaningful to the student? How can we encourage students to value their own ideas and have confidence in the worth of those ideas? How can we move students from simply replicating the ideas or language of others to expressing themselves clearly and thoughtfully in their own voices? How can our instruction encourage students to explore ideas and develop confidence and comfort with open-endedness and unresolved problems or issues?

INCREASING OWNERSHIP BY DIVERSIFYING OPPORTUNITIES FOR WRITING

It should not come as a surprise that many university students see term papers as a strictly academic exercise with no connection to their own lives or needs. What originated in the elite universities of another era as a way to prepare scholars for the world of academic publishing has turned into the default undergraduate assignment, one that is of questionable relevance in the modern, mass multiversity. It is often difficult to rationalize a connection between the ability to apply, say, correct APA format, and the graduate's future role as a music teacher, dentist, or forestry worker. Undergraduates in professional faculties may well be justified in complaining that the traditional term paper is not particularly relevant to their needs. There may be more appropriate written assignments for assessing content knowledge or students' writing and thinking skills in applied disciplines. If we want students to take more ownership of their writing, the first step may be to allow them greater choice in the format that writing takes.

An effective writer owns the ideas, believes in what he or she has to say, and is aware of an obligation to communicate to the reader. Most first-year students, however, write on topics chosen by their instructors for an audience of one (the instructor), and consequently feel little commitment to either the topic or to the opinions they are expressing for the benefit of the marker. Allowing students to freely choose any topic relevant to the course content may significantly increase student ownership. Equally important is providing students with a real audience. Assignments that are to be shared with peers or the public are likely to increase student ownership, and to decrease the tendency to "suck up" to the instructor.

One obvious example of a modern alternative to traditional term paper format that also provides students with a real audience is publishing on the world wide web. A number of instructors, especially in issue-oriented courses, have already experienced considerable success by having groups of students mount a web page related to one of the issues discussed in the course. Knowing that their work is "going public," students take greater ownership for both the content and their ability to communicate it. Although no one would suggest that a web page assignment can assess all of the skills (such as sustained argument) served by a traditional term paper, neither can it be denied that these new communication technologies require new skills (such as non-linear connectedness, layout and graphic design, greater succinctness) that our graduates should also possess. Forcing all students to produce web pages in every course would be as dysfunctional as insisting that term papers are the only appropriate format for undergraduate writing. Rather, written assignments need to be matched as closely as possible to the learning objectives for the particular course.

INCREASING OWNERSHIP, RISK-TAKING, SPECIFICITY, AND TOLERANCE FOR AMBIGUITY BY CLARIFYING CRITERIA

We have argued that it is impossible for students to take ownership of their writing, take risks, or tolerate ambiguity so long as they view the instructor as the locus of control. Somewhat paradoxically, the best way of resolving these problems is to make scoring criteria more explicit and to involve students in their creation. Detailed scoring rubrics serve several purposes.

First, they allow instructors to mark more objectively. By frequently referring back to the scoring rubric, and matching the characteristics of the paper in front of them to these descriptors, the marker is more likely to disregard irrelevant factors that might otherwise bias their assessment. Explicit reference to the descriptors can also be made in the feedback to the students, so that students can confirm that the assessment matched the assignment criteria. By being able to review the descriptors and confirm the assessment of their paper, students are more likely to take responsibility for the grade they have earned, rather than see it as the result of chance or marker bias.

Second, by making the scoring criteria explicit and distributing these rubrics beforehand, there are no surprises for students. Students are less likely to inappropriately apply the lessons learned in one discipline or paradigm to another if each course instructor is explicit about his/her own expectations. More importantly, it forces instructors to examine their own assumptions and hidden criteria, as students can challenge marker's comments that do not correspond to the official rubric. At a minimum, the perceived locus of control is moved from the idiosyncratic and unpredictable biases of individual instructors to the objective application of the scoring rubric. In other words, given explicit criteria for the assignment, it becomes obvious that the nature of the writing task itself differs from paper to paper, and that students need to adapt their approach to accommodate different writing tasks rather than to accommodate the instructors.

Third, once the focus shifts from the instructor to the writing task, it becomes possible to explain the rationale behind the specific demands of each discipline, school, or paradigm. Better yet, by involving students in the actual creation of scoring criteria, we can give them a wider perspective and deeper understanding of the discipline in question. In so doing, we help to develop student metacognition.

Before students can be said to have ownership of their writing, they must not only know what to do, but also why they are doing it. As students are taught why particular approaches best suit the requirements of particular contexts, they are able to build up a toolkit of writing techniques and devices from which they can choose the most appropriate for any specific task. Given ownership of this variable repertoire, students can begin to take more risks, combining and recombining techniques until they achieve a synthesis that represents their own voice over a much wider range of writing tasks.

Of course, in structuring the writing task, the instructor may also be able to address the issues of ambiguity and specificity. Understanding the relationship between the discipline and the writing task, students are less likely to attribute arbitrary motives to instructors, and therefore they are less paranoid about identifying the "correct" answer. And, by specifying the degree of supporting evidence required for successful completion of first-year assignments, one can model and enforce a level of specificity that might not occur spontaneously. Students can be directed to "show not tell," to make connections explicit, and to organize information by classifying and categorizing. Building on student strengths, one moves students from unconsciousness through consciousness to automaticity.

On the other hand, it is important not to structure the assignment to such a degree that it erodes student ownership. While we all recognize the importance of pre-writing, outlining, and drafting to establish context — situation, purpose, and audience — for students, one should resist the impulse to teach any *one correct* approach to the writing process. We have all had the experience of students turning in polished essays, apologizing that they "haven't had a chance to get to the idea web and point outline yet, but will have them ready for next Monday, if that's okay." Clearly, our purpose must be to provide students with a set of useable tools, not to impose an arbitrary set of hoops that bear little relation to the student's actual process.

Similarly, since students at the "3" level often structure their papers to mechanically follow the categories as listed in the scoring rubric, it is important to indicate when analytically distinct elements are intended to be combined into an integrated whole.

INCREASING OWNERSHIP OF LANGUAGE AND VOICE

We have argued that faced with required readings that seem to feature inflated language, hopelessly long or convoluted sentence structures, and a general mind-numbing density, students often try to emulate this style by overly complicating their own writing. Far from teaching first-year students how to become clear writers, the readings set before them often do a disservice by modeling the worst excesses of academic publishing. Pompous, exclusionary, and above all boring, much of what is published in academic journals and texts is inexcusably badly written. No matter how seminal the article, first-year students should not be afflicted with such writing when there are usually better written sources available. Readings should be carefully selected to challenge and stretch first-year students, but not overwhelm them.

Where it is considered absolutely necessary to expose students to seminal but poorly written material, the writing, as well as the content, should be placed in an appropriate context. Take, for example, the infamously bad writing of American sociologist Talcott Parsons. No first-year student should be exposed to this important figure without first being told that Parsons completed his graduate work in Germany, and so retained German syntax even when writing in English. The simple recognition that they are engaged in an act of translation helps undergraduate readers negotiate the convoluted style and also suggests that this is not a style they should seek to emulate. It should be further explained that as one of the founders of modern sociology, Parsons was often driven to obscure the field's initially mundane observations in a sea of redundant jargon. The jargon Parsons created helped distinguish the new discipline from the social philosophers who went before, a crucial step in the creation of a separate sociology department within the university. Deconstructing the political and sociological purposes behind Parson's abominable style allows students to be critical of Parsons' impenetrable writing and so retain confidence in the simple clarity of their own voice.

INCREASING TOLERANCE FOR AMBIGUITY BY INCREASING AMBIGUITY

The selection of readings should also strive to increase the students' tolerance for ambiguity by providing a balanced presentation of differing views. Many instructors are successful at using books of readings in which opposing views are argued in successive chapters. As students complete each reading, are convinced by it, they are immediately confronted by an equally convincing refutation, which is itself overturned in the third reading. If the instructor is cautious not to editorialize as students progress through such materials, students generally develop a critical stance in which each new reading is approached with the implicit question, "I wonder what the loopholes are in this argument." Once "authoritative" statements are accepted as limited, tentative, and open to revision, these students may themselves move away from absolute pronouncements.[vii]

THE "AFTER" PICTURE

If the range exhibited by freshman writers is that described in Table 1, then one purpose of undergraduate education must be to move those who enter at the "3" level to the "5" category. Table 2 (on the following page) presents a checklist of the preconditions necessary for students to achieve beyond satisfactory writing. We believe that there are four attitudinal changes required of instructors to achieve these goals.

First, *instructors in all disciplines need to attend more closely to the writing process.* For some students, achieving a *Satisfactory* (3) level of performance is a great accomplishment. For others, that level of achievement is only the beginning of what is possible. In many subjects, however, instructors take the students' writing skills as a given, and feel little or no responsibility for helping to improve them. Fixated on subject content, these instructors feel that the writing process is outside their purview. Consequently, students writing at the "3" level are progressively marginalized as they advance to their second and third years with their writing difficulties unaddressed. It is generally left to teachers of rhetoric, English literature, and so on to accept the full burden of instruction in the writing process. We believe this is an error, and that *all* undergraduate instructors bear responsibility for all aspects of student learning, including (perhaps especially) the writing and thinking skills that are

Table 2. Instructional Focus

---

1. The Importance of Establishing an Appropriate State of Mind
   - A willingness to take personal ownership of ideas
   - A feeling of confidence that these ideas are worthwhile/important
   - A desire to communicate these ideas meaningfully
   - A feeling of acceptance of ambiguity/paradox/dilemma

---

2. The Importance of Pre-writing, Outlining, and Drafting
   (Establishing Situation, Purpose, and Audience)
   - An understanding of and a comfort with the topic
   - An ability to formulate and maintain a controlling idea
   - An awareness of readers' needs and a willingness to meet those needs

---

3. The Importance of Providing Details for the Reader
   - An ability to "show" rather than merely "tell"

---

4. The Importance of Organizing Information
   - An ability to abstract (categorize, classify)
   - An ability to connect

---

5. The Importance of Making Effective Choices
   - An understanding of rhetorical effects
   - An ability to create effects

---

6. The Importance of Reducing Writing Errors
   - A desire to meet readers' needs
   - An awareness of frequently made errors
   - An ability to proofread

---

7. Beginning with Students' Strengths
   - Developing metacognition
   - From unconsciousness through consciousness to automaticity

---

basic to mastery in any discipline. Assignment structures, scoring criteria, and marker attention all have to be directed to the writing process (as well as to the subject content) in every course in which written assignments are set.

Second, instructors need to provide students with *constructive feedback that makes sense within the students' own frame of reference.* Grades alone are insufficient, since these often appear arbitrary, even random, to students. We are all familiar with the student complaint that papers that were dashed off in a single evening may do as well or better than those in which the student invested inordinate time and energy. Students need extensive written feedback, explicitly linked to clear scoring criteria, to be able to make sense of their grades. For students in the "3" category, this feedback must focus on the writing process at least as much as on content weaknesses. Equally important, however, is that these comments be linked to the requirements of the particular writing task as shaped by the discipline, school, or paradigm. Instructors need to recognize that these students may well be receiving contradictory advice in another class, and without a discipline-based rationale, students have no context in which to interpret this conflicting feedback as other than marker bias.

Instructors also have a bad habit of making only negative comments. Taking student strengths for granted, they tend to focus their comments on those areas where they see the student needs help. But that approach reflects the instructor's perspective, not the student's. All the student sees is a sea of red ink, a litany of complaints and criticisms that undermine confidence and do not promote learning. For students to successfully integrate the feedback they receive, it needs to be balanced with at least as many comments on what they have done right as suggestions for improvement. Given the occasionally contradictory feedback from different disciplines, it is extremely useful for students to have their strengths identified so that they know what to do over again.

Furthermore, feedback is *most* effective when it begins with student strengths and then moves to the corresponding weaknesses. For example, it is not uncommon for a student to use three examples in building their argument. If the first example is well developed, the second less so, and the third much weaker — perhaps even off topic, as the student desperately casts around to build his/her case — one's feedback should begin by identifying what made the first example so powerful, before turning to demonstrate the lack of those same qualities in the third example. Similarly, students who have used parallel structures to good effect in one part of their essay, but suffered breakdowns in parallelism elsewhere, will be better able to understand what they should have done when the marker starts by explaining what went right in the first instance. By building on student strengths, by making students conscious of what they are doing right, one is able to move them from unconsciousness to consciousness and so towards the ultimate goal of automaticity.

Third, instructors need to provide students with greater opportunities to undertake *writing tasks that are meaningful within the context of the students' careers and lives.* It is difficult to see how students are to take ownership for their writing when they are seldom given topic choice or a real audience to address.

Finally, instructors need to *structure written assignments and scoring criteria to elicit desirable characteristics in their students' writing.* They also need to provide direct instruction on the writing process as it relates to their discipline.

Notes

i.   L. Walker, Dean, Faculty of Education, University of Lethbridge. Personal communication, concerning his experience as part of a mentoring program for first year student writers.

ii. E. Scraba, Patterns & Processes: Approaches to Writing by Grade 12 Students Student Evaluation Branch, Alberta Education, pp. 1-22.

iii. R. Runté, following a recent "Social Issues in Education" class.

iv. R. Runté, in his second year of university teaching.

v.   M. Runté, Instructor, Lethbridge Community College. Personal communication concerning her experiences teaching a marketing management course.

vi. R. Runté, in a 2nd year undergraduate class.

vii. See, for example, Taylor, Gerald and Robert Runté. "Sociology, Student Directed Inquiry, and the First Practicum," Curriculum and Teaching, 6 (1), 1991.

References

Anyon, J. (1981). Elementary schooling and distinctions of social class. Interchange on Educational Policy, 12(2-3), 118-132.

Bowles, S. & Gintis, H. (1976). Schooling in capitalist America. NY: Basic Books.

Dunn, T. & Jonas, B. (1994). Moving students beyond satisfactory writing. Summer Institute on Student Assessment in the Classroom. Calgary, AB.

Runté, R. (1990). On giving professors what they want to hear: I'm not boring you am I? FAPA, 1(8), 212.

————. (2000). Feedback they can use: Understanding the undergraduate's frame of reference. Paper presented to Society for Teaching and Learning in Higher Education Conference.

————. (1998). Replacing the term paper with a website: Some practical considerations. Society for Teaching and Learning.

Scraba, E. (1990). Patterns and processes: Approaches to writing by Grade 12 students. Edmonton, AB: Student Evaluation Branch, Alberta Education.

Taylor, G. & Runté, R. (1991). Sociology, student directed inquiry, and the first practicum. Curriculum and Teaching, 6(1).

Second Chances: A Study of the Coping Strategies of Undergraduate University Students

Robert C. Twigg
University of Regina

INTRODUCTION

In Winter term of the 1996-97 academic year, a group of 79 undergraduate students at a major Canadian University who, based on their grades for the Fall term, should have been required to withdraw from university for two semesters, were allowed to register. The official reason for this extension of grace was a "computer programming error." Of this group, 31 did not re-register and one registered as a part-time student. Of those who registered full time, 21 successfully completed the Winter term and were admitted with clear standing for the Fall 1997 term; 26 were required to withdraw.

This author felt that the 47 students who took advantage of this "computer error" and registered for the 1997 Winter term (the Second Chance group) would provide an interesting cohort for study, especially at a time when the University was at the same time raising its admission standards and struggling with finding ways to reduce the undergraduate student drop-out rate. Studying the Second Chance group provided the University with a chance to determine at least the appropriateness of requiring students who did not complete at least half their classes with an average of 50% in any semester to drop out for two semesters.

The University Registrar's Office had in place the mechanisms necessary to track students' academic records. The thrust of the Second Chance research project was to determine the coping strategies used by these students, whether these strategies changed from the Fall to Winter term, and how these strategies compared with a Control Group of students who had met the University's criteria for continuing their academic studies.

To achieve this goal, the 47 members of the Second Chance group who enrolled for the Winter semester and a group of 88 students of similar demographic background were sent a survey. Return of this survey indicated that the students understood both the purpose of the study and the relevant ethical issues that accompany this type of research. Six members of the Study Group and five Control Group members returned the survey forms.

LIMITATIONS OF THE STUDY

The design of this project included focus groups to be held following the compilation of data from the surveys. No respondents indicated an interest in such groups. For this reason, the meaning of several responses is not as clear as had been intended. Although the small return limits the generalizability of this study, the two groups of students who responded were close enough demographically that comparisons between the two groups can be made. Although both the Second Chance and the Control Group mirror the demographic characteristics of the larger cohorts of students each represents, those from both groups who chose to respond were self-selected. There is therefore no way to determine if they differ in any significant way from other members of their cohorts. Finally, as this study is based on self-report, there is no way to determine the accuracy of the responses. Because the study was totally anonymous, there was no apparent reason for respondents to report falsely. As no attempt was made to compare this study group to students at other Canadian universities, it is impossible to know if these findings are generalizable to other universities.

FINDINGS

Demographics

The six students in the Second Chance group included three males and three females, all single with no dependants. Three listed their home addresses as the city in which the University is located, two from outside the city but within its economic catchment area, and one from a significant distance from the university city. All had completed secondary school in their home communities.

Two males and three females from the Control Group responded to the survey. All were single with no dependants. Two were from the university city, two from a fair distance from the city, and one from out of province. All had completed secondary school in their home communities.

Residence at time of study

In the fall of 1996, three members of the Second Chance group were living at home, two off campus and one on campus. One of those living at home moved to the campus for the Winter term. This student's responses suggest that living at home had been very stressful and that the move to campus was an attempt to alleviate that stress. Three members of the Control Group lived at home, one on campus, and one off campus. Their place of residence did not change between terms.

Work/Volunteer Activities

Two members of the Second Chance group worked off campus during the Fall term, one working more than 20 hours a week and the other between 11 and 15 hours. Two were working in the Winter term: one on and one off campus, one working 11-15 hours a week and the other over 20 hours a week. Four, including one of the employed, were also volunteering their time, three less than 10 hours and one 11-15 hours a week. One did volunteer work on campus; three volunteered off campus. During the Winter term, one student left volunteer work; two volunteered less than 10 hours and one 11-15. In the Winter, one volunteered on campus and two off campus.

Two members of the Control Group worked during the Fall term. Both worked off campus, one 11-15 hours a week and the other over 20. One volunteered off campus for less than 10 hours a week during the Fall term and for 11-15 hours a week in the Winter. No member of the Control Group had both a job and a volunteer position.

Academics

The Second Chance group reported taking 17 courses in the Fall (average 3.4 courses per student) with a GPA of 50.7%. They reported averaging 10.2 hours of study time per week (average 0.6 hours per course per week). The Second Chance group took 13 courses in the Winter (average 2.6 courses per student) with a GPA of 54.2%, studying 17.2 hours a week (average 1.3 hours per course per week). These data are based on the responses of five students as one gave no indication of academic performance.

The Control Group took 18 courses in the Fall (average 3.6 per student) with a GPA of 63%, and reported studying 8.6 hours a week (average 0.5 hours per course per week). In the Winter they took 20 courses (average 4 per student) with a GPA of 63.5%, studying on average 25.2 hours a week (average 1.3 hours per course per week).

Removing the student with the highest marks in the Control Group in the Fall term (4 courses, GPA 77.5%) reduced that group's GPA for the Fall term to 58.7%. As student marks in the Winter term were more uniform, removing the student with the highest marks (not the same student as in the fall) made minimal difference in the GPA. Similarly, removing the Second Chance student with the lowest marks in the Fall term (4 courses, GPA 41.3%) gave this group a GPA of 53.6%. Given the University requirement that marks be recorded in multiples of 5, this difference in marks (58.7 versus 53.6) becomes meaningless. Again, for the Second Chance group there was less within-group variance in the Winter marks.

Use of Resources

Respondents were given a list of services and resources available to students at the University and asked to rate their use of them on a five-point Likert-type scale, with one meaning never used and 5 used a great deal.

The groups reported using the following services and resources (numbers indicate average score — fall term/winter term):

Service	Second Chance	Control
ON CAMPUS		
Library	3.7 / 4.4	3.4 / 3.2
Advising Centre	1.4 / 2.3	1.0 / 1.0
Counselling Centre	2.0 / 1.2	1.0 / 1.0
Help Centres	1.8 / 1.6	1.0 / 1.4
Clubs and Societies	2.2 / 1.6	1.4 / 1.5
Instructor Office Hours	1.8 / 2.3	2.2 / 2.6
OFF CAMPUS		
Off Campus Help	2.5 / 2.4	1.5 / 2.5
Peer Support	3.0 / 2.8	2.0 / 2.5
Family Support	2.0 / 2.0	2.5 / 3.0

Discussion

The first impression one has in reviewing this data is that there was a significant difference between the Fall and Winter terms for both groups. Neither group devoted a significant amount of time to studying in the Fall, with the differences in reported hours of weekly study being almost totally dependent on one Control Group student's work habits (most of the between-group difference in marks in the Fall term was attributable to the same student). Both groups worked harder in the Winter term. The Control Group took additional courses while the Second Chance group took a reduced course load (in both cases this amounted to an average change of less than one course per student). Both groups spent the same amount of time studying per course taken in the Winter term.

Differences existed in the two groups' use of resources, both on campus and off. Both groups used the library most. One of the goals of the focus groups would have been to gain a better understanding of the type of use made of each resource. In the case of library use, for example, the focus groups would have been used to clarify whether respondents reported time spent studying within the walls of the library building or time spent making use of the support services provided by the library.

Student use of the other campus resources varied from minimal to no use. Further research needs to be done to determine the reason for this. Questions to be asked should include:

1. are students aware of the resources available to them
2. are these resources seen as meeting student needs

For example, while instructor office hours was the second most used on-campus resource, students still rarely made use of the time instructors made available to them. Was this because students were not aware of office hours and the support they could receive from their instructors or because their instructors made it clear that they had neither time nor interest in consulting with students? This researcher is aware of university instructors whose posted office hours are late in the evening, on weekends, and over mealtimes. I also heard stories of university instructors who intimidated students who approached them and in various ways made it clear that they were not to be bothered by students.

Students in the Second Chance group made more use of resources off campus than they did of on-campus resources except for the library, clubs, and societies. If clubs and societies are seen as forms of peer support, peer support becomes this group's most used resource.

It is evident that neither group "hit the books" with great diligence in the Fall term. While both groups more than doubled the hours a week spent studying in the winter term, 1.3 hours of study time per course per week still reflects a minimal investment in academic activities. For the Control Group, the number of hours spent studying per week directly correlated with GPA (high of 40 hours of study generated a 77.5 GPA; low of 2 hours of study generated a GPA of 57). A negative correlation between hours studied and marks was found in the Second Chance group (high of 25 hours of study generated a GPA of 46.7; the low 3 hours of study generated a GPA of 53.3).

NEED FOR FUTURE RESEARCH

This research suggests that if universities wish to become student friendly and create an academic environment that maximizes the learning experiences of their students, the following issues need to be addressed:

- To the extent that the respondents to this study accurately represent the Canadian university student body, this study suggests that the student body is not oriented to academic study. This is shown in the amount of time spent studying, the use of support services, and marks — the bottom line.
- Research needs to be done to determine the study skills students enter university with. Such research would determine whether secondary schools in the province need to improve their training in this area or whether universities need to be more proactive in promoting study skills.
- The impact of the financial cost of university education on student life, and specifically academic life, needs to be measured. To what extent does the additional pressure of raising funds for university education impact on students' ability to cope with university life? This question was especially relevant to the students who were studied as they came from one of Canada's most "have not" provinces. Should scholarships be increased, more on campus jobs be created, student loan payment schedules be changed, more loan forgiveness be provided, etc.?
- Student motivation needs to be studied. While this sample was too small to generalize from, it was apparent from the responses that some students attended university to party. While it is important that students have an active social life, perhaps university recruitment and secondary school preparation needs to reflect the academic rigor of university life.
- The performance expectations and marking skills of university instructors should be studied.
- The degree to which students are aware of the various support systems that do exist on campus and the student perception of their value needs to be studied. This study showed a minimal use of all services except the library. The method of data collection and the lack of response to the invitation to participate in focus groups made it impossible to tell

whether students who reported using the library were using it as a place of study or whether they were actually making use of the service resources housed in the library.

- Students coming from outside the university's home city reported being intimidated by life in the big city. Although it is known that the adjustment from rural to urban centres has a negative impact on student achievement, none of these students reported coming from isolated communities. It might be of value for universities which service rural populations to focus more energy on assisting rural students to make the adjustment to the big city during the orientation process.

Contributors

NEIL J. ANDERSON is a teacher educator in the MA TESOL program at Brigham Young University, Provo, Utah, USA. He received his MA in TESL from Brigham Young University and his Ph.D. from the University of Texas at Austin. He has worked in Intensive English programs at Brigham Young University, The University of Texas at Austin, and Ohio University. He worked as the Program Associate for Measurement and Evaluation for the Overseas Refugee Training Program in Southeast Asia for the Center for Applied Linguistics. He has presented papers and workshops at various conferences internationally, including: Brazil, Costa Rica, Egypt, Honduras, Indonesia, Japan, Malaysia, Morocco, Namibia, Panama, The Philippines, South Africa, Thailand, and Venezuela. His research interests include second-language reading and writing, language learning strategies, teaching and learning styles, and second-language evaluation and testing. He is the author of a teacher education text in the TeacherSource series entitled *Exploring Second Language Reading: Issues and Strategies* (1999, Heinle & Heinle) and a new EFL reading series *ACTIVE Skills for Reading* (2002, Heinle & Heinle). He served as President of Teachers of English to Speakers of Other Languages, Inc. 2001-2002.

WENDY CARSE is Associate Professor of English at Indiana University of Pennsylvania. Her interests include the study of the horror genre as it has evolved through the ages, feminist theory and practice, and the uses of popular culture in the composition classroom.

TOM DUNN received his B.A., Professional Diploma in Education (PD/AD), Graduate Diploma in Education, and M.Ed. from the University of Alberta between 1971 and 1982. He taught senior high English language arts in Brooks and in Sherwood Park, Alberta before joining Alberta Learning as a Test Development Specialist in 1981. He has held a variety of positions with Alberta Learning, including English 33 Diploma Examination Manager, Senior High English Language Arts Curriculum Consultant, and, most recently, Assistant Director, Examination Administration, Learner Assessment Branch. As English 33 Diploma Examination Manager, he worked closely with teachers from across Alberta to develop and mark the diploma examinations in English 33. As Senior High English Language Arts Curriculum Consultant, he worked with Alberta teachers and colleagues from Alberta Learning to develop the province's new Program of Studies for Senior High School English Language Arts. His current work, as Assistant Director, Examination Administration, Learner Assessment Branch, involves creation and interpretation of examination administration policies and procedures and direction of the administration of achievement tests and diploma examinations throughout Alberta.

KIM FEDDERSON is Professor of English at Lakehead University. His field is rhetorical studies, with particular emphasis on Renaissance rhetoric and classic and contemporary rhetorical theory. He has published various articles on the history of rhetoric in the *Historisches Worterbuch der Rhetorike* and *The Dictionary of Literary Biography*. He has written on pedagogy and rhetoric in *Works and Days* and in *Contextual Literacy*, and is the co-author of *A Case for Writing*. Work continues on a collaborative project with J.M. Richardson on Shakespeare in popular culture.

BILL HEATH is Professor of English at Lakehead University. His primary field is American literature. He teaches both graduate and undergraduate courses in American poetry and prose, with an emphasis on Nineteenth-century New England writers. He has published articles on Emerson, Thoreau, Dickinson, and Frost. His most recent publication is the chapter on Cyrus Augustus Bartol in the volume on The American Renaissance in New England in the *Dictionary of Literary Biography*. Bill began using learning journals in his classes about ten years ago and continues to use a variation of this activity in his classes today.

FREDERICK M. HOLMES is Professor of English at Lakehead University. His area of expertise is twentieth-century British literature, with special emphasis on contemporary fiction and narrative theory. He has a secondary interest in Victorian literature. He has published numerous articles and a book titled *The Historical Imagination: Postmodernism and the Treatment of the Past in Contemporary British Fiction*. He is a past recipient of Lakehead University's Distinguished Instructor Award.

JUDY HUNTER is Assistant Professor of English and Coordinator of the Language Centre at Ryerson University in Toronto, where she has taught and developed course curriculum in English as a Second Language, composition, and literacy in society. Her research and writing interests include ethnographic studies of literacy and language use and development in school, university, and workplace settings.

BARRY JONAS attended both the University of Calgary and the University of Alberta, receiving undergraduate degrees in History and Political Science and a graduate diploma in Education. He taught senior high school social studies in Calgary from 1966 to 1981. Moving to Alberta Education in Edmonton, he served as a test development specialist and, subsequently, examination manager for the Social Studies 30 Provincial Diploma Examination program. In this capacity, he was primarily responsible for the development of the examinations by coordinating and refining teacher input and for supervising the marking of the written component of the examinations. He also assisted in the development and validation of the provincial achievement tests for social studies in grades 3, 6 and 9, as well as the English 30 and 33 diploma examinations. During the course of this career, he presented numerous evaluation in-services for social studies across Alberta. He retired in 2000.

JULIE JUNG is an Assistant Professor of English at Illinois State University, where she teaches courses in rhetorical theory, composition theory, and writing, with an emphasis on theories and practices of revision. Her publications have appeared in the *Journal of Advanced Composition, Composition Studies,* and *Living Languages: Contexts for Reading and Writing.* Currently she is at work on her book-length project, "On the Borders of Belonging: Revisionary Rhetoric and Multigenre Texts."

ROBERT LUKE is Curriculum Coordinator at the Special Needs Opportunity Windows (SNOW) Projects (http://snow.utoronto.ca), an initiative of the Adaptive Technology Resource Centre at the University of Toronto. He is also a PhD candidate in Social Justice and Cultural Studies at the Ontario Institute for Studies in Education of the University of Toronto. His research focuses on digital identity formulation, policy for online learning and governance, and issues of online access and accessibility.

JEANETTE LYNES is currently Associate Professor of English at St. Francis Xavier University, where she teaches Canadian literature and creative writing. She taught in the English Department at Lakehead University from 1991 to 1998. She is the author of the poetry collection *A Woman Alone on the Atikokan Highway* (Wolsak and Wynn, 1999), editor of the anthology *Words Out There: Women Poets in Atlantic Canada* (Roseway, 1999), and co-editor (with John Fell and David Antilla) of the anthology *Paradise Frost: The Thunder Bay Poetry Renaissance* (Edgy Writers, 1999).

JAQUELINE MCLEOD ROGERS is Associate Professor in the Centre for Academic Writing at the University of Winnipeg. She works with a number of first-year students who enrol in Academic Writing, a university-mandated writing course that encourages students to become aware of academic and disciplinary conventions and to develop an effective writing process that involves elements of staging and collaboration. She notes that students come to the first class with attitudes ranging from enthusiasm to fear, to disdain, but that most appear to leave with a sense of satisfaction linked to accomplishment. She was awarded a Spencer Foundation (Chicago) Grant to study interdisciplinary narrative writing, and is currently completing a book-length study that examines the uses of academic narrrative. She has taught several courses centred on narrative inquiry, The Teacher Researcher (for Education students), and Narrative Thinking and Writing. She was delighted to have her narrative "Grace After Pressure" included in *Dropped Threads* (Vintage), a recently published anthology of women's stories about silences.

CARRIE E. NARTKER teaches composition in the English Department at the University of Toledo, as well as composition, basic writing, and sociology at Monroe County Community College in Michigan. She graduated from the University of

Toledo, Ohio, with an M.A. in English Literature. Future plans include pursuing a Ph.D. in Renaissance and Restoration Literature.

RANDALL L. POPKEN was Professor of English and Director of the Writing Program at Tarleton State University, Stephenville, Texas. His primary research interests were discourse analysis and genre acquisition; his articles have appeared in Composition Studies, English for Specific Purposes, Focuses, Issues in Writing, Journalism of Advanced Composition, Journal of Teaching Writing, Journal of Technical Writing and Communication, Technical Writing Teacher, Written Communication, Writing Instructor, and Writing on the Edge.

ROBERT RUNTÉ is Associate Professor in the Faculty of Education at the University of Lethbridge, where he teaches courses in both sociology and student evaluation. He was born and raised in Edmonton and received his B.A., Professional Diploma in Education, M.Ed., and Ph.D. from the University of Alberta. Prior to joining the University of Lethbridge, he worked as a Test Development Specialist for Alberta Learning where he was primarily responsible for the Social Studies Achievement Tests for grades 3, 6, and 9 and assisted with the Social Studies 30 Diploma Examinations. His Ph.D. provided a sociological analysis of the ideological proletarianization of educators, and is summarized in part in "The Impact of Centralized Examinations on Teacher Professionalism," *Canadian Journal of Education* Vol. 23, no. 2 (Spring 1998) 166-181. He is co-editor (with Gerald Taylor) of *Thinking About Teaching: An Introduction* (Harcourt Brace, 1995) and co-editor (with Yves Meynard) of an anthology of Canadian speculative fiction, *Tesseracts5* (1995). His interest in the miscommunication between markers and students emerged out of a four-year study of the grade appeal process at post-secondary institutions across Canada, in which it became apparent that what students thought they were hearing was not the same as what markers thought they were saying. He currently offers workshops on student-oriented grading to universities across Canada. Dr. Runté's web page is http://www.edu.uleth.ca/~runte/.

ANDREW STUBBS is Associate Professor of English at the University of Regina, where he teaches courses in advanced and introductory composition, professional writing, history and theory of rhetoric, and creative writing. He has co-edited, with Judy Chapman, *The Other Harmony: The Collected Poetry of Eli Mandel* (CPRC, 2000). His investigation of Eli Mandel's poetry and poetics, *Myth, Origins, Magic*, was published in 1993 (Turnstone, CFH). In addition to publications and conference papers on writing theory and pedagogy, psychoanalysis, literary theory, postmodern poetry and poetics, he has conducted studies of a range of contemporary Canadian authors, including Sandra Birdsell, Clark Blaise, Dennis Cooley, Hugh Hood, Anne Marriott, Alice Munro, John Newlove, and Sharon Thesen. Intrigued by linkages between rhetoric and psychoanalysis, he has just competed an examination of William Styron's *Darkness Visible*, to be published in a collection of essays on writing and addiction.

WILLIAM H. THELIN is Director of Composition at the University of Akron and is interested in critical pedagogy, response practices, and theory. His first book, a co-edited volume titled *Blundering for a Change: Errors and Expectations in Critical Pedagogy*, examines teacher error and is available through Boynton-Cook Heinemann.

ROBERT TWIGG is Associate Professor with the Faculty of Social Work at the University of Regina. His areas of interest include child welfare, clinical practice, law and ethics, and cultural diversity. Prior to entering academia, he worked in a private foster care program for 10 years and has consulted, published and made presentations on that topic. As this chapter shows, he is also interested in facilitating university education.

ROBERT VUCKOVICH is slowly working towards a Master's degree in philosophy at Brock University and is completing his thesis, "Marcus Aurelius' meditations on suicide". He intends on earning a PhD in philosophy, specializing in stoicism and existentialism. His interest in rhetoric relates to the contrary and covert approaches found in speech. His paper, "Evangelion and Existentialism: the Case of Shinji Ikari", is slated for publication in the forthcoming, but tentatively, titled collection, *The Uses of Science Fiction Genre*, by Cambridge Scholars Publishing.

MICHAEL WHITEHEAD lives in Prince Edward Island, where he is completing a thesis on the Canadian/Maritime writer David Adams Richards. His background is in Canadian and American literature, as well as eighteenth-century poetry and poetics. A graduate of St. Francis Xavier University in Antigonish, Nova Scotia, he has pursued graduate studies at the University of Regina, where he has also worked as an assistant program coordinator, instructor, editor, and writing consultant for First Year Services. He has been a contributing editor for the collaborative writing journal *Textshop*.